Garfield SHOVELS IT IN

BY JIM DAVIS

Ballantine Books • New York

A Ballantine Books Trade Paperback Original

Published in the United States by Ballantine Books, an imprint of The Random House Publishing Group,
a division of Random House, Inc., New York.

BALLANTINE and colophon are registered trademarks of Random House, Inc.

ISBN 978-0-345-52419-5

Printed in the United States of America

www.ballantinebooks.com

9 8 7 6 5 4 3

Garfield's FURRY TALES

Hansel and Gobbler

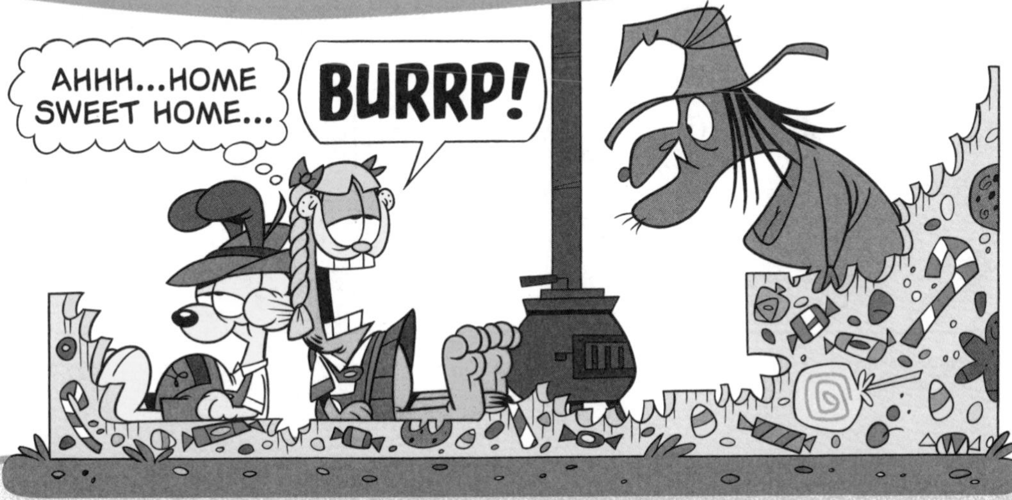
AHHH...HOME SWEET HOME...
BURRP!

Little Red Riding Dog

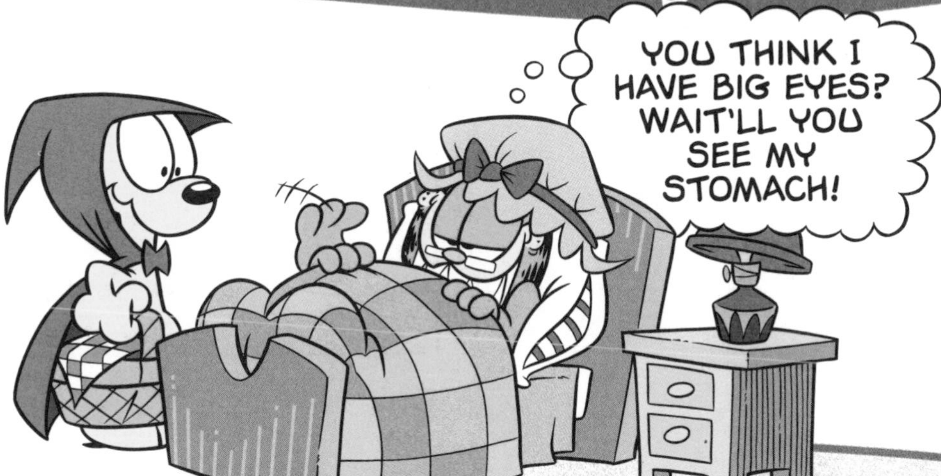
YOU THINK I HAVE BIG EYES? WAIT'LL YOU SEE MY STOMACH!

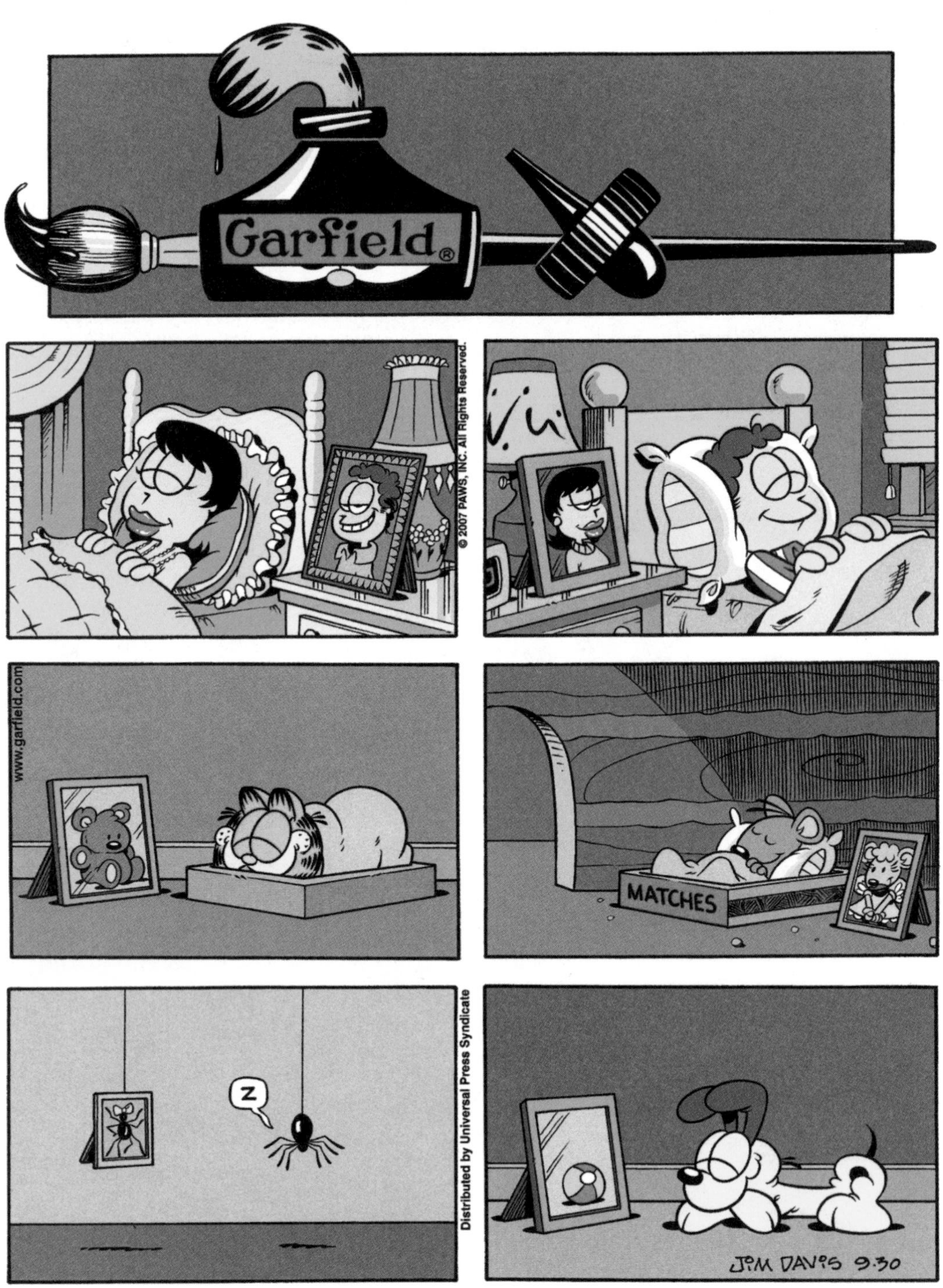
Garfield®
© 2007 PAWS, INC. All Rights Reserved.
www.garfield.com
MATCHES
Z
Distributed by Universal Press Syndicate
JIM DAVIS 9-30

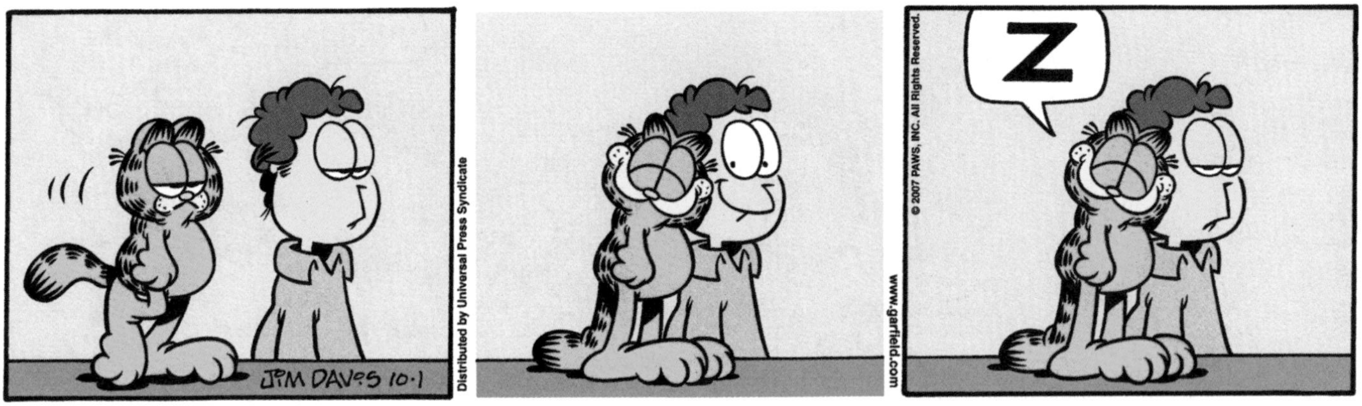
JPM DAVPS 10·1
Distributed by Universal Press Syndicate
www.garfield.com
© 2007 PAWS, INC. All Rights Reserved.
Z

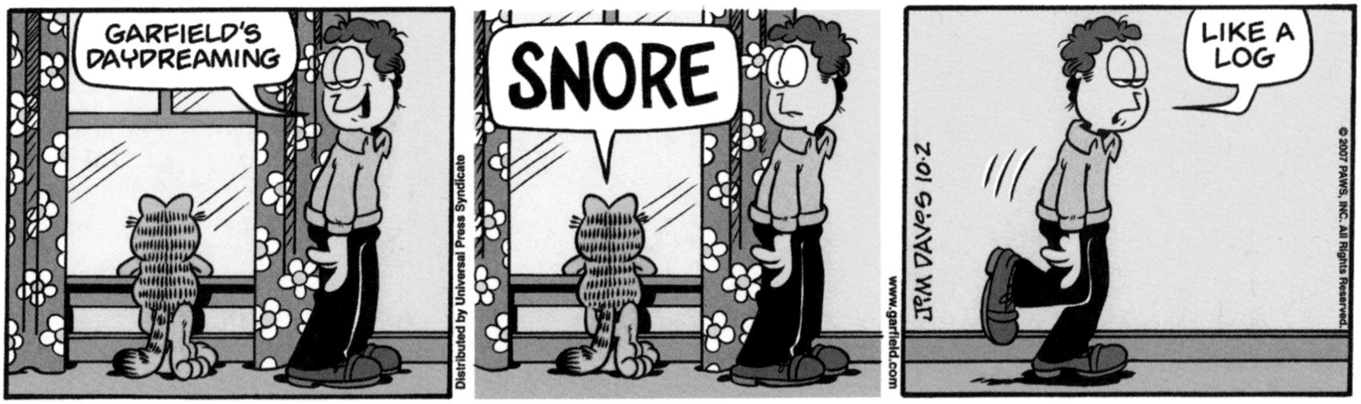
GARFIELD'S DAYDREAMING
Distributed by Universal Press Syndicate
SNORE
www.garfield.com
JPM DAVPS 10·2
LIKE A LOG
© 2007 PAWS, INC. All Rights Reserved.

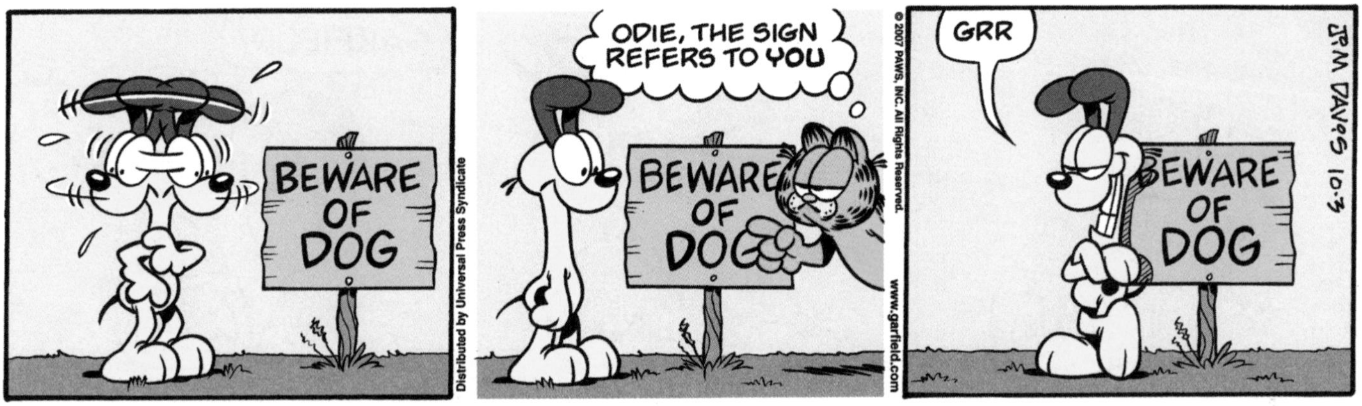
BEWARE OF DOG
Distributed by Universal Press Syndicate
ODIE, THE SIGN REFERS TO YOU
BEWARE OF DOG
© 2007 PAWS, INC. All Rights Reserved.
www.garfield.com
GRR
BEWARE OF DOG
JPM DAVPS 10·3

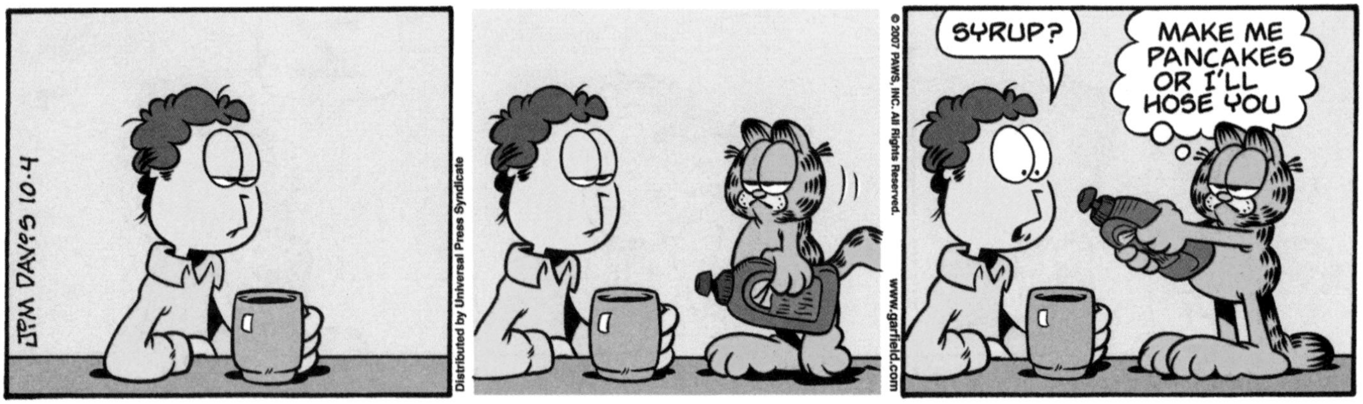
JIM DAVIS 10-4
Distributed by Universal Press Syndicate
© 2007 PAWS, INC. All Rights Reserved.
www.garfield.com
SYRUP?
MAKE ME PANCAKES OR I'LL HOSE YOU

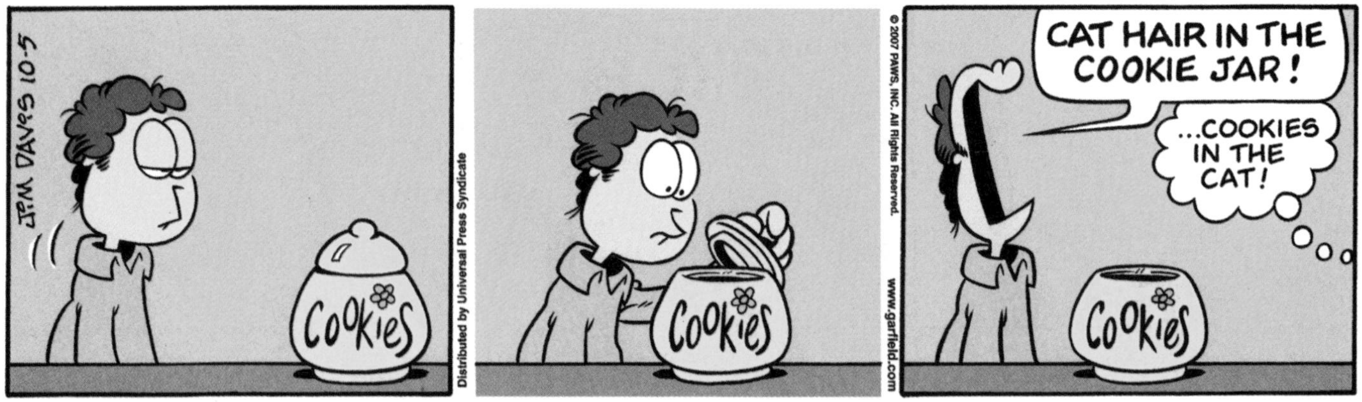
JIM DAVIS 10-5
COOKIES
Distributed by Universal Press Syndicate
COOKIES
© 2007 PAWS, INC. All Rights Reserved.
www.garfield.com
CAT HAIR IN THE COOKIE JAR!
...COOKIES IN THE CAT!
COOKIES

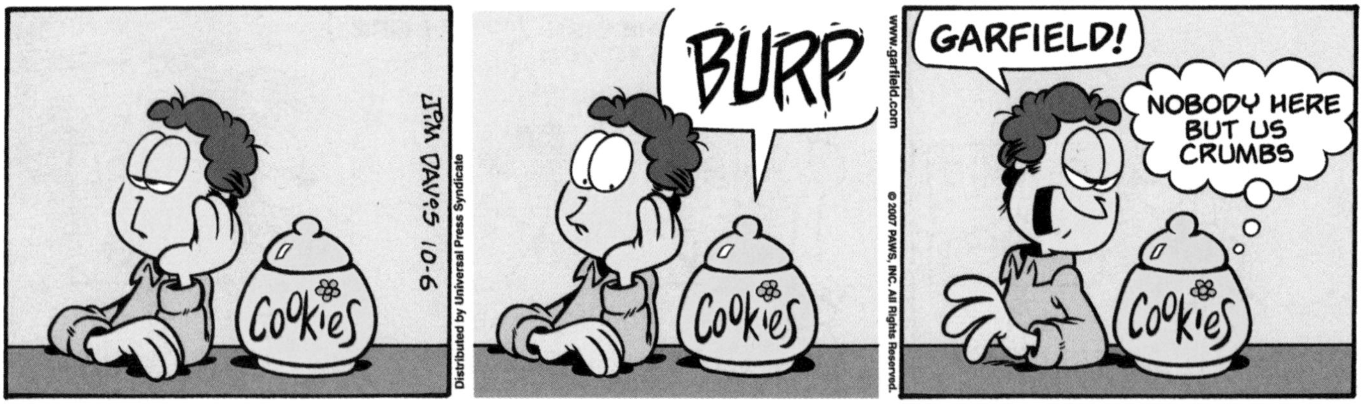
JIM DAVIS 10-6
COOKIES
Distributed by Universal Press Syndicate
BURP
COOKIES
www.garfield.com
© 2007 PAWS, INC. All Rights Reserved.
GARFIELD!
NOBODY HERE BUT US CRUMBS
COOKIES

GARFIELD®

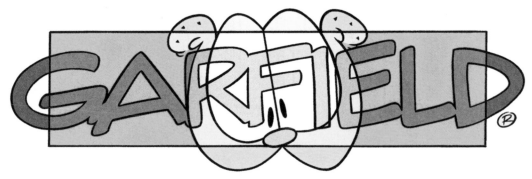

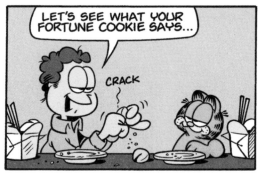

LET'S SEE WHAT YOUR FORTUNE COOKIE SAYS...
CRACK
© 2007 PAWS, INC. All Rights Reserved.
"YOU ARE KIND, LOVING, CREATIVE, AND ORIGINAL. GOOD THINGS ARE BEING SAID ABOUT YOU..."
"...SUNSHINE, HAPPINESS, GREAT SUCCESS, AND TRUE LOVE ALL AWAIT YOU IN THE NEAR FUTURE..."
"...YOU ARE WONDERFUL BEYOND MEASURE, AND EVERYONE TREASURES YOU DEARLY"
KIND OF FLOWERY, BUT NOT BAD. NOW LET'S SEE WHAT MINE SAYS...
CRACK
JPM DAVIS 10-7
Distributed by Universal Press Syndicate
"IT STINKS TO BE YOU"
I LIKE MINE BETTER

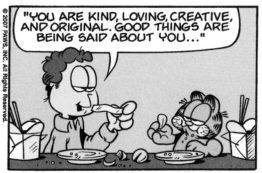

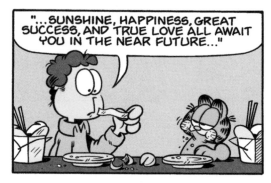

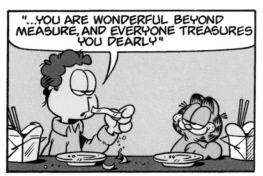

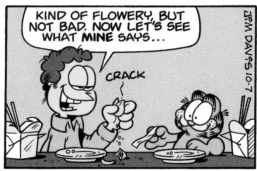

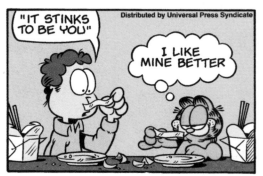

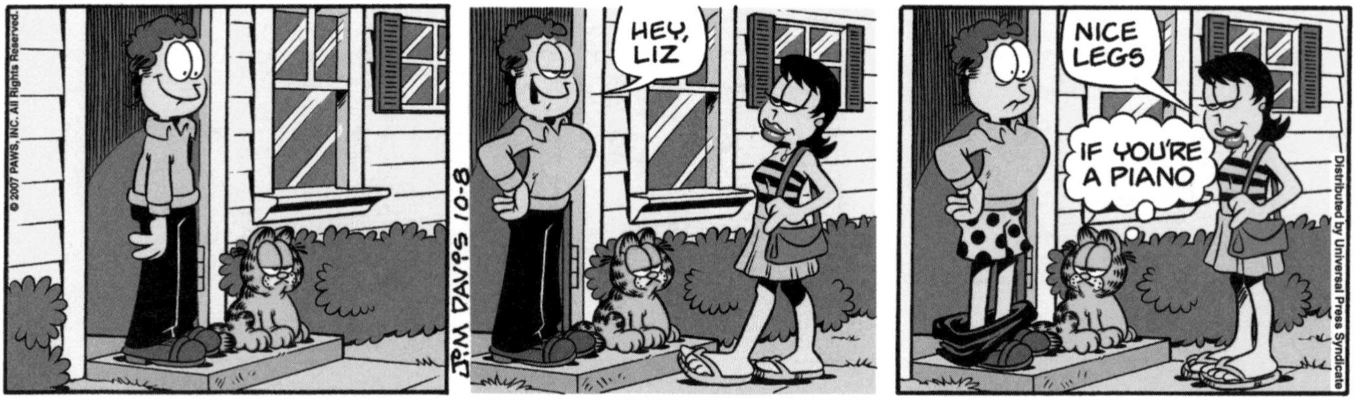
© 2007 PAWS, INC. All Rights Reserved.
HEY, LIZ
JIM DAVIS 10-8
NICE LEGS
IF YOU'RE A PIANO
Distributed by Universal Press Syndicate

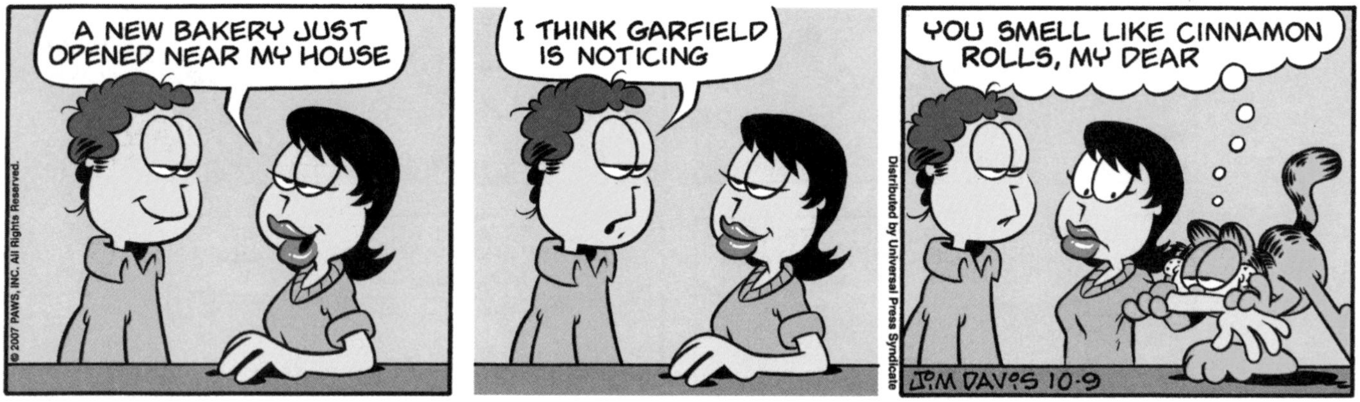
© 2007 PAWS, INC. All Rights Reserved.
A NEW BAKERY JUST OPENED NEAR MY HOUSE
I THINK GARFIELD IS NOTICING
Distributed by Universal Press Syndicate
YOU SMELL LIKE CINNAMON ROLLS, MY DEAR
JIM DAVIS 10-9

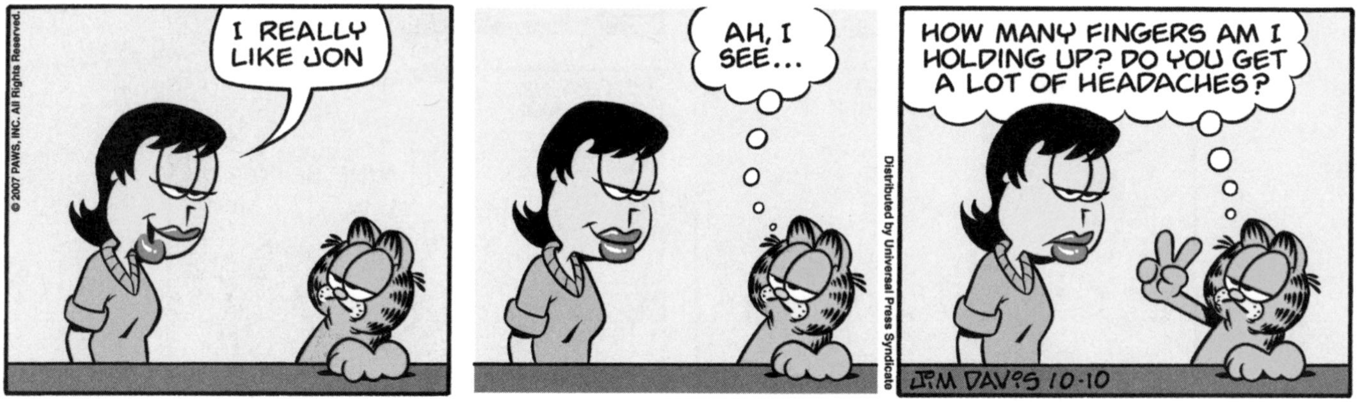
© 2007 PAWS, INC. All Rights Reserved.
I REALLY LIKE JON
AH, I SEE...
Distributed by Universal Press Syndicate
HOW MANY FINGERS AM I HOLDING UP? DO YOU GET A LOT OF HEADACHES?
JIM DAVIS 10-10

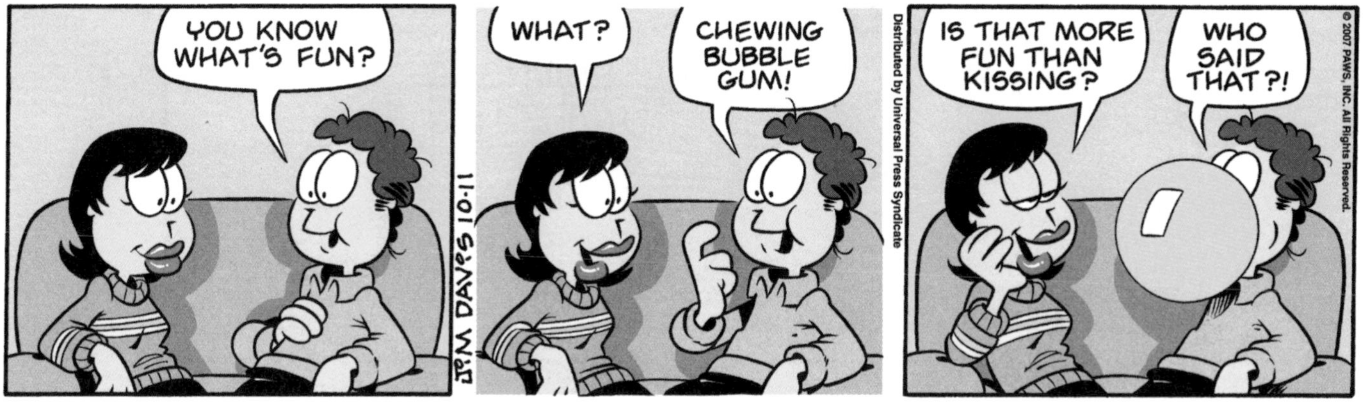
YOU KNOW WHAT'S FUN?
WHAT?
CHEWING BUBBLE GUM!
IS THAT MORE FUN THAN KISSING?
WHO SAID THAT?!
JIM DAVIS 10-11
Distributed by Universal Press Syndicate
© 2007 PAWS, INC. All Rights Reserved.

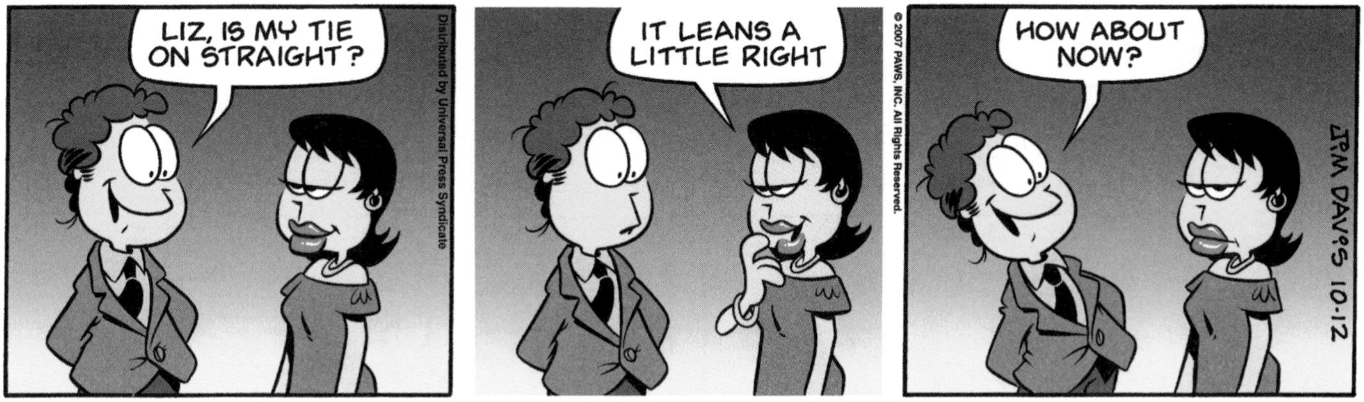
LIZ, IS MY TIE ON STRAIGHT?
IT LEANS A LITTLE RIGHT
HOW ABOUT NOW?
JIM DAVIS 10-12
Distributed by Universal Press Syndicate
© 2007 PAWS, INC. All Rights Reserved.

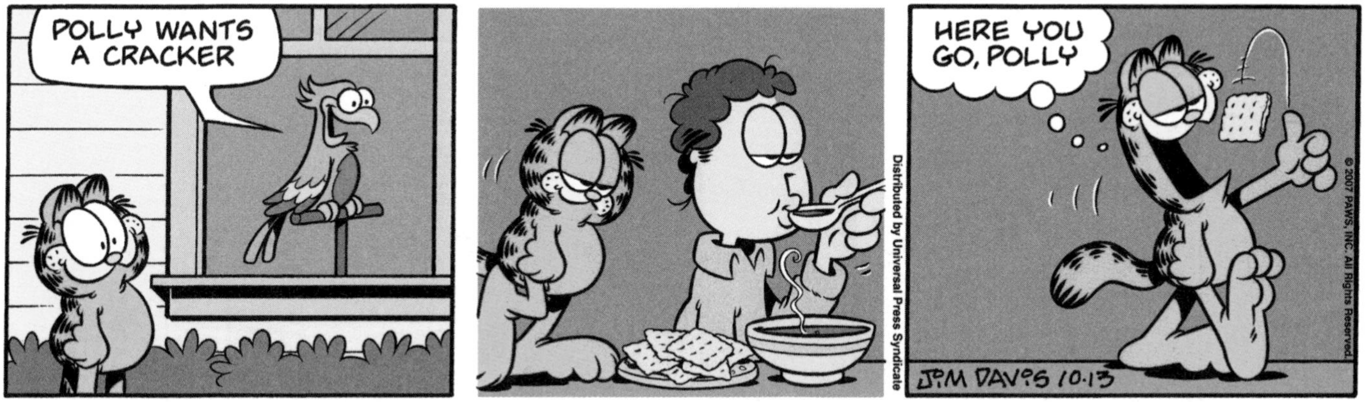
POLLY WANTS A CRACKER
HERE YOU GO, POLLY
JIM DAVIS 10-13
Distributed by Universal Press Syndicate
© 2007 PAWS, INC. All Rights Reserved.

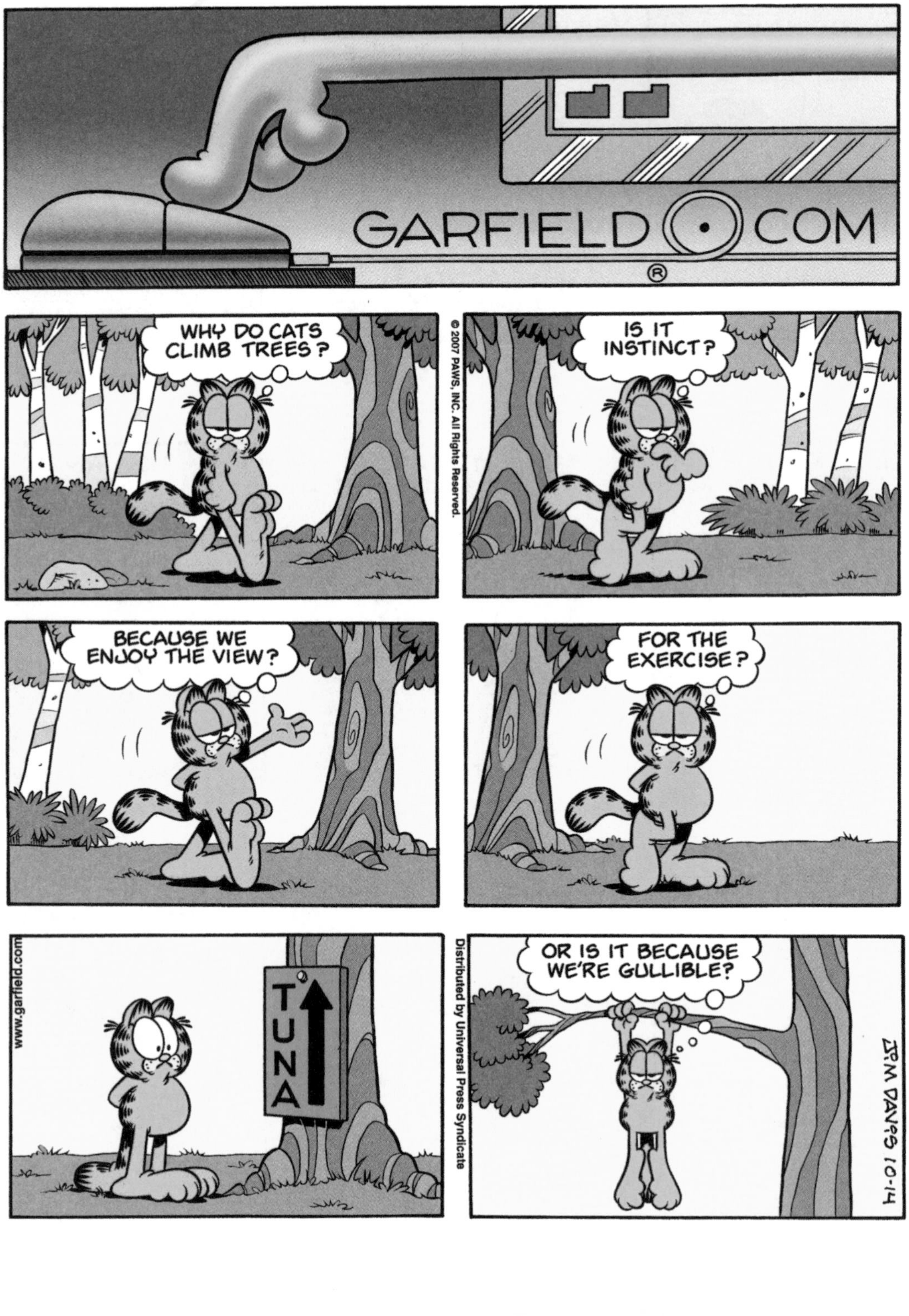
GARFIELD.COM
©
© 2007 PAWS, INC. All Rights Reserved.
WHY DO CATS CLIMB TREES?
IS IT INSTINCT?
BECAUSE WE ENJOY THE VIEW?
FOR THE EXERCISE?
www.garfield.com
TUNA
Distributed by Universal Press Syndicate
OR IS IT BECAUSE WE'RE GULLIBLE?
JPM DAVIS 10-14

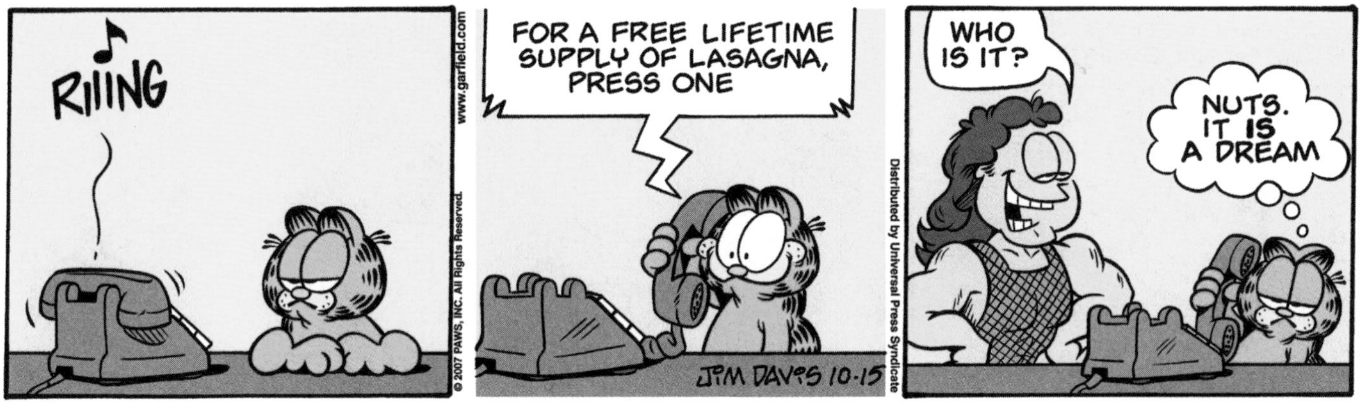
RIIING
FOR A FREE LIFETIME SUPPLY OF LASAGNA, PRESS ONE
JIM DAVIS 10-15
WHO IS IT?
NUTS. IT IS A DREAM
© 2007 PAWS, INC. All Rights Reserved. www.garfield.com
Distributed by Universal Press Syndicate

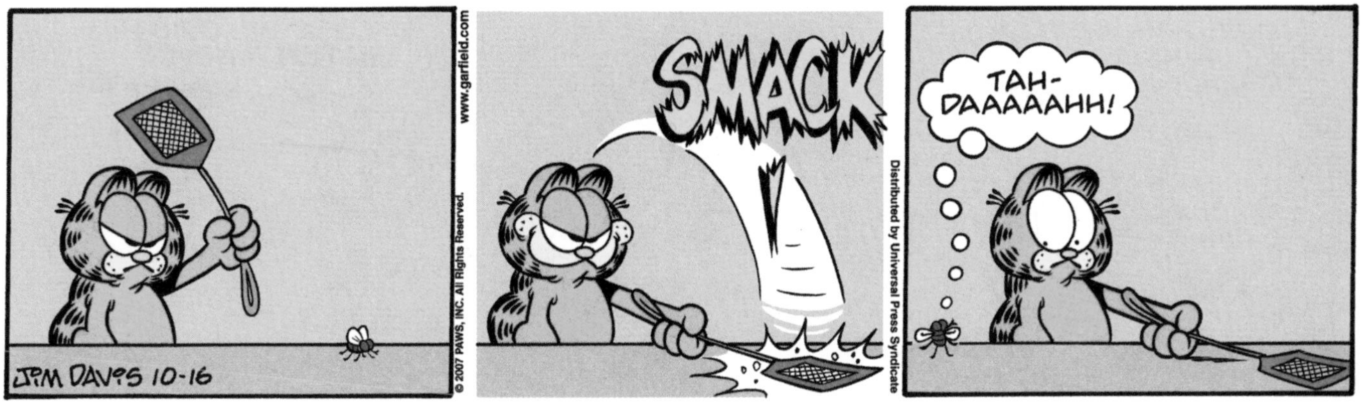
JIM DAVIS 10-16
SMACK
TAH-DAAAAAHH!
© 2007 PAWS, INC. All Rights Reserved. www.garfield.com
Distributed by Universal Press Syndicate

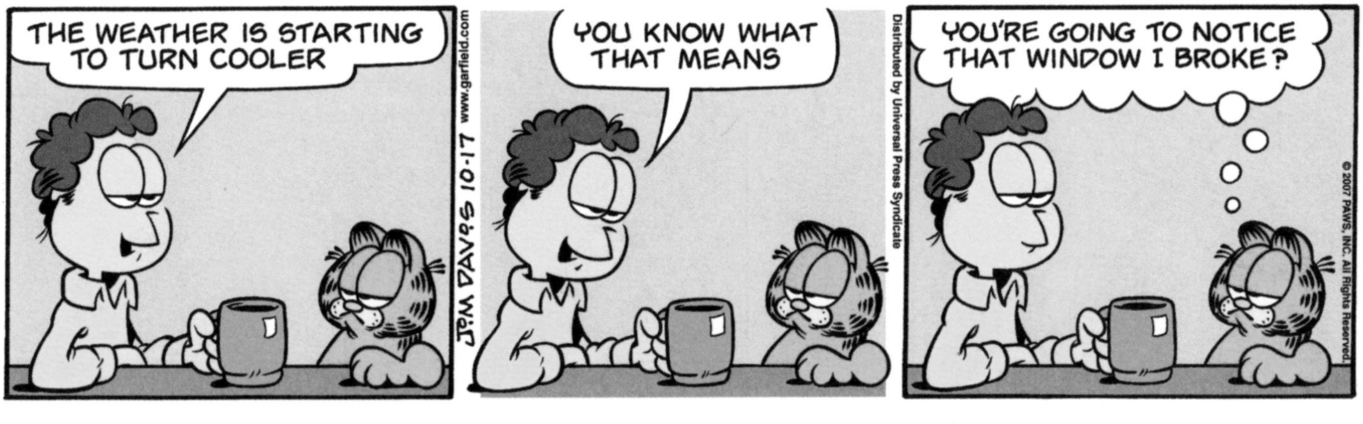
THE WEATHER IS STARTING TO TURN COOLER
JIM DAVIS 10-17
YOU KNOW WHAT THAT MEANS
YOU'RE GOING TO NOTICE THAT WINDOW I BROKE?
www.garfield.com
Distributed by Universal Press Syndicate
© 2007 PAWS, INC. All Rights Reserved.

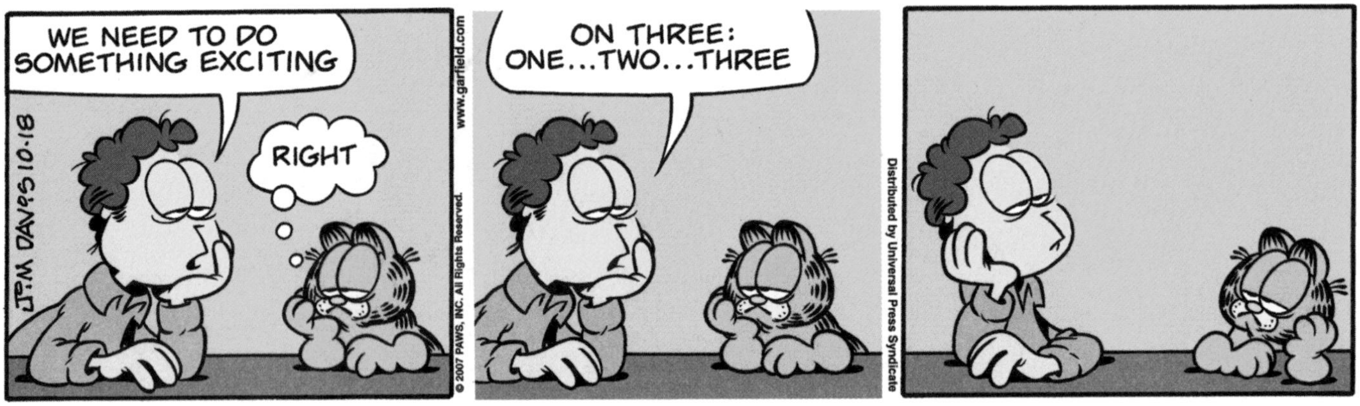
WE NEED TO DO SOMETHING EXCITING
RIGHT
JIM DAVIS 10-18
© 2007 PAWS, INC. All Rights Reserved. www.garfield.com
ON THREE: ONE...TWO...THREE
Distributed by Universal Press Syndicate

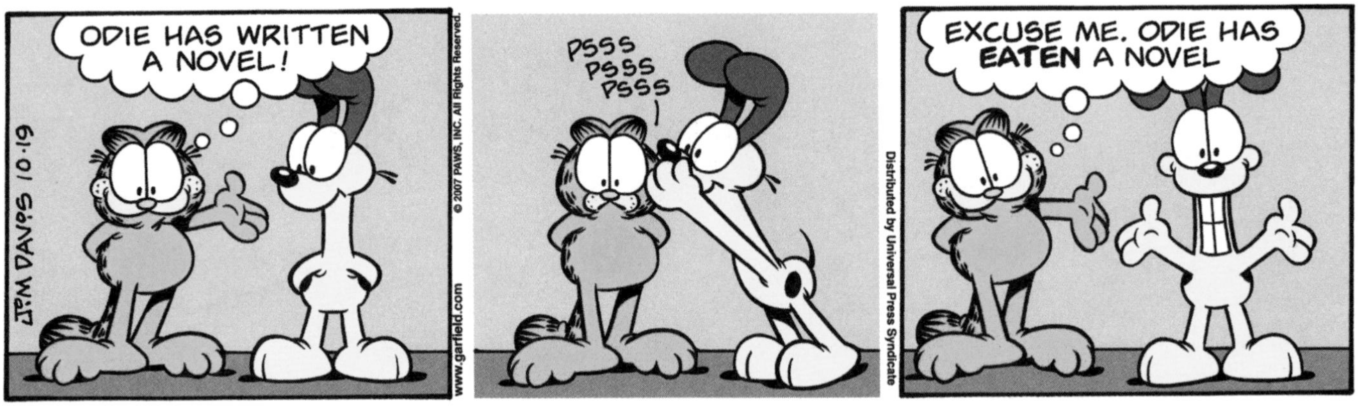
ODIE HAS WRITTEN A NOVEL!
JIM DAVIS 10-19
© 2007 PAWS, INC. All Rights Reserved. www.garfield.com
PSSS PSSS PSSS
EXCUSE ME. ODIE HAS EATEN A NOVEL
Distributed by Universal Press Syndicate

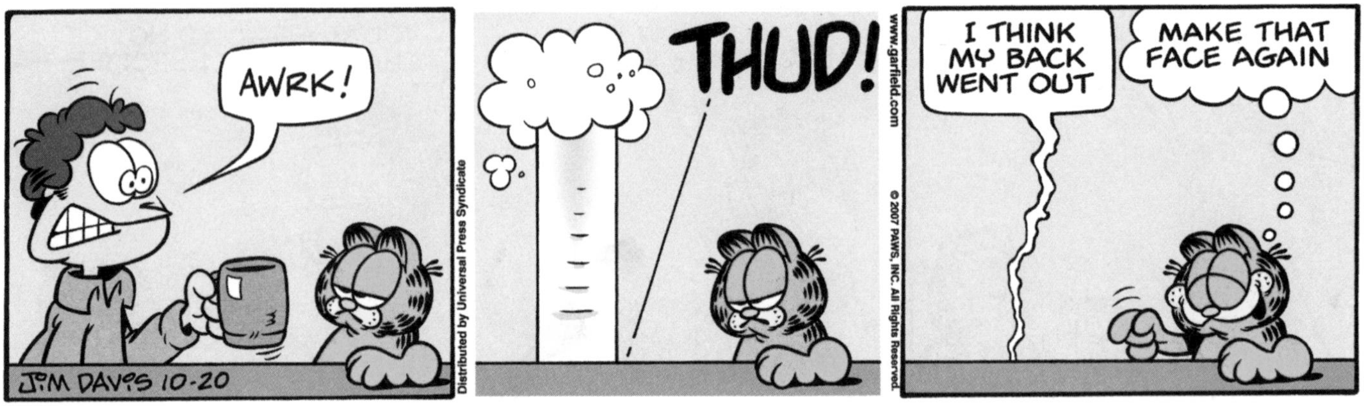
AWRK!
JIM DAVIS 10-20
Distributed by Universal Press Syndicate
THUD!
www.garfield.com © 2007 PAWS, INC. All Rights Reserved.
I THINK MY BACK WENT OUT
MAKE THAT FACE AGAIN

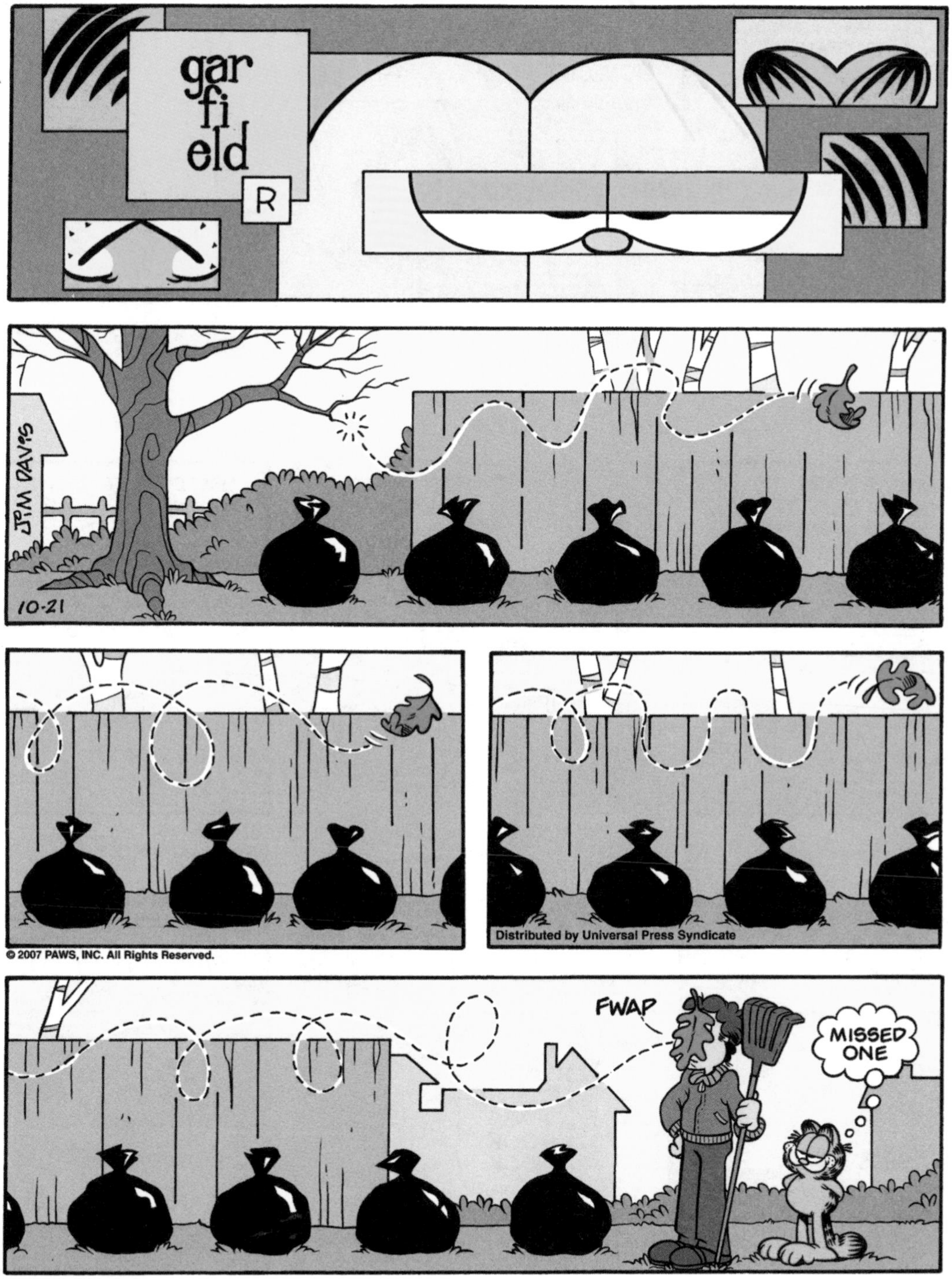
garfield
R
JIM DAVIS
10-21
© 2007 PAWS, INC. All Rights Reserved.
Distributed by Universal Press Syndicate
FWAP
MISSED ONE

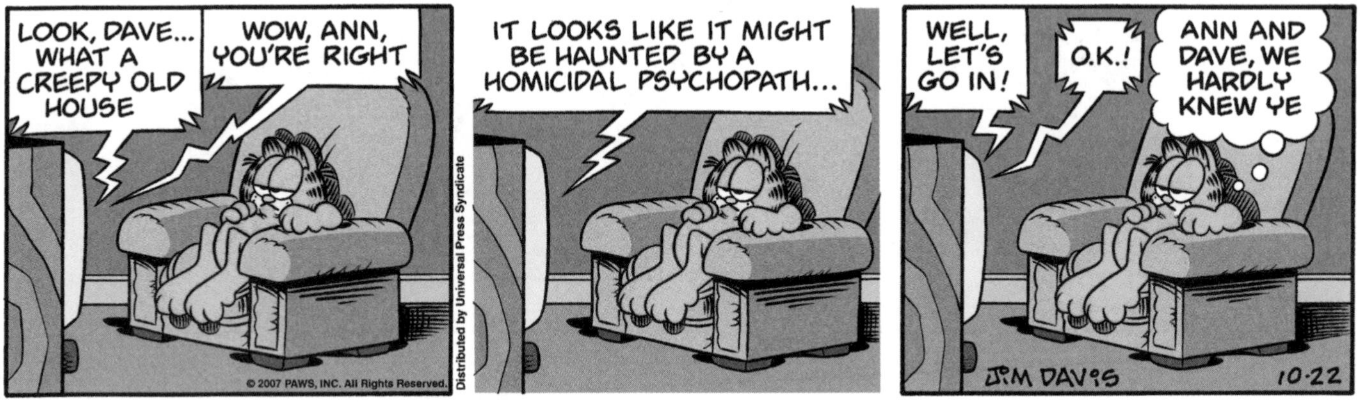
LOOK, DAVE... WHAT A CREEPY OLD HOUSE
WOW, ANN, YOU'RE RIGHT
© 2007 PAWS, INC. All Rights Reserved.
Distributed by Universal Press Syndicate
IT LOOKS LIKE IT MIGHT BE HAUNTED BY A HOMICIDAL PSYCHOPATH...
WELL, LET'S GO IN!
O.K.!
ANN AND DAVE, WE HARDLY KNEW YE
JIM DAVIS 10·22

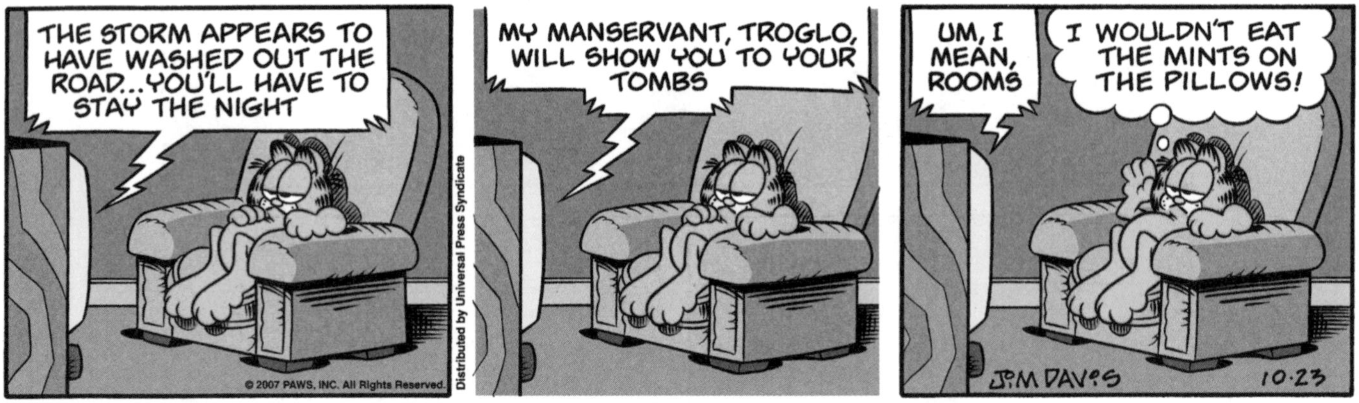
THE STORM APPEARS TO HAVE WASHED OUT THE ROAD...YOU'LL HAVE TO STAY THE NIGHT
© 2007 PAWS, INC. All Rights Reserved.
Distributed by Universal Press Syndicate
MY MANSERVANT, TROGLO, WILL SHOW YOU TO YOUR TOMBS
UM, I MEAN, ROOMS
I WOULDN'T EAT THE MINTS ON THE PILLOWS!
JIM DAVIS 10·23

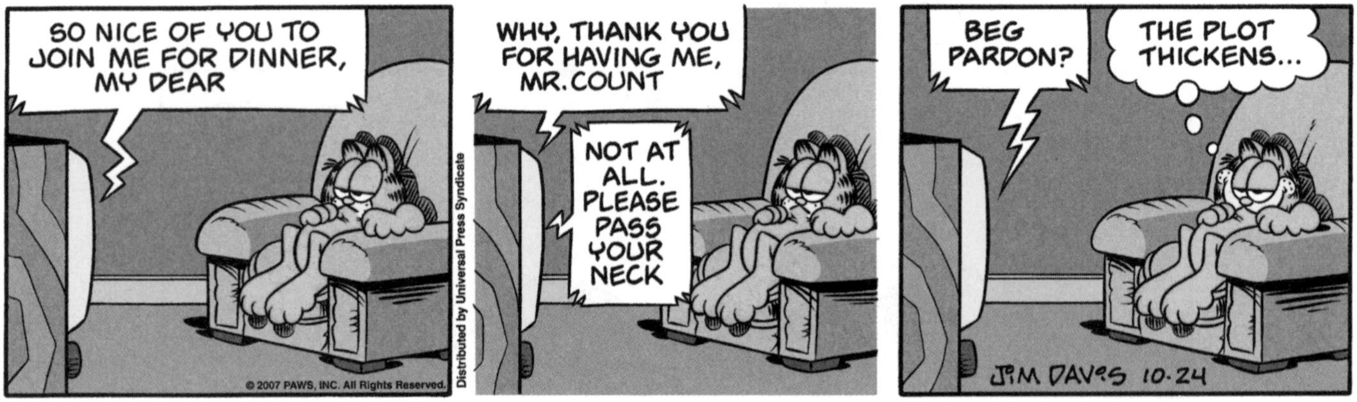
SO NICE OF YOU TO JOIN ME FOR DINNER, MY DEAR
© 2007 PAWS, INC. All Rights Reserved.
Distributed by Universal Press Syndicate
WHY, THANK YOU FOR HAVING ME, MR.COUNT
NOT AT ALL. PLEASE PASS YOUR NECK
BEG PARDON?
THE PLOT THICKENS...
JIM DAVIS 10·24

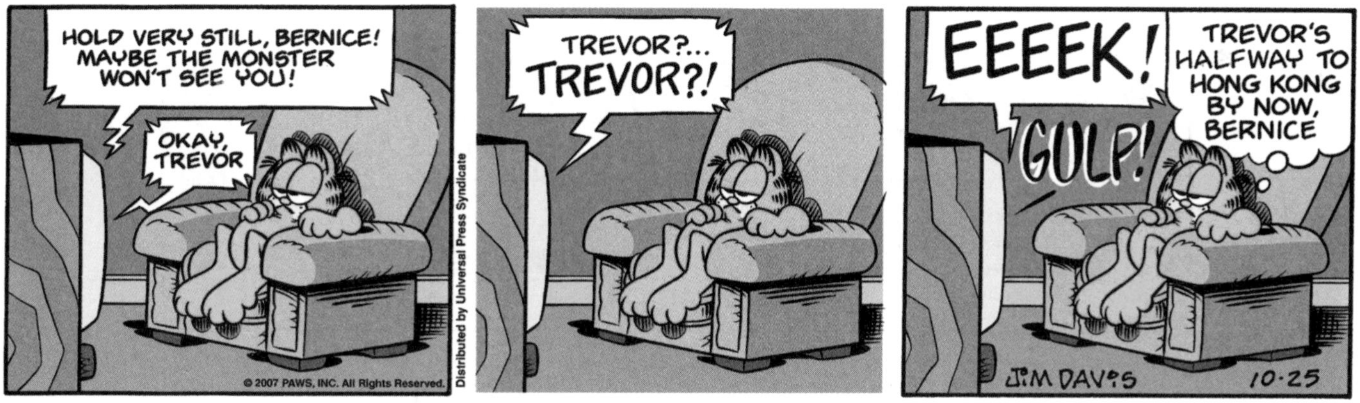
HOLD VERY STILL, BERNICE! MAYBE THE MONSTER WON'T SEE YOU!
OKAY, TREVOR
© 2007 PAWS, INC. All Rights Reserved.
Distributed by Universal Press Syndicate
TREVOR?... TREVOR?!
EEEEK!
GULP!
TREVOR'S HALFWAY TO HONG KONG BY NOW, BERNICE
JIM DAVIS
10-25

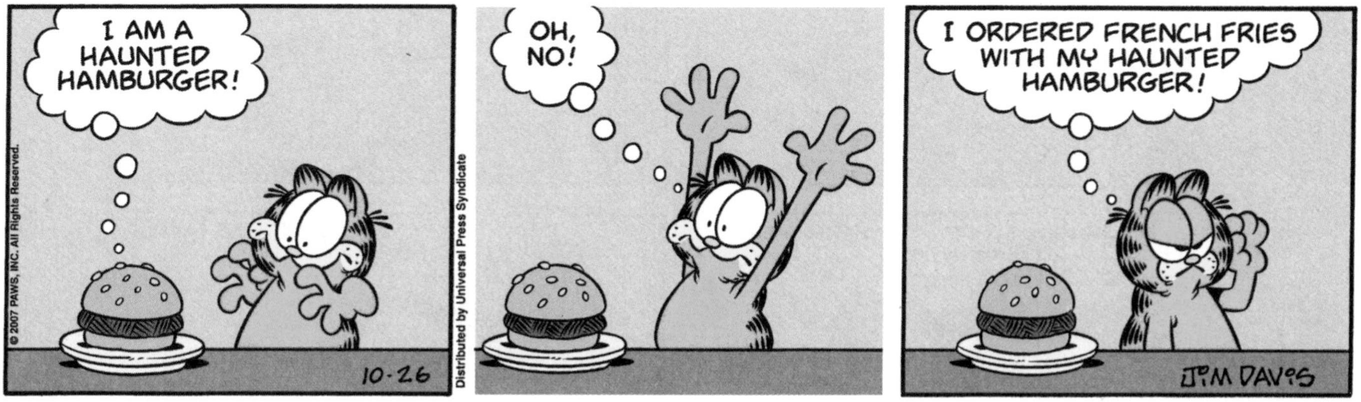
I AM A HAUNTED HAMBURGER!
© 2007 PAWS, INC. All Rights Reserved.
10-26
Distributed by Universal Press Syndicate
OH, NO!
I ORDERED FRENCH FRIES WITH MY HAUNTED HAMBURGER!
JIM DAVIS

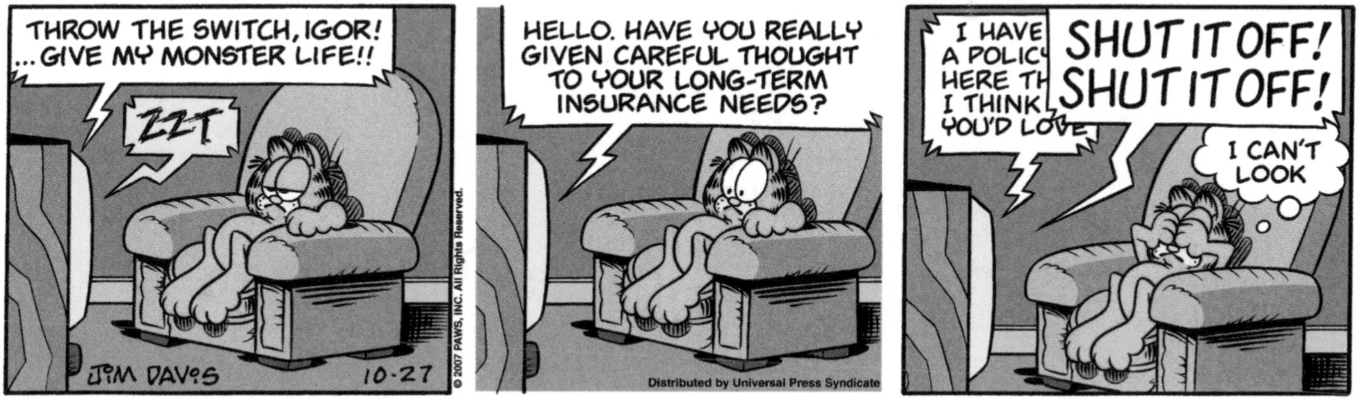
THROW THE SWITCH, IGOR! ...GIVE MY MONSTER LIFE!!
ZZT
JIM DAVIS
10-27
© 2007 PAWS, INC. All Rights Reserved.
HELLO. HAVE YOU REALLY GIVEN CAREFUL THOUGHT TO YOUR LONG-TERM INSURANCE NEEDS?
Distributed by Universal Press Syndicate
I HAVE A POLIC HERE TH I THINK YOU'D LOVE
SHUT IT OFF! SHUT IT OFF!
I CAN'T LOOK

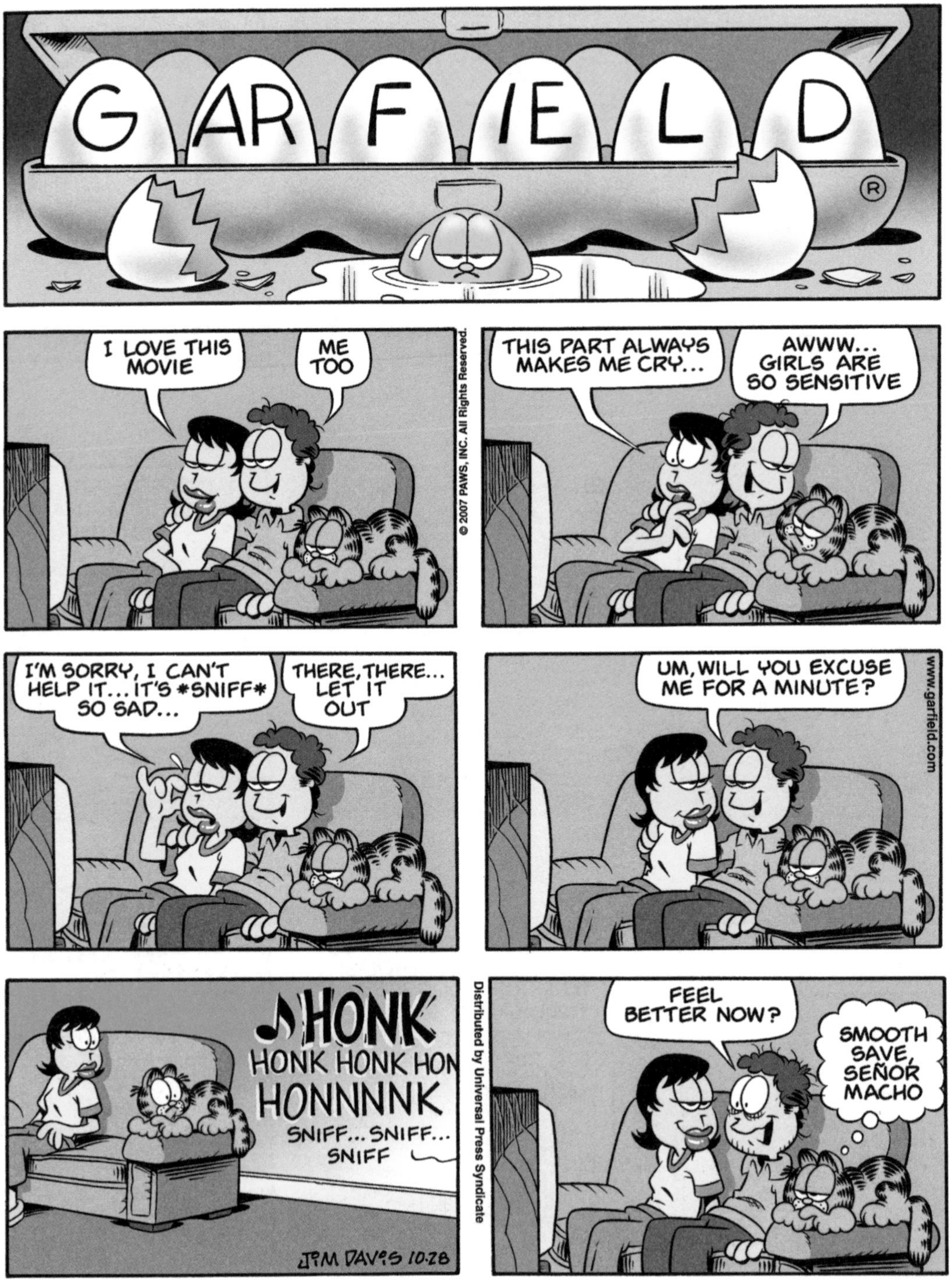
GARFIELD
I LOVE THIS MOVIE
ME TOO
© 2007 PAWS, INC. All Rights Reserved.
THIS PART ALWAYS MAKES ME CRY...
AWWW... GIRLS ARE SO SENSITIVE
I'M SORRY, I CAN'T HELP IT... IT'S *SNIFF* SO SAD...
THERE, THERE... LET IT OUT
UM, WILL YOU EXCUSE ME FOR A MINUTE?
www.garfield.com
HONK
HONK HONK HON
HONNNNK
SNIFF... SNIFF... SNIFF
JIM DAVIS 10-28
Distributed by Universal Press Syndicate
FEEL BETTER NOW?
SMOOTH SAVE, SEÑOR MACHO

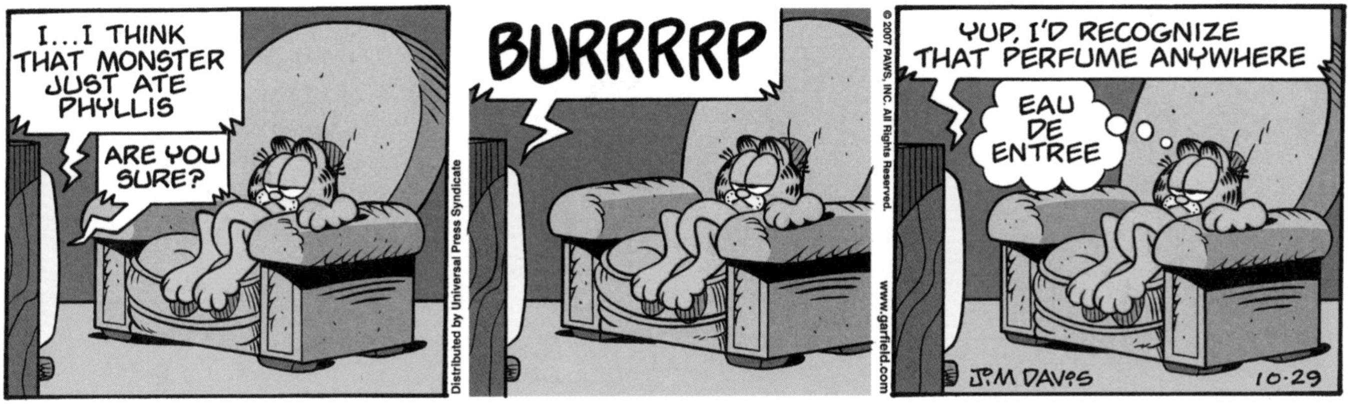
I...I THINK THAT MONSTER JUST ATE PHYLLIS
ARE YOU SURE?
BURRRRP
YUP, I'D RECOGNIZE THAT PERFUME ANYWHERE
EAU DE ENTREE
JIM DAVIS 10-29
Distributed by Universal Press Syndicate
© 2007 PAWS, INC. All Rights Reserved.
www.garfield.com

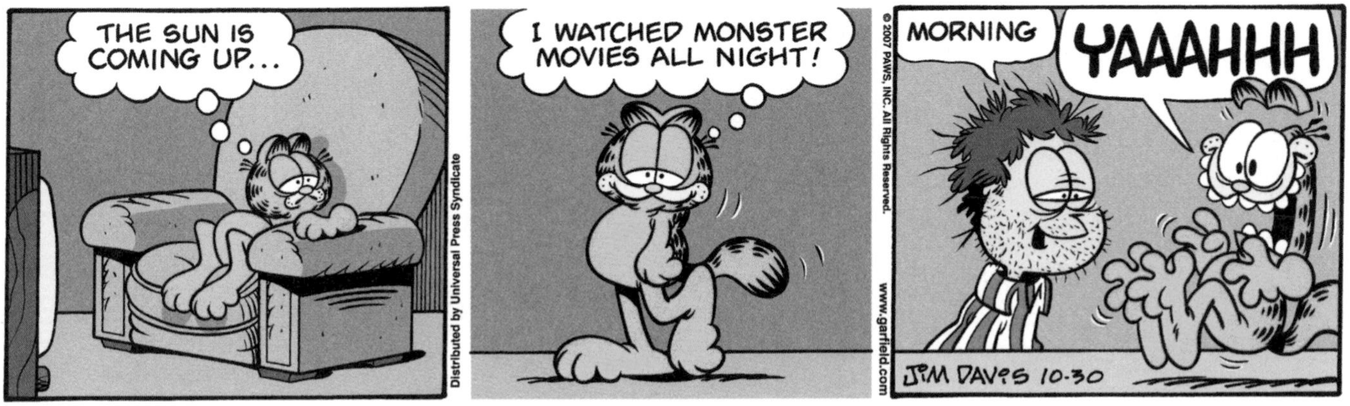
THE SUN IS COMING UP...
I WATCHED MONSTER MOVIES ALL NIGHT!
MORNING
YAAAHHH
JIM DAVIS 10-30
Distributed by Universal Press Syndicate
© 2007 PAWS, INC. All Rights Reserved.
www.garfield.com

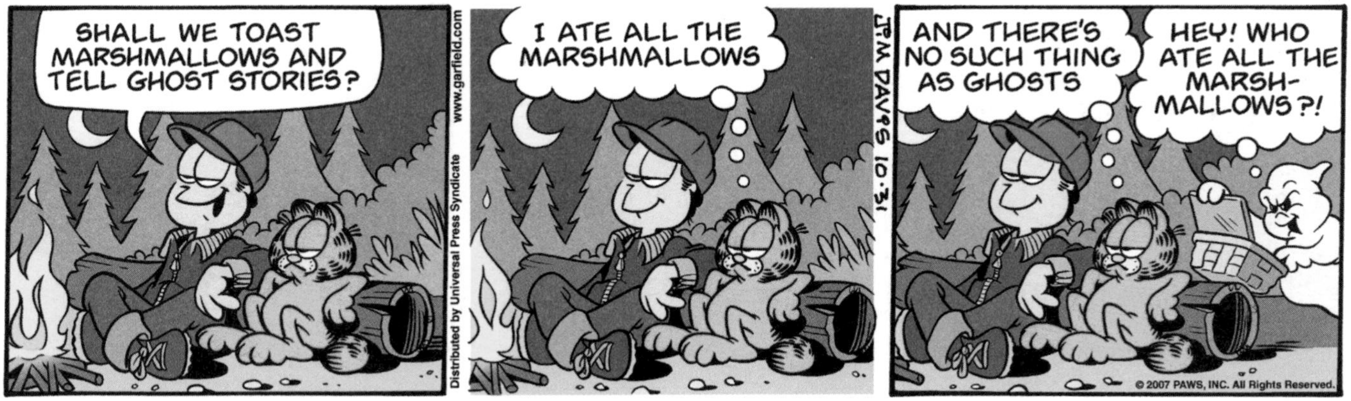
SHALL WE TOAST MARSHMALLOWS AND TELL GHOST STORIES?
I ATE ALL THE MARSHMALLOWS
AND THERE'S NO SUCH THING AS GHOSTS
HEY! WHO ATE ALL THE MARSH-MALLOWS?!
JIM DAVIS 10-31
www.garfield.com
Distributed by Universal Press Syndicate
© 2007 PAWS, INC. All Rights Reserved.

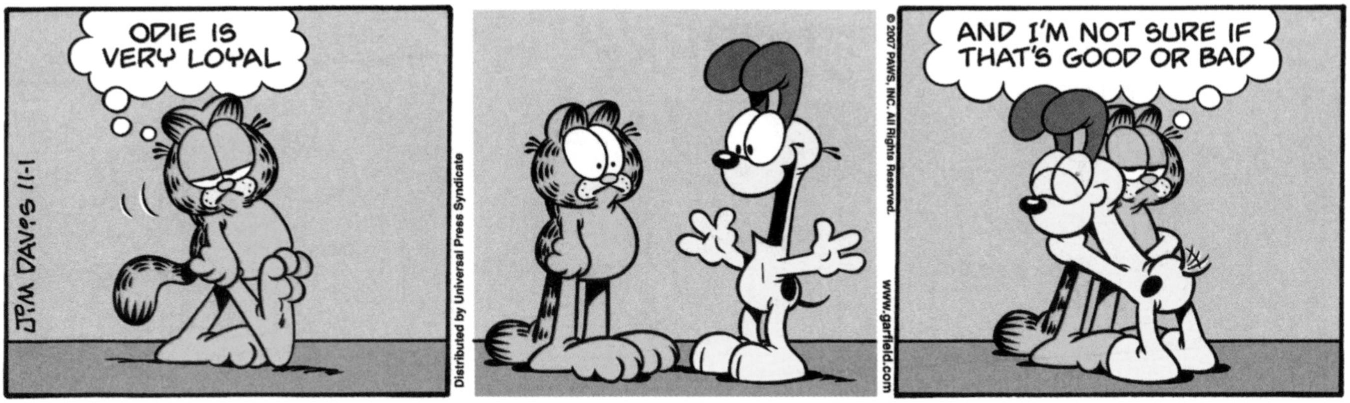
ODIE IS VERY LOYAL
JIM DAVIS 11-1
Distributed by Universal Press Syndicate
© 2007 PAWS, INC. All Rights Reserved.
www.garfield.com
AND I'M NOT SURE IF THAT'S GOOD OR BAD

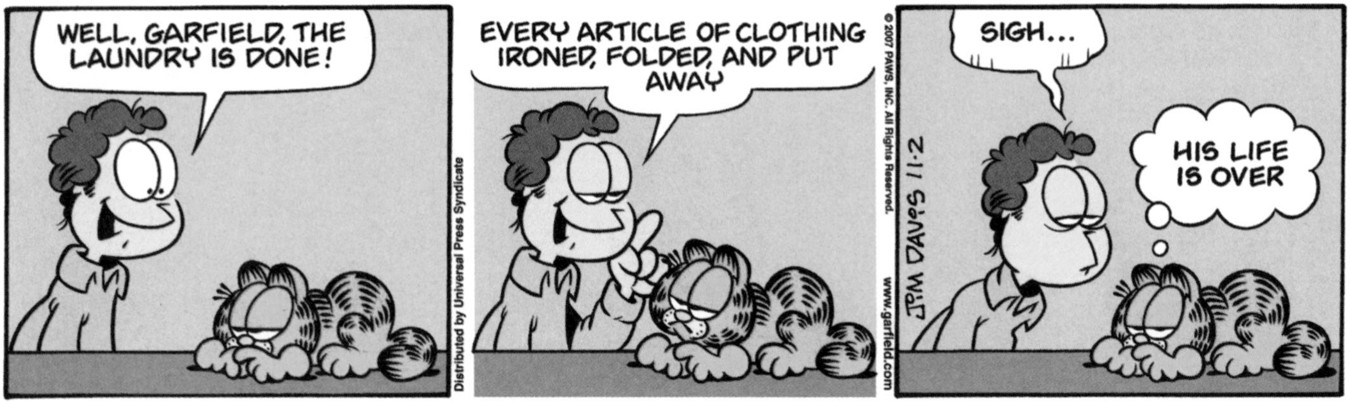
WELL, GARFIELD, THE LAUNDRY IS DONE!
Distributed by Universal Press Syndicate
EVERY ARTICLE OF CLOTHING IRONED, FOLDED, AND PUT AWAY
© 2007 PAWS, INC. All Rights Reserved.
www.garfield.com
JIM DAVIS 11-2
SIGH...
HIS LIFE IS OVER

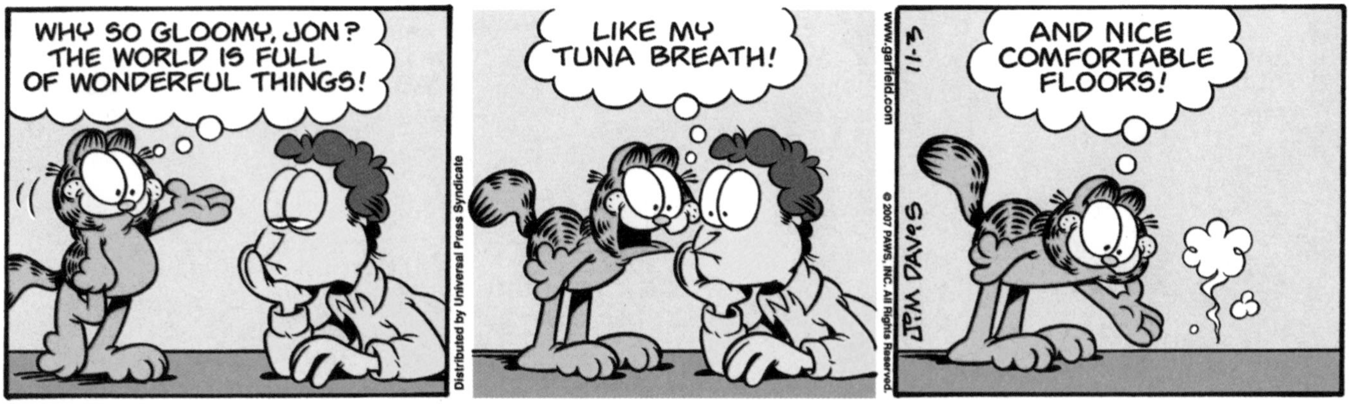
WHY SO GLOOMY, JON? THE WORLD IS FULL OF WONDERFUL THINGS!
Distributed by Universal Press Syndicate
LIKE MY TUNA BREATH!
www.garfield.com
11-3
JIM DAVIS
© 2007 PAWS, INC. All Rights Reserved.
AND NICE COMFORTABLE FLOORS!

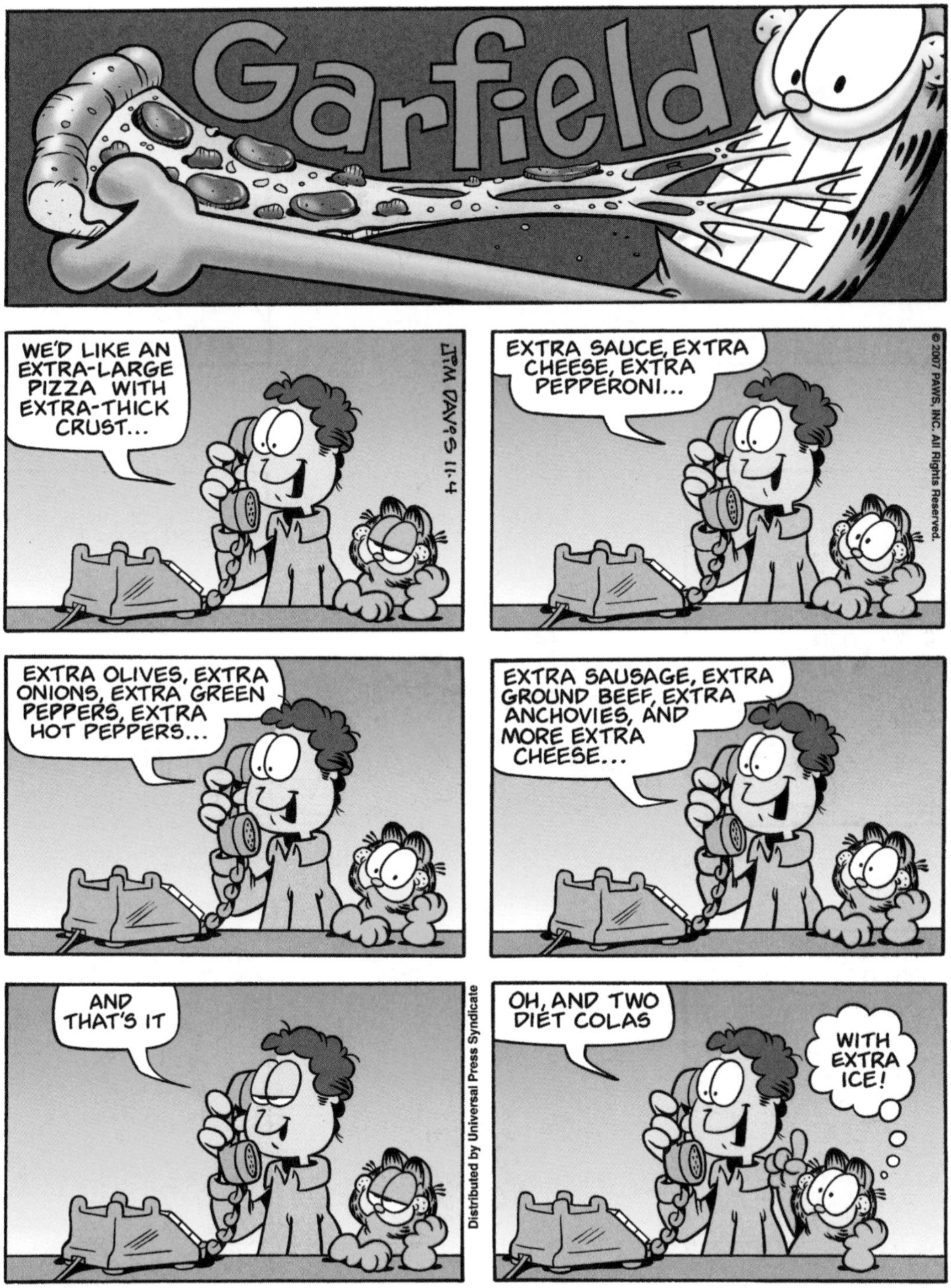
Garfield
JIM DAVIS 11-4
© 2007 PAWS, INC. All Rights Reserved.
WE'D LIKE AN EXTRA-LARGE PIZZA WITH EXTRA-THICK CRUST...
EXTRA SAUCE, EXTRA CHEESE, EXTRA PEPPERONI...
EXTRA OLIVES, EXTRA ONIONS, EXTRA GREEN PEPPERS, EXTRA HOT PEPPERS...
EXTRA SAUSAGE, EXTRA GROUND BEEF, EXTRA ANCHOVIES, AND MORE EXTRA CHEESE...
AND THAT'S IT
Distributed by Universal Press Syndicate
OH, AND TWO DIET COLAS
WITH EXTRA ICE!

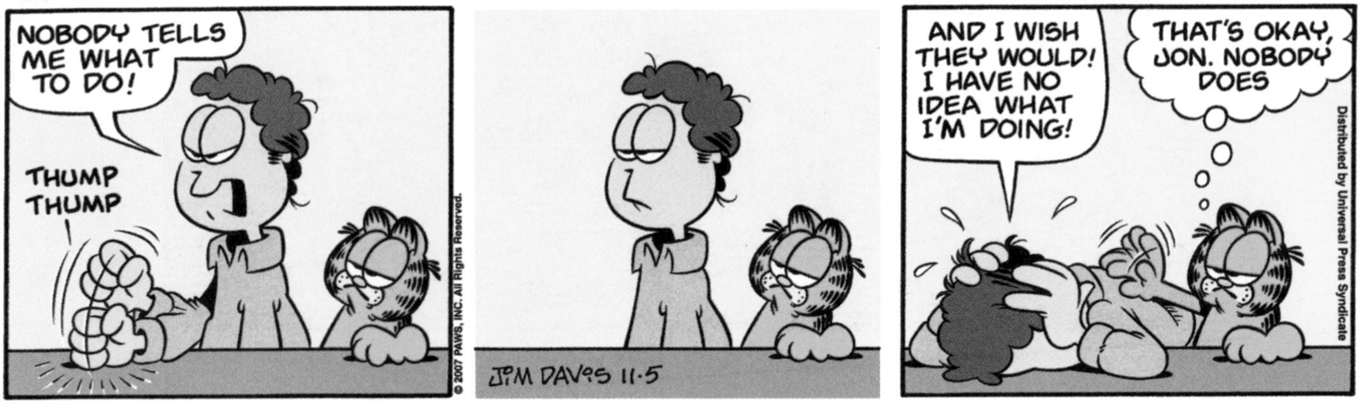
NOBODY TELLS ME WHAT TO DO!
THUMP THUMP
© 2007 PAWS, INC. All Rights Reserved.
JIM DAVIS 11-5
AND I WISH THEY WOULD! I HAVE NO IDEA WHAT I'M DOING!
THAT'S OKAY, JON. NOBODY DOES
Distributed by Universal Press Syndicate

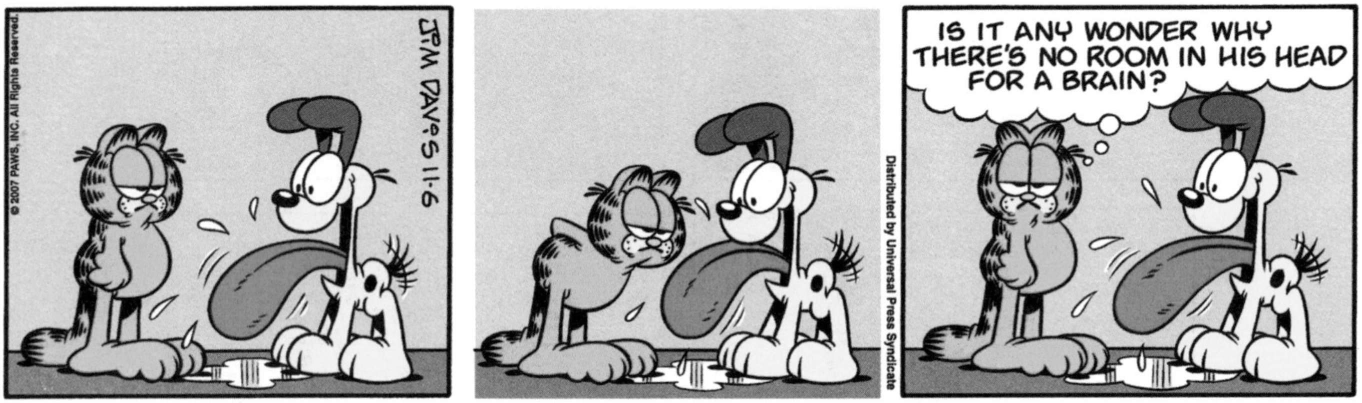
© 2007 PAWS, INC. All Rights Reserved.
JIM DAVIS 11-6
Distributed by Universal Press Syndicate
IS IT ANY WONDER WHY THERE'S NO ROOM IN HIS HEAD FOR A BRAIN?

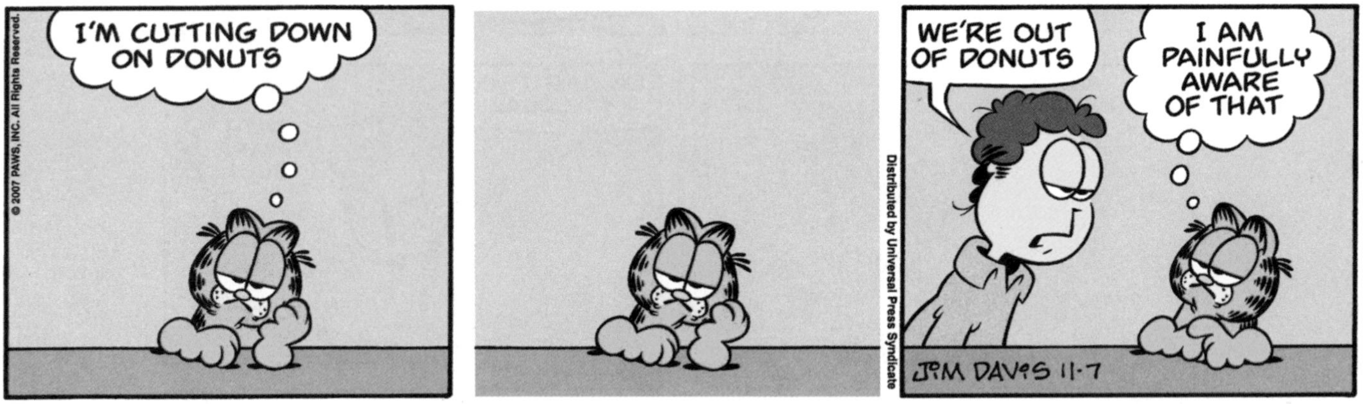
© 2007 PAWS, INC. All Rights Reserved.
I'M CUTTING DOWN ON DONUTS
Distributed by Universal Press Syndicate
WE'RE OUT OF DONUTS
I AM PAINFULLY AWARE OF THAT
JIM DAVIS 11-7

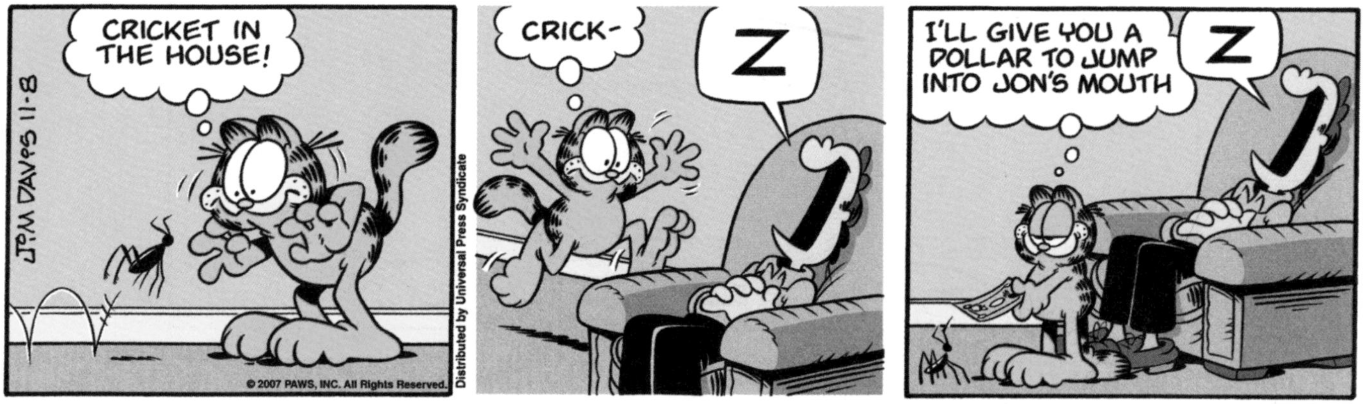
CRICKET IN THE HOUSE!
JPM DAVPS 11-8
© 2007 PAWS, INC. All Rights Reserved.
Distributed by Universal Press Syndicate
CRICK-
Z
I'LL GIVE YOU A DOLLAR TO JUMP INTO JON'S MOUTH
Z

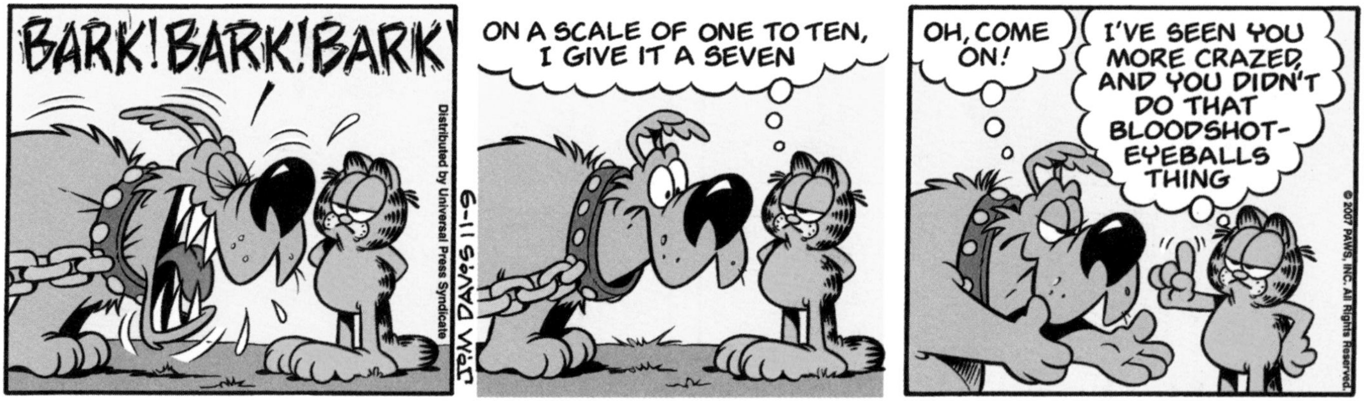
BARK! BARK! BARK!
Distributed by Universal Press Syndicate
JPM DAVPS 11-9
ON A SCALE OF ONE TO TEN, I GIVE IT A SEVEN
OH, COME ON!
I'VE SEEN YOU MORE CRAZED, AND YOU DIDN'T DO THAT BLOODSHOT-EYEBALLS THING
© 2007 PAWS, INC. All Rights Reserved.

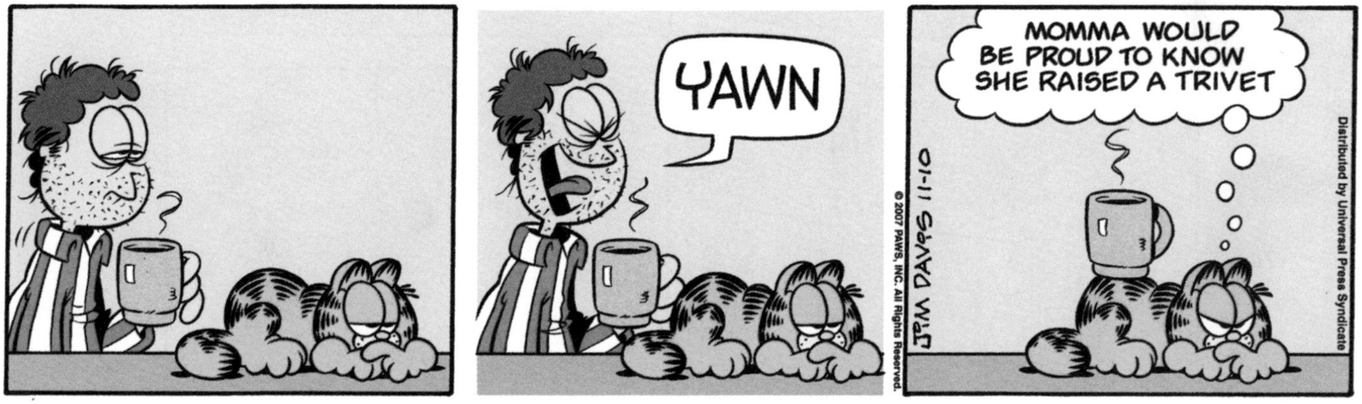
YAWN
JPM DAVPS 11-10
© 2007 PAWS, INC. All Rights Reserved.
MOMMA WOULD BE PROUD TO KNOW SHE RAISED A TRIVET
Distributed by Universal Press Syndicate

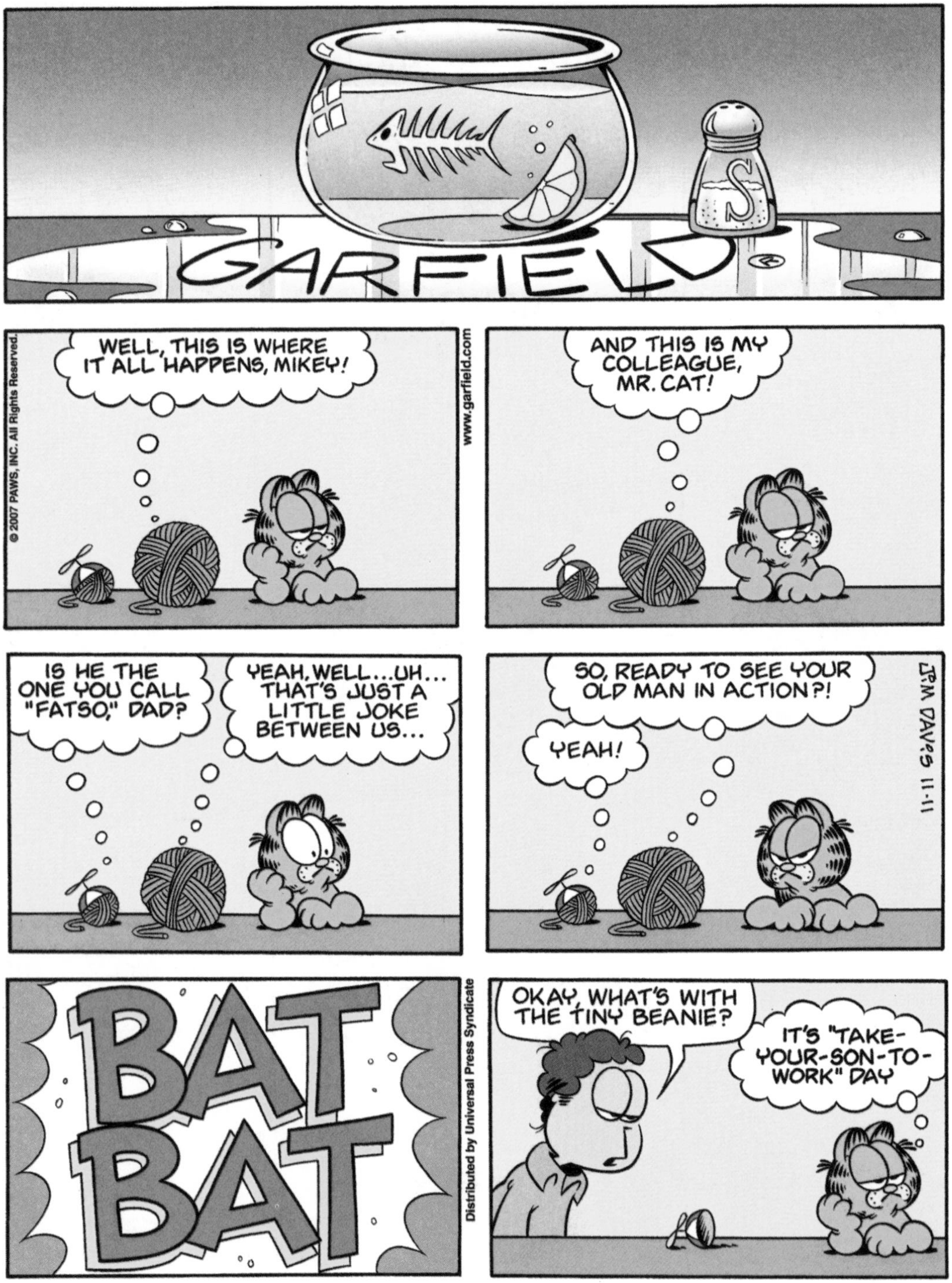
GARFIELD®
© 2007 PAWS, INC. All Rights Reserved.
www.garfield.com
WELL, THIS IS WHERE IT ALL HAPPENS, MIKEY!
AND THIS IS MY COLLEAGUE, MR. CAT!
IS HE THE ONE YOU CALL "FATSO," DAD?
YEAH, WELL...UH... THAT'S JUST A LITTLE JOKE BETWEEN US...
SO, READY TO SEE YOUR OLD MAN IN ACTION?!
YEAH!
JPM DAVIS 11-11
BAT BAT
Distributed by Universal Press Syndicate
OKAY, WHAT'S WITH THE TINY BEANIE?
IT'S "TAKE-YOUR-SON-TO-WORK" DAY

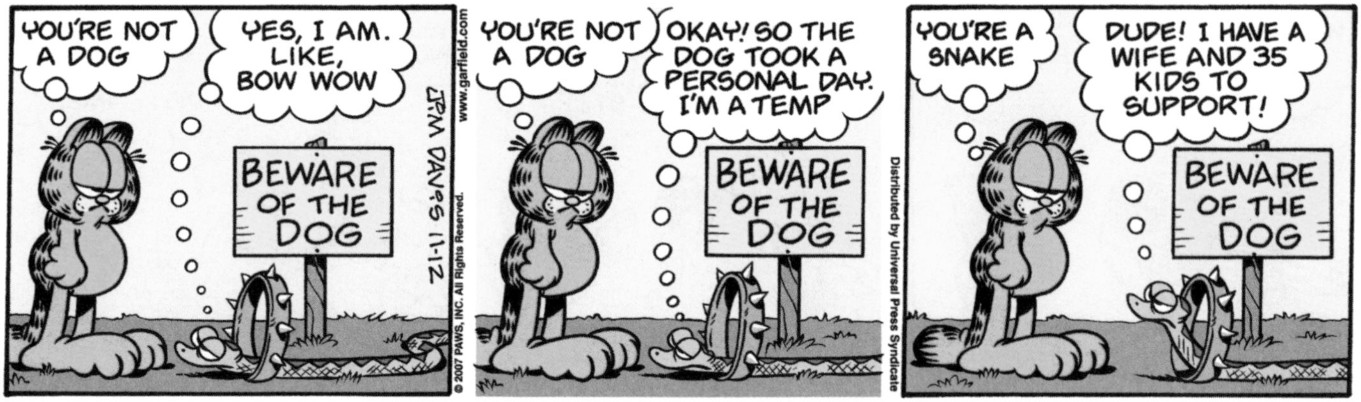
YOU'RE NOT A DOG
YES, I AM. LIKE, BOW WOW
BEWARE OF THE DOG
JIM DAVIS 11-12
www.garfield.com
© 2007 PAWS, INC. All Rights Reserved.
YOU'RE NOT A DOG
OKAY! SO THE DOG TOOK A PERSONAL DAY. I'M A TEMP
BEWARE OF THE DOG
Distributed by Universal Press Syndicate
YOU'RE A SNAKE
DUDE! I HAVE A WIFE AND 35 KIDS TO SUPPORT!
BEWARE OF THE DOG

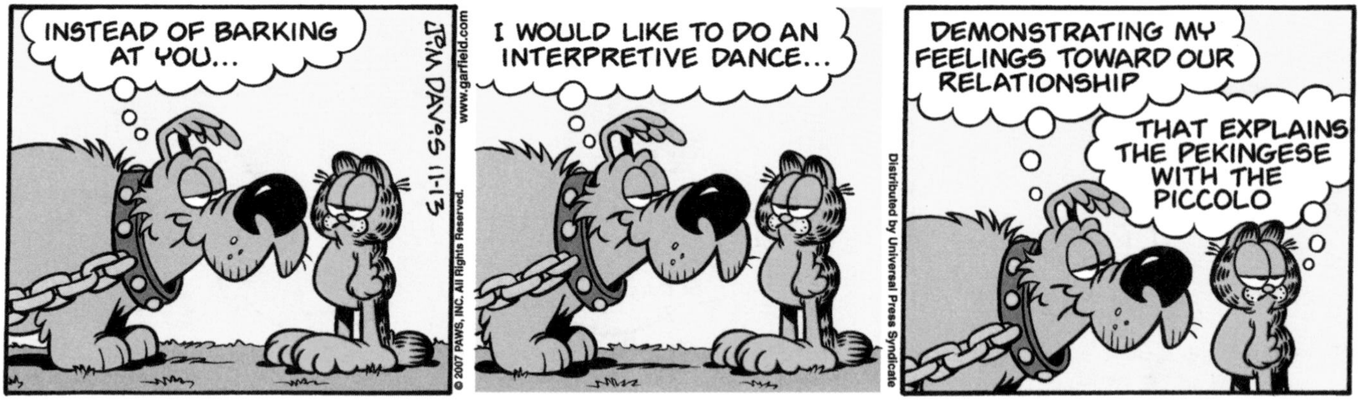
INSTEAD OF BARKING AT YOU...
JIM DAVIS 11-13
www.garfield.com
© 2007 PAWS, INC. All Rights Reserved.
I WOULD LIKE TO DO AN INTERPRETIVE DANCE...
Distributed by Universal Press Syndicate
DEMONSTRATING MY FEELINGS TOWARD OUR RELATIONSHIP
THAT EXPLAINS THE PEKINGESE WITH THE PICCOLO

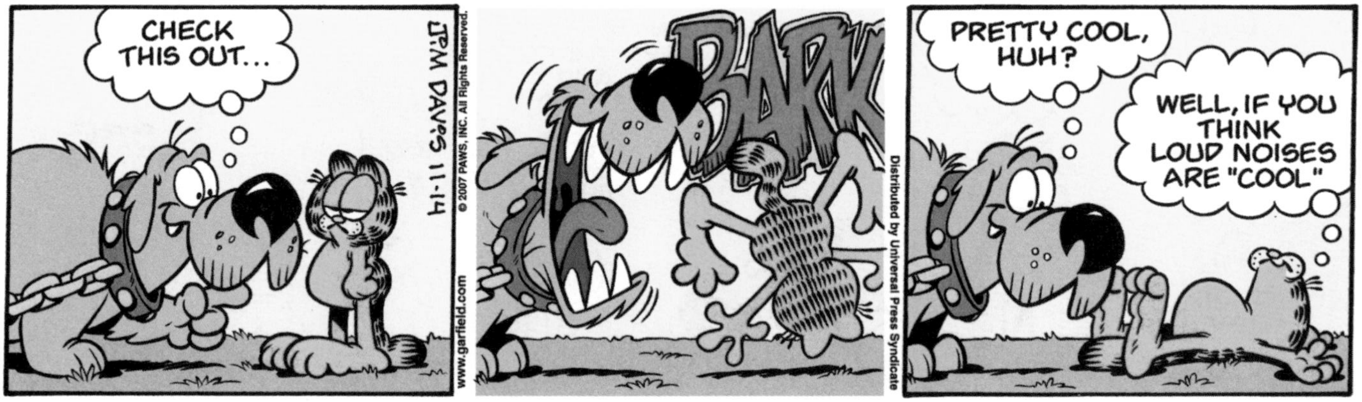
CHECK THIS OUT...
JIM DAVIS 11-14
© 2007 PAWS, INC. All Rights Reserved.
www.garfield.com
BARK
Distributed by Universal Press Syndicate
PRETTY COOL, HUH?
WELL, IF YOU THINK LOUD NOISES ARE "COOL"

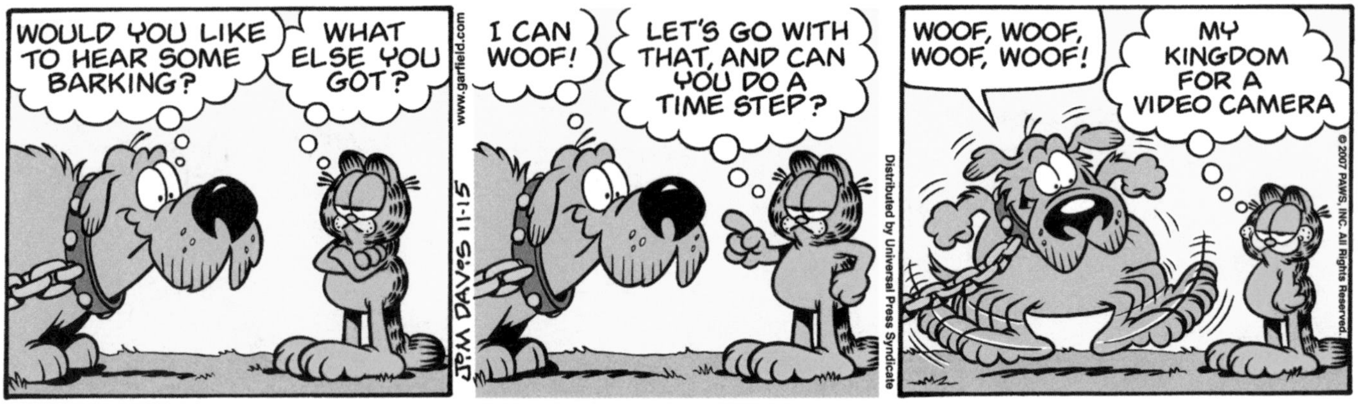
WOULD YOU LIKE TO HEAR SOME BARKING?
WHAT ELSE YOU GOT?
www.garfield.com
JIM DAVIS 11-15
I CAN WOOF!
LET'S GO WITH THAT, AND CAN YOU DO A TIME STEP?
Distributed by Universal Press Syndicate
WOOF, WOOF, WOOF, WOOF!
MY KINGDOM FOR A VIDEO CAMERA
© 2007 PAWS, INC. All Rights Reserved.

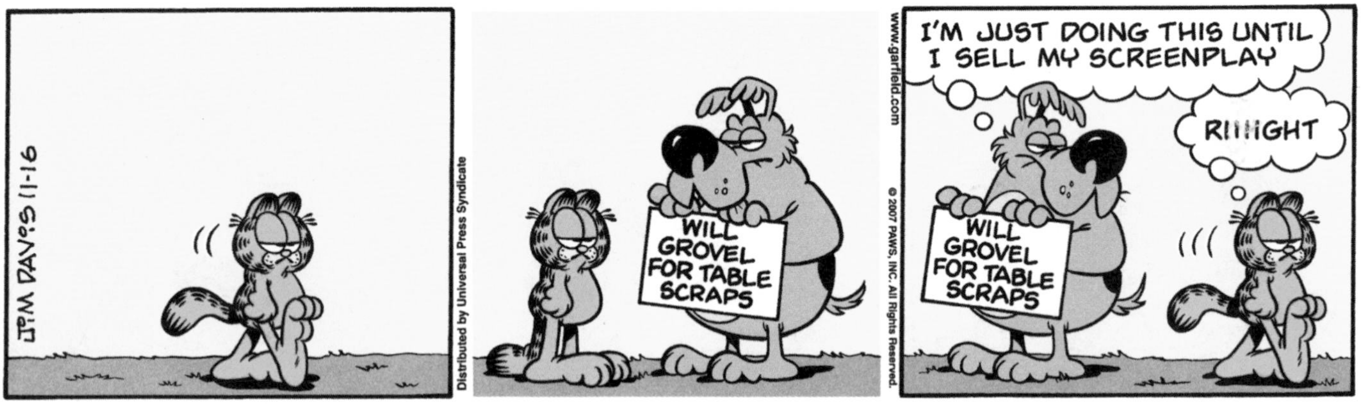
JIM DAVIS 11-16
Distributed by Universal Press Syndicate
WILL GROVEL FOR TABLE SCRAPS
www.garfield.com
© 2007 PAWS, INC. All Rights Reserved.
I'M JUST DOING THIS UNTIL I SELL MY SCREENPLAY
WILL GROVEL FOR TABLE SCRAPS
RIIIIGHT

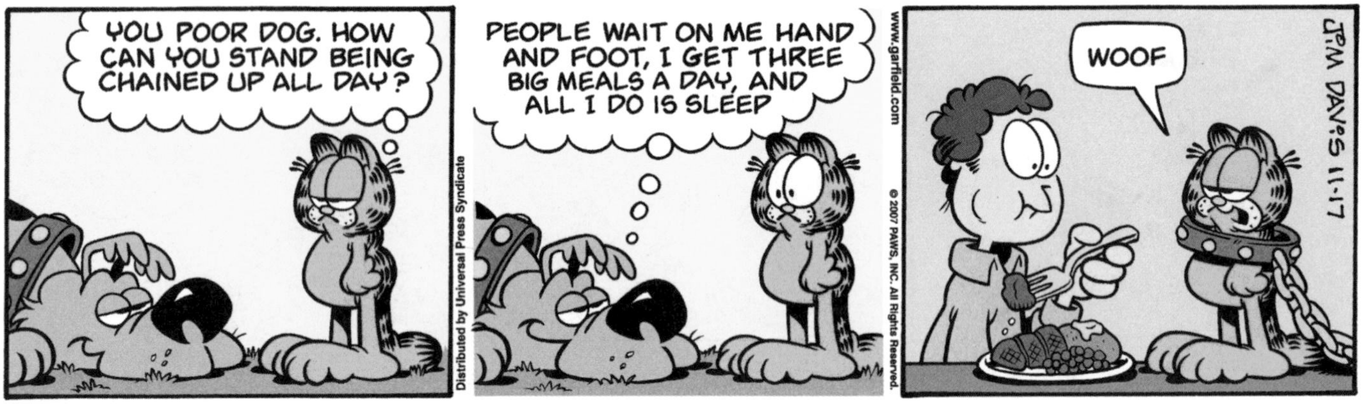
YOU POOR DOG. HOW CAN YOU STAND BEING CHAINED UP ALL DAY?
Distributed by Universal Press Syndicate
PEOPLE WAIT ON ME HAND AND FOOT, I GET THREE BIG MEALS A DAY, AND ALL I DO IS SLEEP
www.garfield.com
© 2007 PAWS, INC. All Rights Reserved.
WOOF
JIM DAVIS 11-17

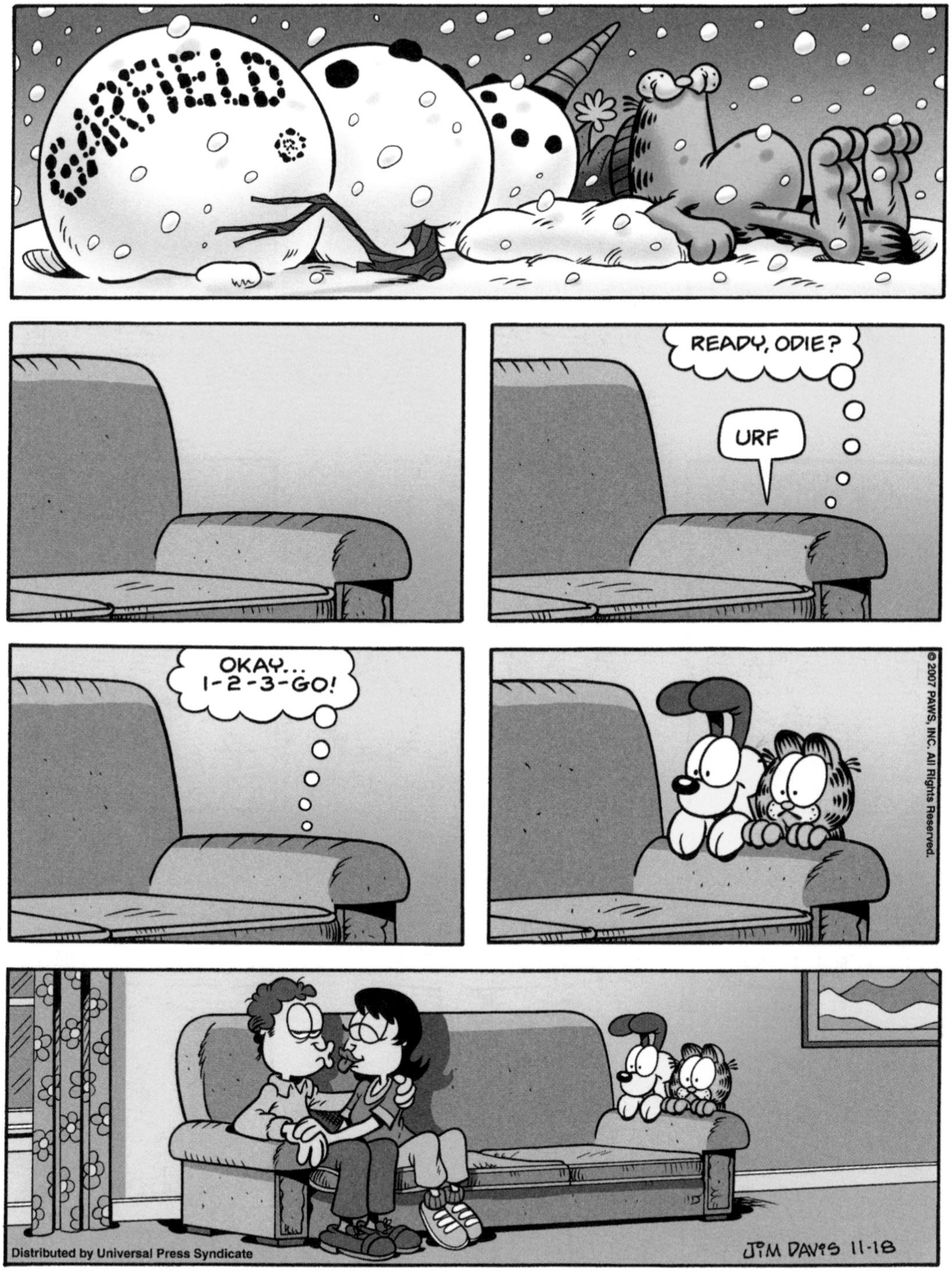
GARFIELD
READY, ODIE?
URF
OKAY... 1-2-3-GO!
© 2007 PAWS, INC. All Rights Reserved.
Distributed by Universal Press Syndicate
JIM DAVIS 11-18

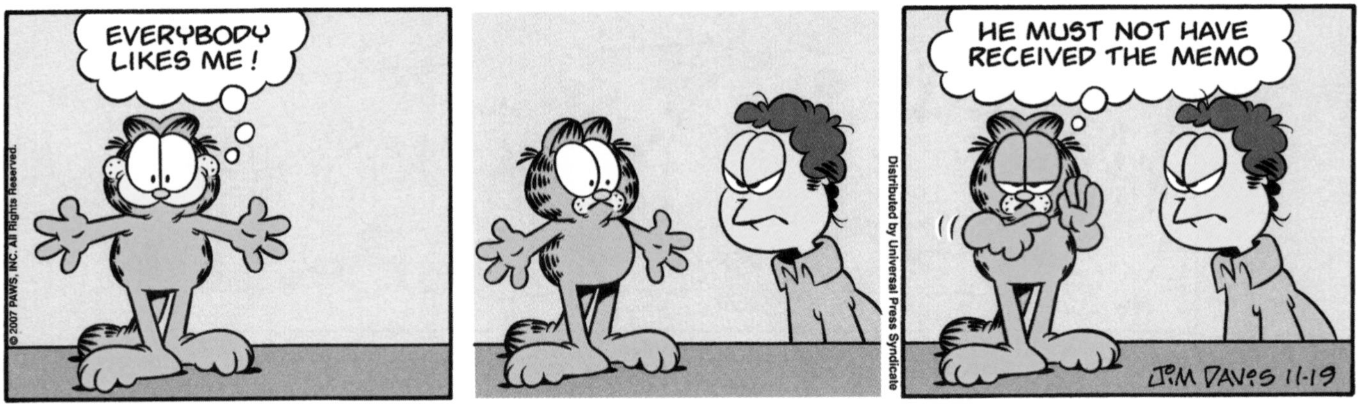
© 2007 PAWS, INC. All Rights Reserved.
EVERYBODY LIKES ME!
Distributed by Universal Press Syndicate
HE MUST NOT HAVE RECEIVED THE MEMO
JIM DAVIS 11-19

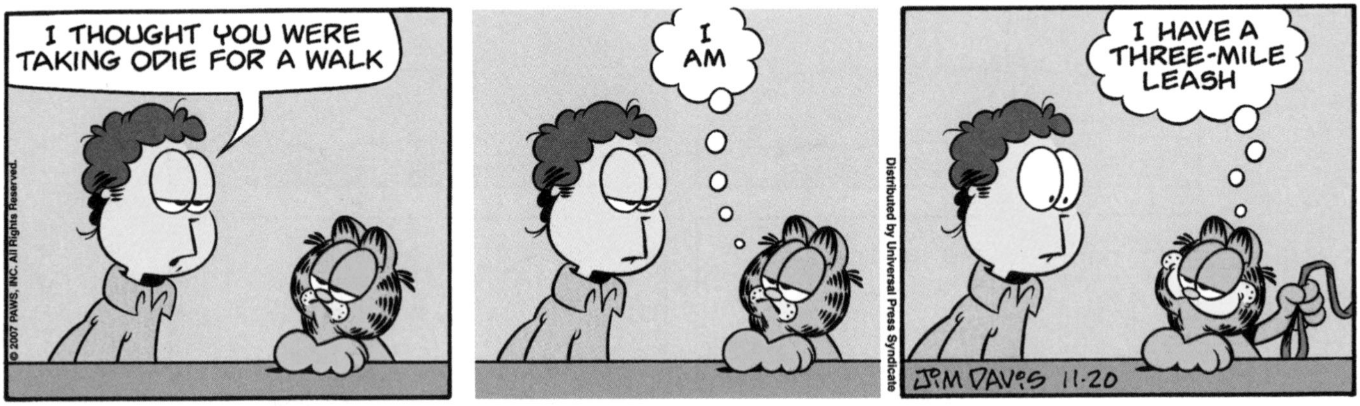
© 2007 PAWS, INC. All Rights Reserved.
I THOUGHT YOU WERE TAKING ODIE FOR A WALK
I AM
Distributed by Universal Press Syndicate
I HAVE A THREE-MILE LEASH
JIM DAVIS 11-20

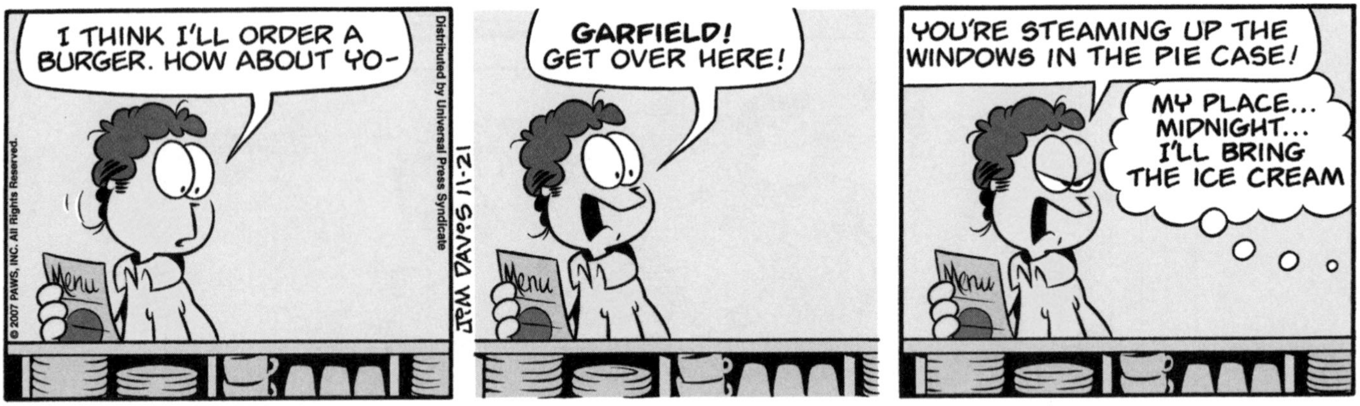
© 2007 PAWS, INC. All Rights Reserved.
I THINK I'LL ORDER A BURGER. HOW ABOUT YO-
Menu
Distributed by Universal Press Syndicate
JIM DAVIS 11-21
GARFIELD! GET OVER HERE!
Menu
YOU'RE STEAMING UP THE WINDOWS IN THE PIE CASE!
MY PLACE... MIDNIGHT... I'LL BRING THE ICE CREAM
Menu

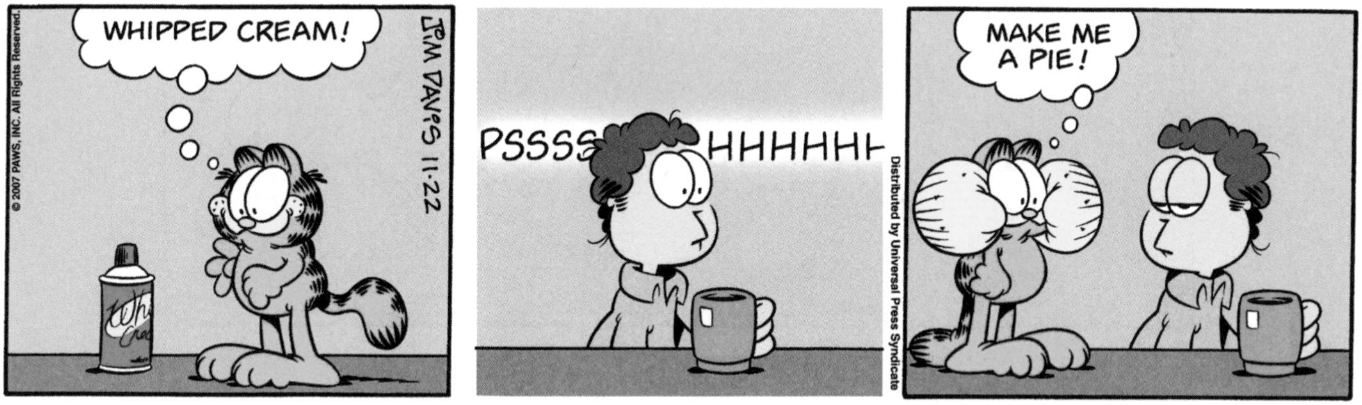
WHIPPED CREAM!
© 2007 PAWS, INC. All Rights Reserved.
JIM DAVIS 11-22
PSSSSSHHHHHH
Distributed by Universal Press Syndicate
MAKE ME A PIE!

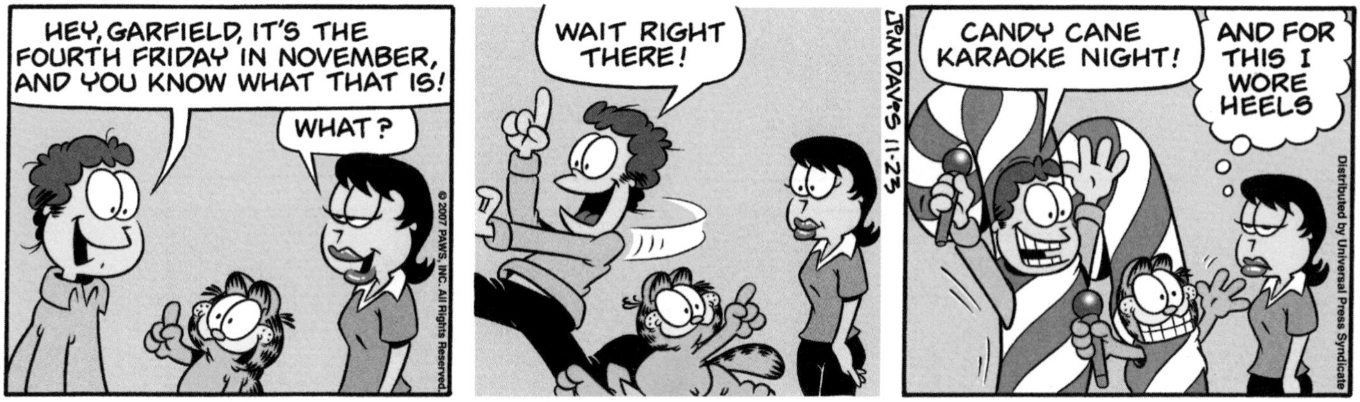
HEY, GARFIELD, IT'S THE FOURTH FRIDAY IN NOVEMBER, AND YOU KNOW WHAT THAT IS!
WHAT?
© 2007 PAWS, INC. All Rights Reserved.
WAIT RIGHT THERE!
JIM DAVIS 11-23
CANDY CANE KARAOKE NIGHT!
AND FOR THIS I WORE HEELS
Distributed by Universal Press Syndicate

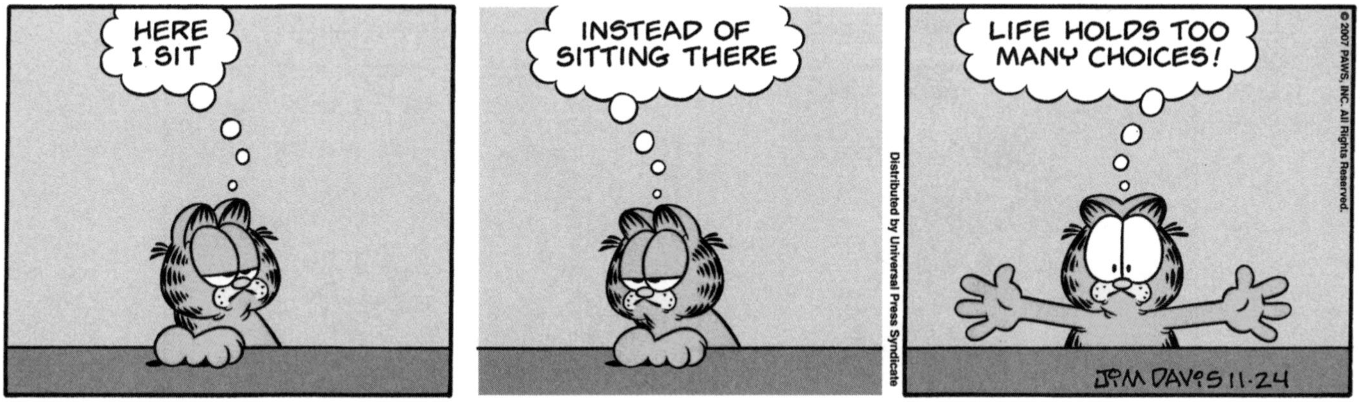
HERE I SIT
INSTEAD OF SITTING THERE
Distributed by Universal Press Syndicate
LIFE HOLDS TOO MANY CHOICES!
© 2007 PAWS, INC. All Rights Reserved.
JIM DAVIS 11-24

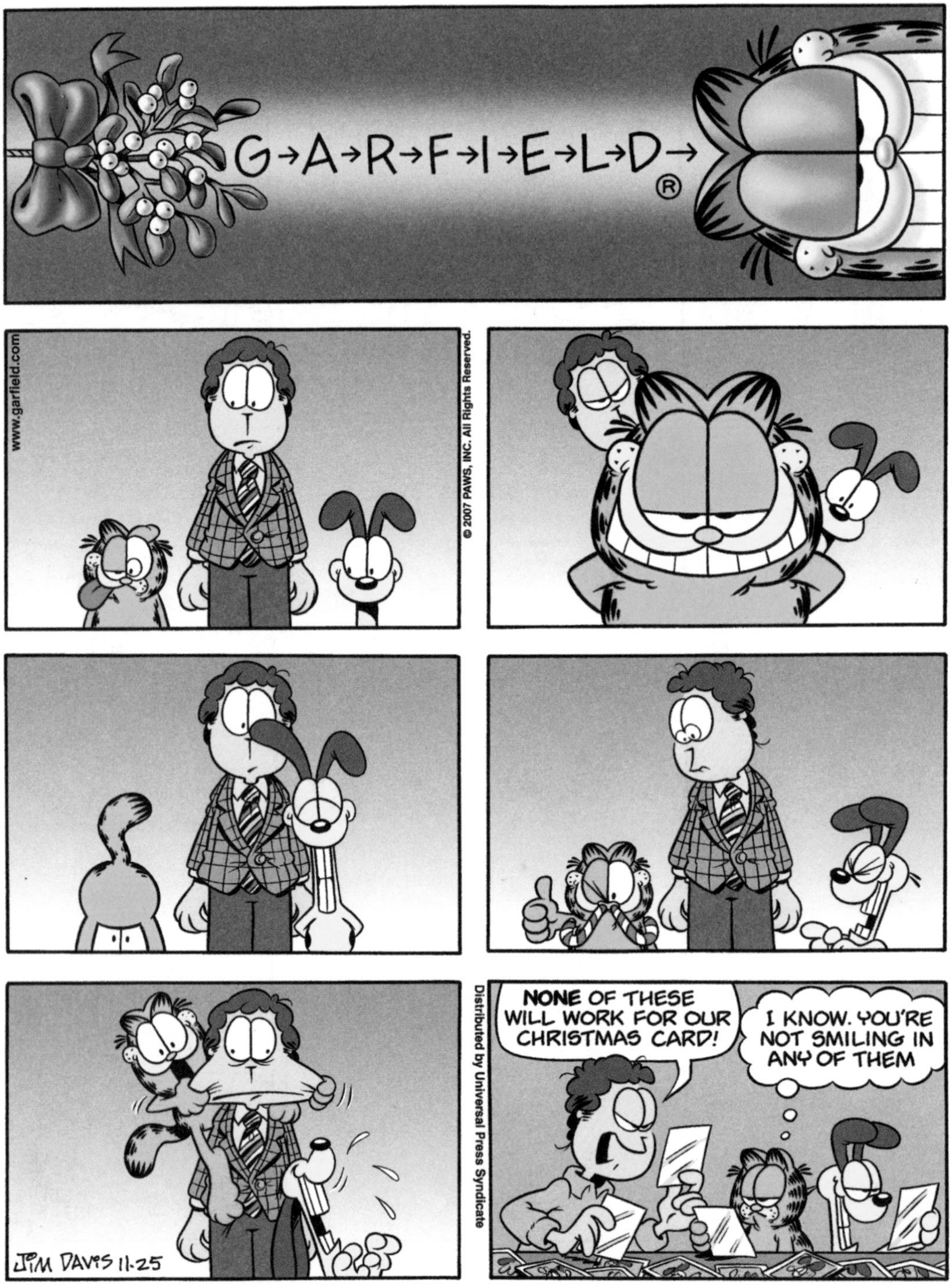
G→A→R→F→I→E→L→D→ ®
www.garfield.com
© 2007 PAWS, INC. All Rights Reserved.
JIM DAVIS 11-25
Distributed by Universal Press Syndicate
NONE OF THESE WILL WORK FOR OUR CHRISTMAS CARD!
I KNOW. YOU'RE NOT SMILING IN ANY OF THEM

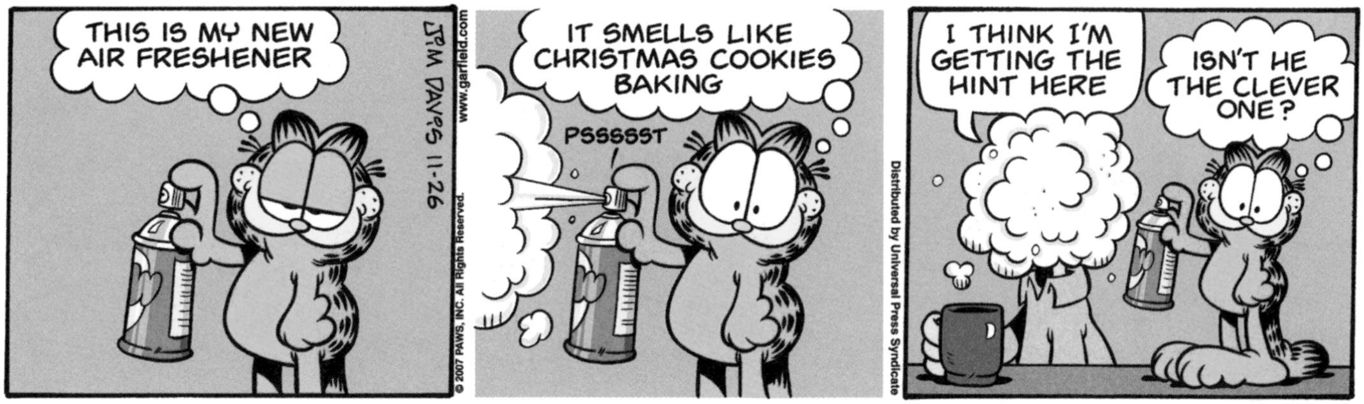
THIS IS MY NEW AIR FRESHENER
JPM DAVPS 11-26
www.garfield.com
© 2007 PAWS, INC. All Rights Reserved.
IT SMELLS LIKE CHRISTMAS COOKIES BAKING
PSSSSST
Distributed by Universal Press Syndicate
I THINK I'M GETTING THE HINT HERE
ISN'T HE THE CLEVER ONE?

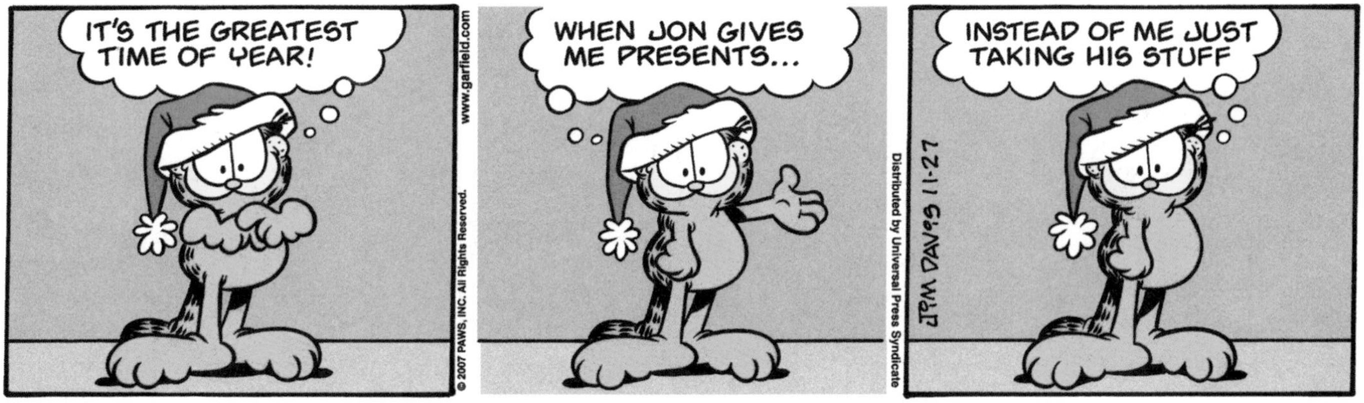
IT'S THE GREATEST TIME OF YEAR!
www.garfield.com
© 2007 PAWS, INC. All Rights Reserved.
WHEN JON GIVES ME PRESENTS...
Distributed by Universal Press Syndicate
JPM DAVPS 11-27
INSTEAD OF ME JUST TAKING HIS STUFF

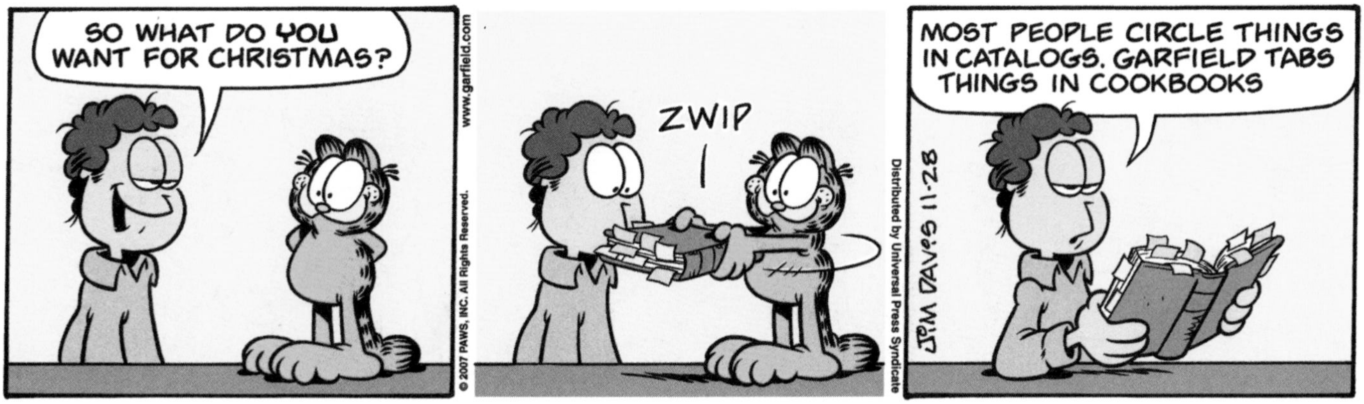
SO WHAT DO YOU WANT FOR CHRISTMAS?
www.garfield.com
© 2007 PAWS, INC. All Rights Reserved.
ZWIP
Distributed by Universal Press Syndicate
JPM DAVPS 11-28
MOST PEOPLE CIRCLE THINGS IN CATALOGS. GARFIELD TABS THINGS IN COOKBOOKS

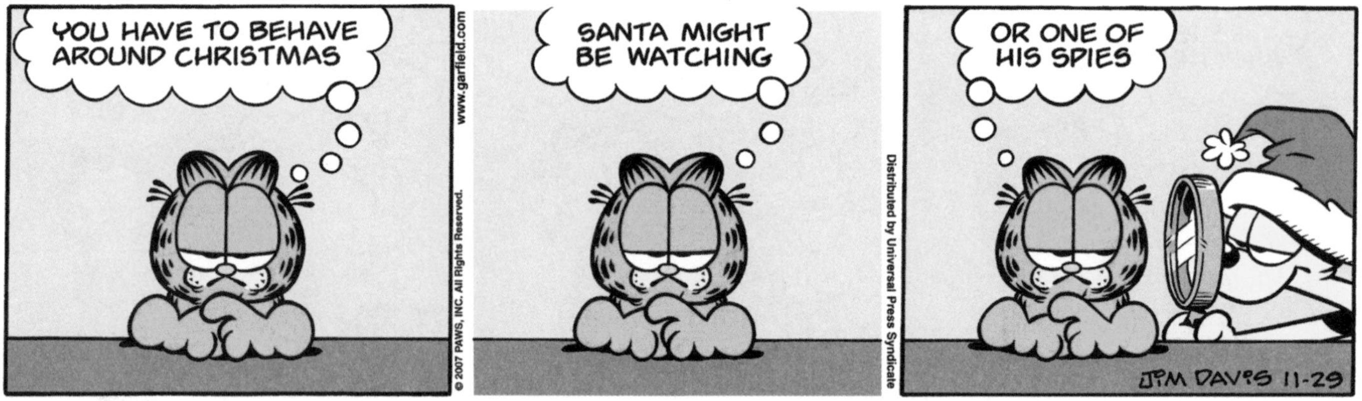
YOU HAVE TO BEHAVE AROUND CHRISTMAS
© 2007 PAWS, INC. All Rights Reserved. www.garfield.com
SANTA MIGHT BE WATCHING
Distributed by Universal Press Syndicate
OR ONE OF HIS SPIES
JIM DAVIS 11-29

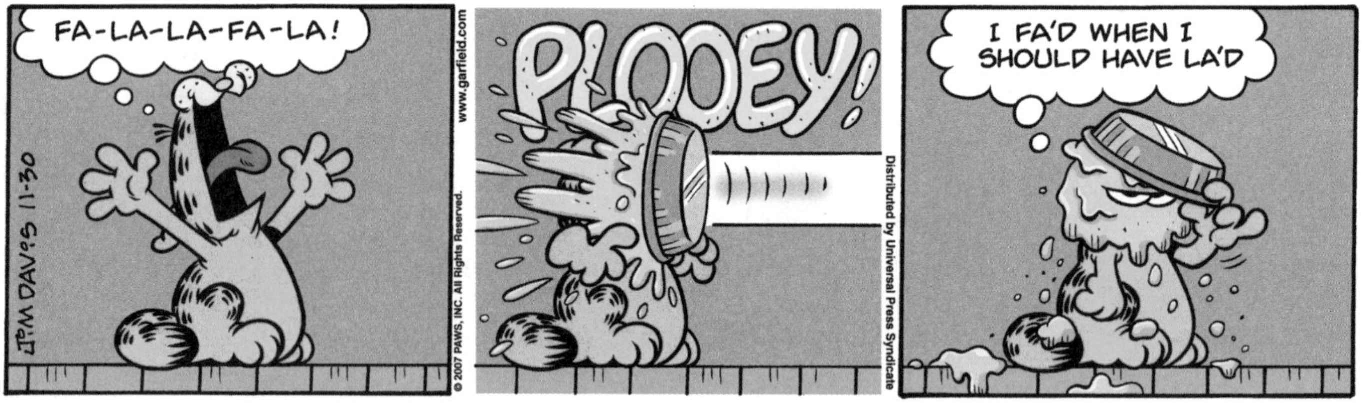
FA-LA-LA-FA-LA!
JIM DAVIS 11-30
© 2007 PAWS, INC. All Rights Reserved. www.garfield.com
PLOOEY!
Distributed by Universal Press Syndicate
I FA'D WHEN I SHOULD HAVE LA'D

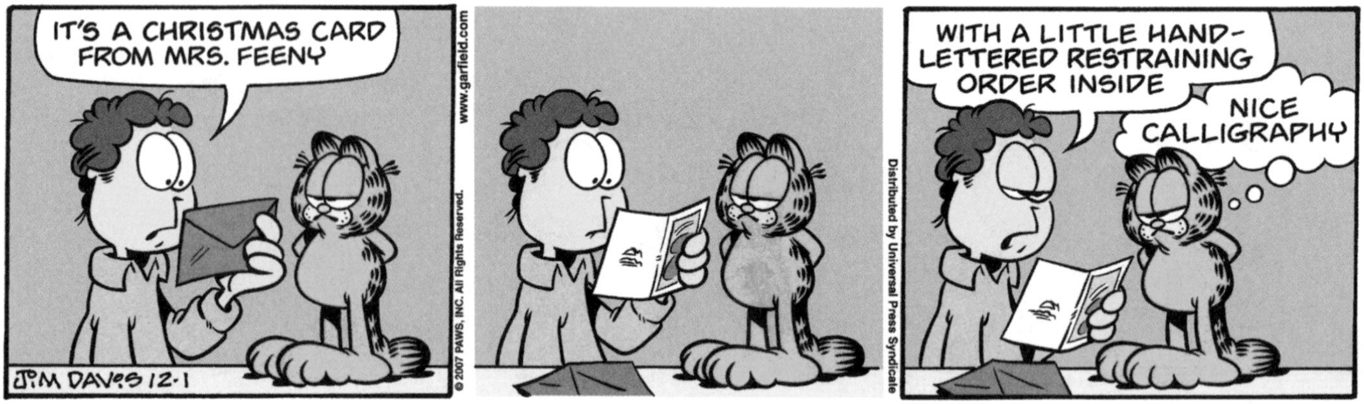
IT'S A CHRISTMAS CARD FROM MRS. FEENY
JIM DAVIS 12-1
© 2007 PAWS, INC. All Rights Reserved. www.garfield.com
Distributed by Universal Press Syndicate
WITH A LITTLE HAND-LETTERED RESTRAINING ORDER INSIDE
NICE CALLIGRAPHY

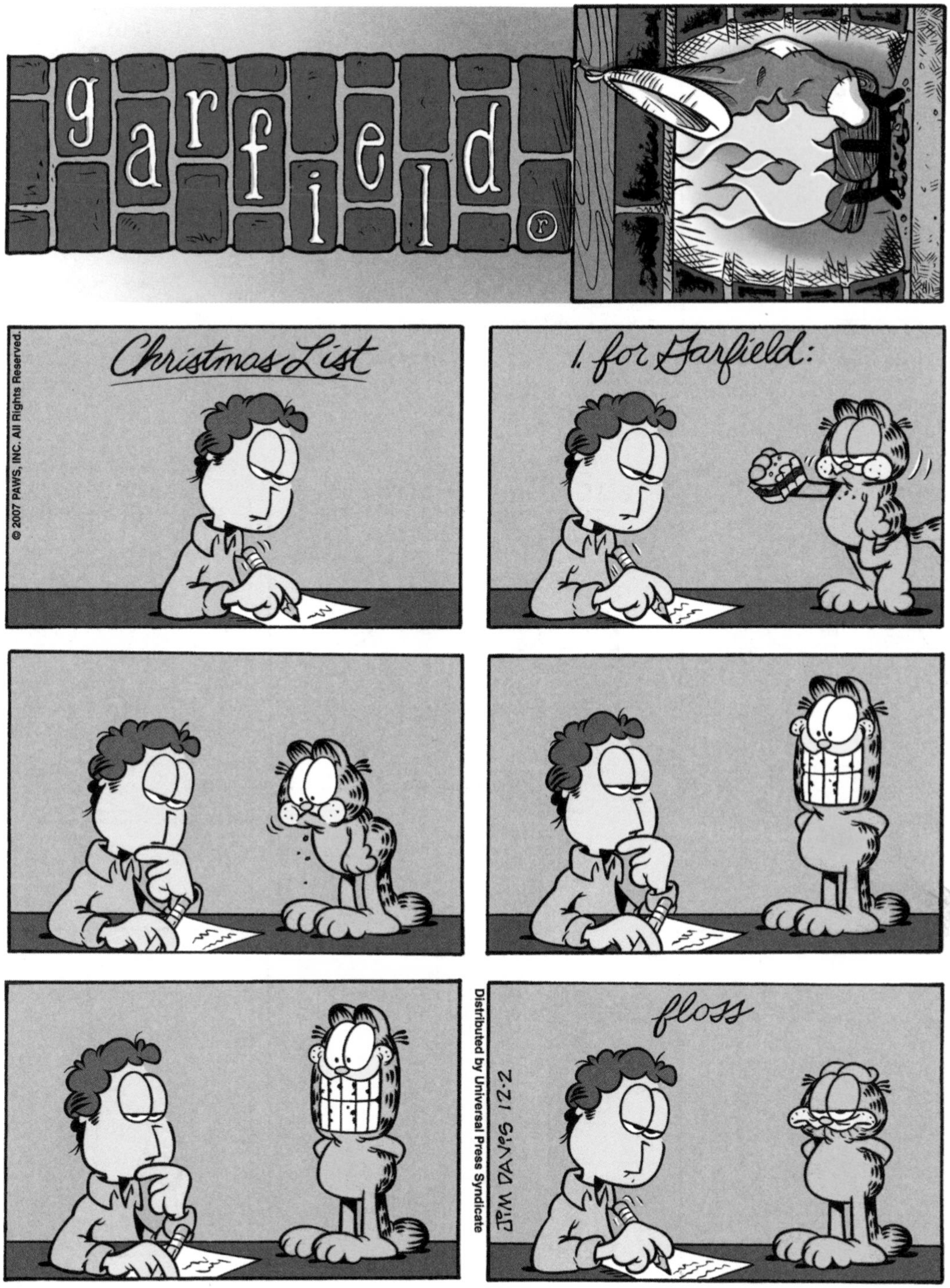
garfield®
© 2007 PAWS, INC. All Rights Reserved.
Christmas List
1. for Garfield:
Distributed by Universal Press Syndicate
JIM DAVIS 12-2
floss

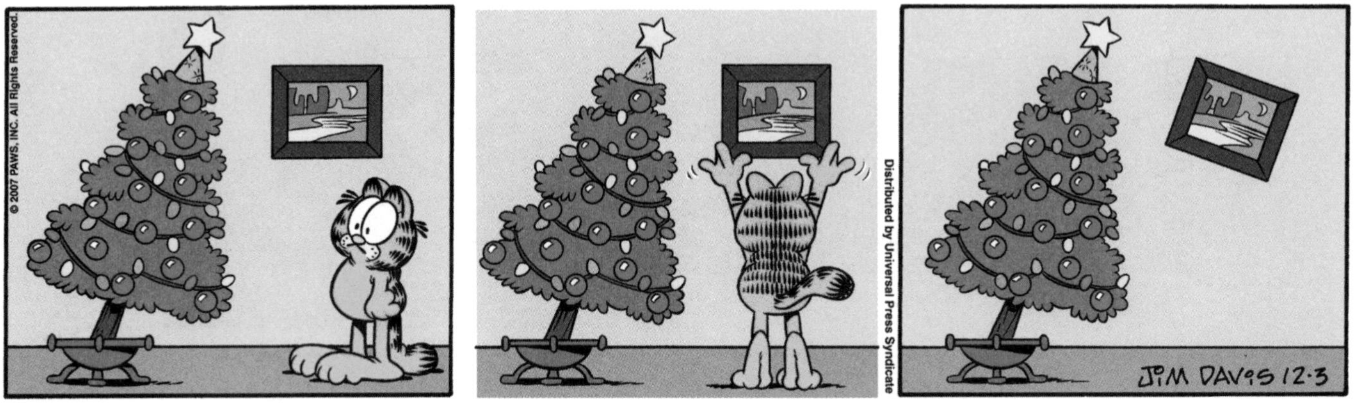
© 2007 PAWS, INC. All Rights Reserved.
Distributed by Universal Press Syndicate
JIM DAVIS 12-3

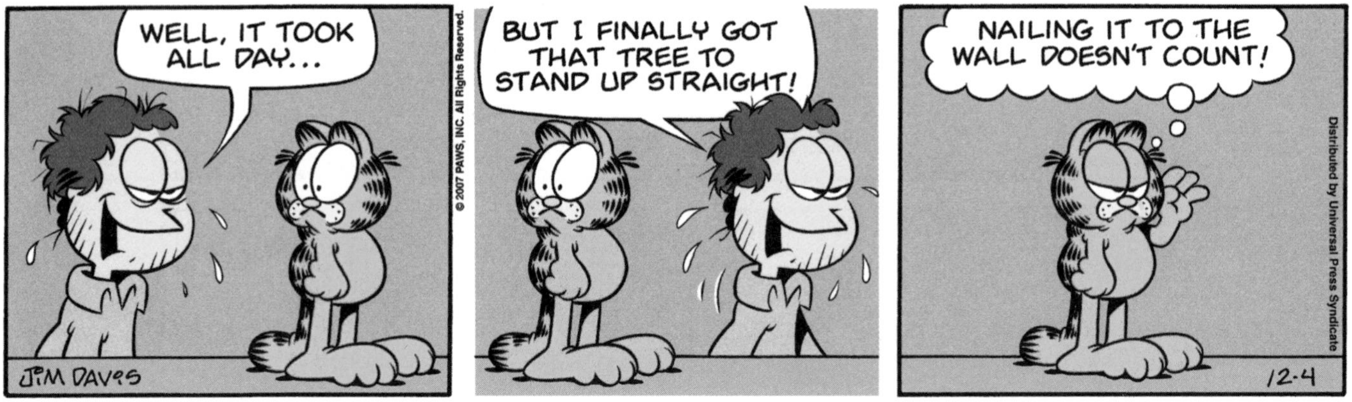
WELL, IT TOOK ALL DAY...
JIM DAVIS
© 2007 PAWS, INC. All Rights Reserved.
BUT I FINALLY GOT THAT TREE TO STAND UP STRAIGHT!
NAILING IT TO THE WALL DOESN'T COUNT!
Distributed by Universal Press Syndicate
12-4

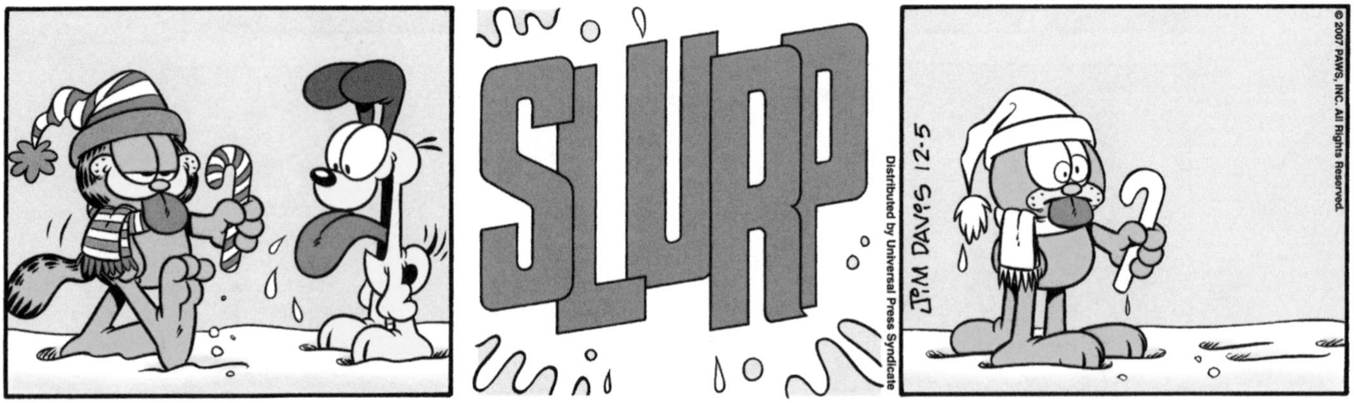
SLURP
Distributed by Universal Press Syndicate
JIM DAVIS 12-5
© 2007 PAWS, INC. All Rights Reserved.

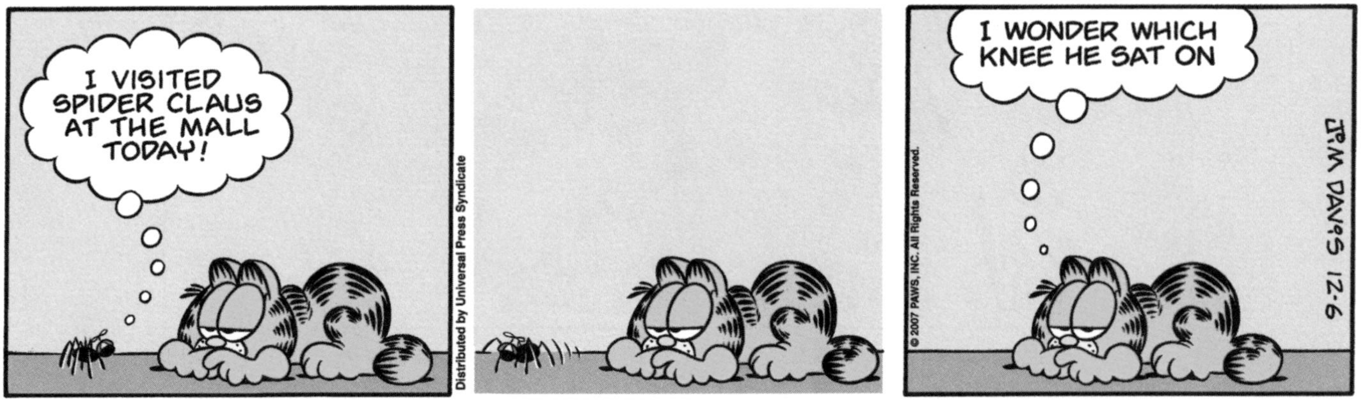
I VISITED SPIDER CLAUS AT THE MALL TODAY!
Distributed by Universal Press Syndicate
© 2007 PAWS, INC. All Rights Reserved.
I WONDER WHICH KNEE HE SAT ON
JIM DAVIS 12-6

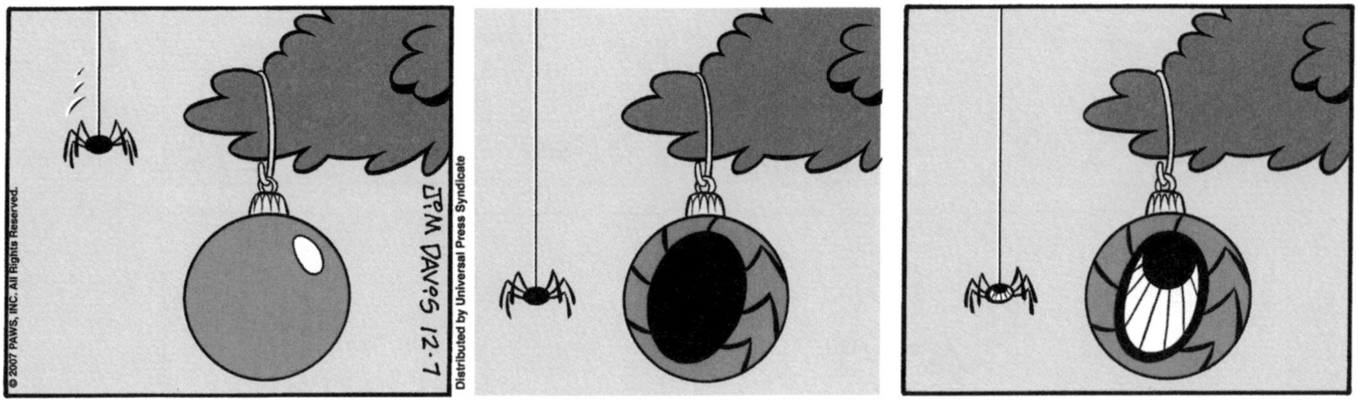
© 2007 PAWS, INC. All Rights Reserved.
JIM DAVIS 12-7
Distributed by Universal Press Syndicate

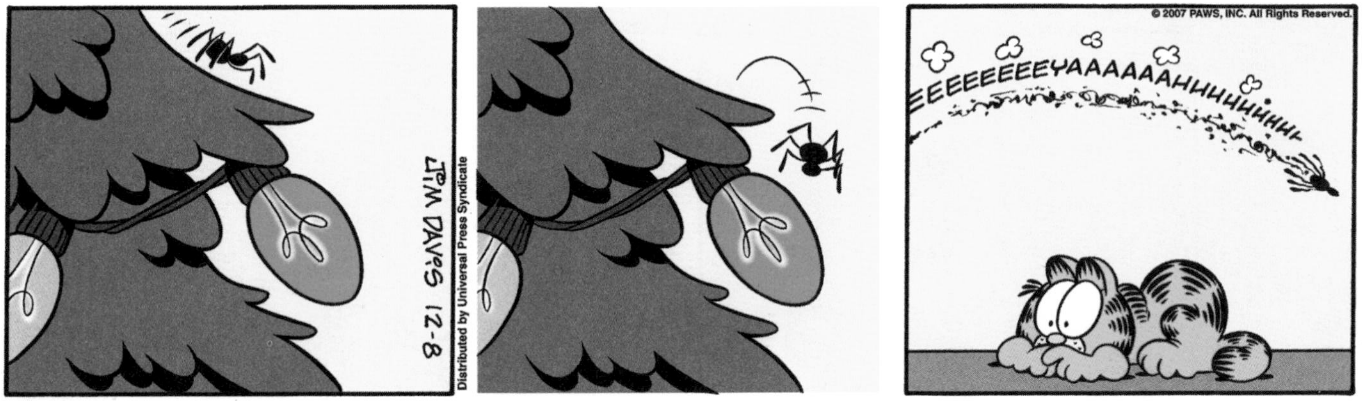
JIM DAVIS 12-8
Distributed by Universal Press Syndicate
© 2007 PAWS, INC. All Rights Reserved.
EEEEEEEEYAAAAAAAHHHHHHHH!

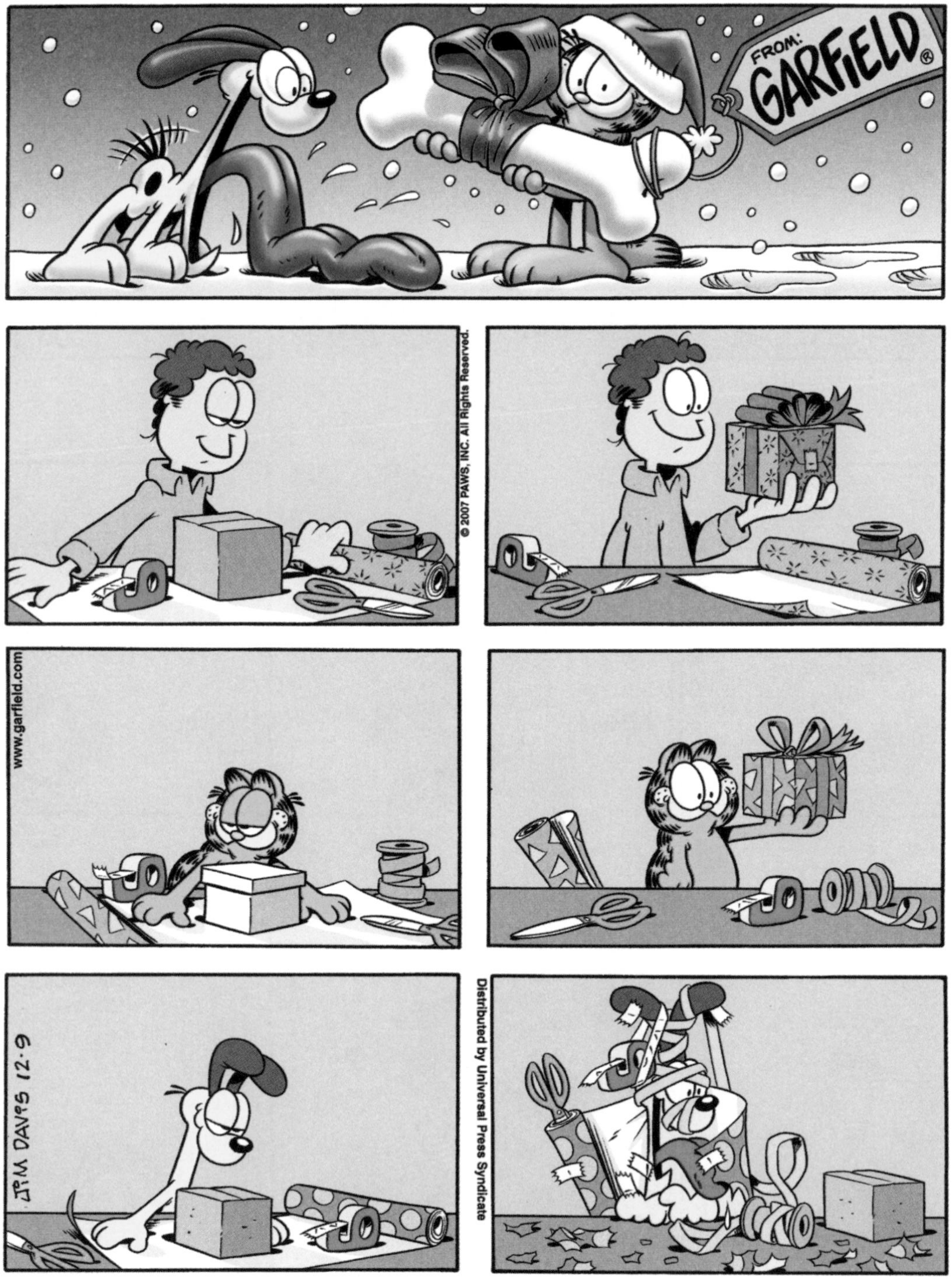
FROM:
GARFIELD®
© 2007 PAWS, INC. All Rights Reserved.
www.garfield.com
JIM DAVIS 12-9
Distributed by Universal Press Syndicate

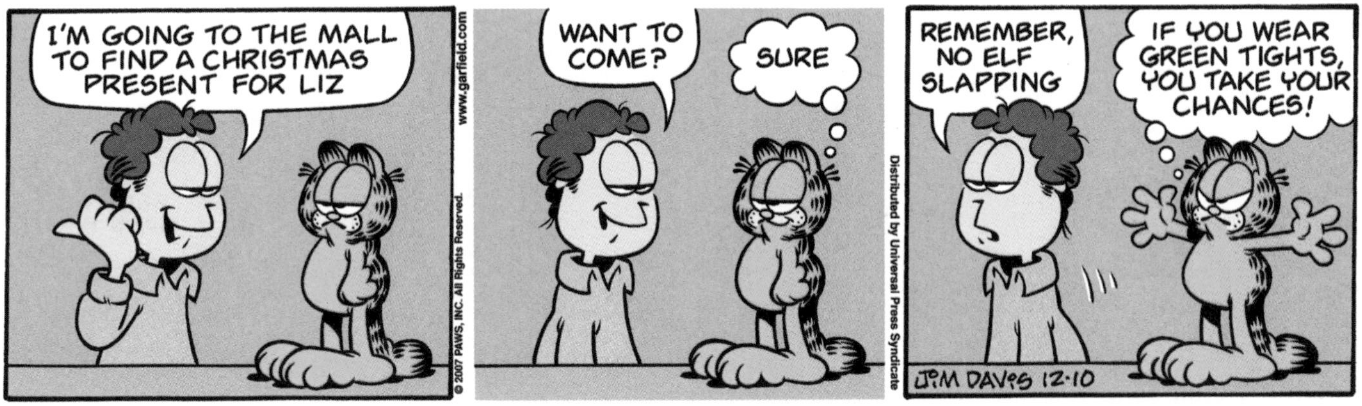
I'M GOING TO THE MALL TO FIND A CHRISTMAS PRESENT FOR LIZ
© 2007 PAWS, INC. All Rights Reserved.
www.garfield.com
WANT TO COME?
SURE
Distributed by Universal Press Syndicate
REMEMBER, NO ELF SLAPPING
IF YOU WEAR GREEN TIGHTS, YOU TAKE YOUR CHANCES!
JIM DAVIS 12-10

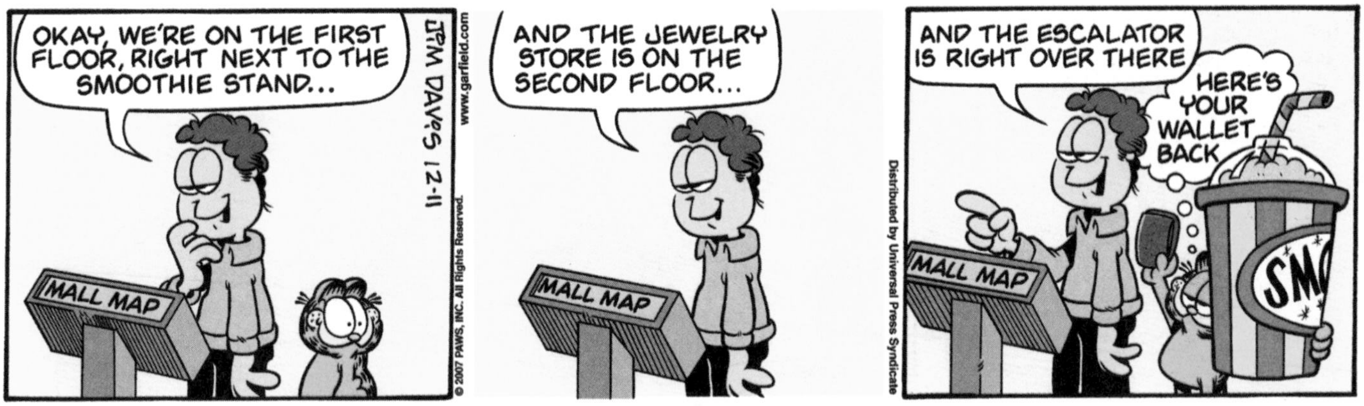
OKAY, WE'RE ON THE FIRST FLOOR, RIGHT NEXT TO THE SMOOTHIE STAND...
MALL MAP
JIM DAVIS 12-11
© 2007 PAWS, INC. All Rights Reserved.
www.garfield.com
AND THE JEWELRY STORE IS ON THE SECOND FLOOR...
MALL MAP
Distributed by Universal Press Syndicate
AND THE ESCALATOR IS RIGHT OVER THERE
HERE'S YOUR WALLET BACK
MALL MAP
SM

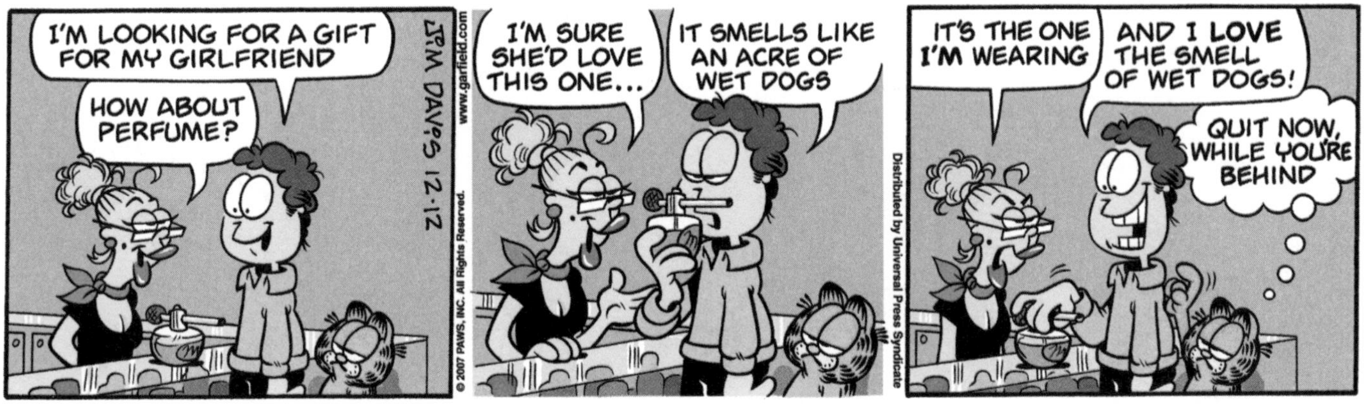
I'M LOOKING FOR A GIFT FOR MY GIRLFRIEND
HOW ABOUT PERFUME?
JIM DAVIS 12-12
© 2007 PAWS, INC. All Rights Reserved.
www.garfield.com
I'M SURE SHE'D LOVE THIS ONE...
IT SMELLS LIKE AN ACRE OF WET DOGS
Distributed by Universal Press Syndicate
IT'S THE ONE **I'M** WEARING
AND I **LOVE** THE SMELL OF WET DOGS!
QUIT NOW, WHILE YOU'RE BEHIND

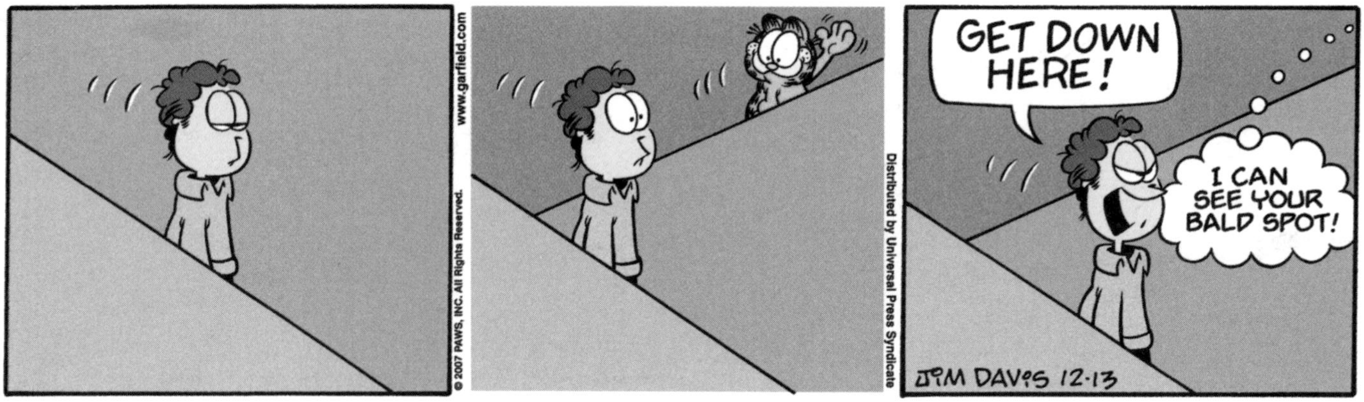
www.garfield.com
© 2007 PAWS, INC. All Rights Reserved.
Distributed by Universal Press Syndicate
GET DOWN HERE!
I CAN SEE YOUR BALD SPOT!
JIM DAVIS 12-13

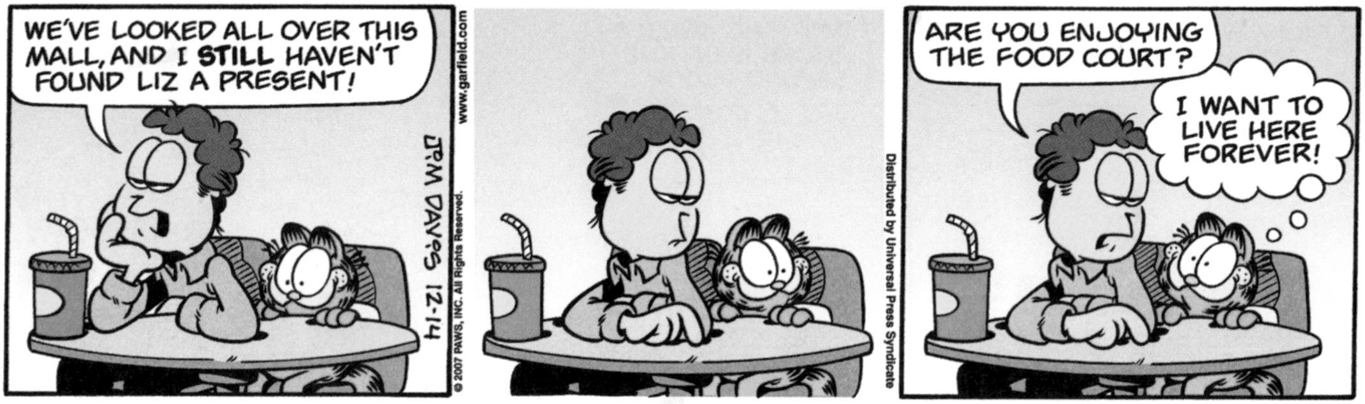
WE'VE LOOKED ALL OVER THIS MALL, AND I **STILL** HAVEN'T FOUND LIZ A PRESENT!
JIM DAVIS 12-14
www.garfield.com
© 2007 PAWS, INC. All Rights Reserved.
Distributed by Universal Press Syndicate
ARE YOU ENJOYING THE FOOD COURT?
I WANT TO LIVE HERE FOREVER!

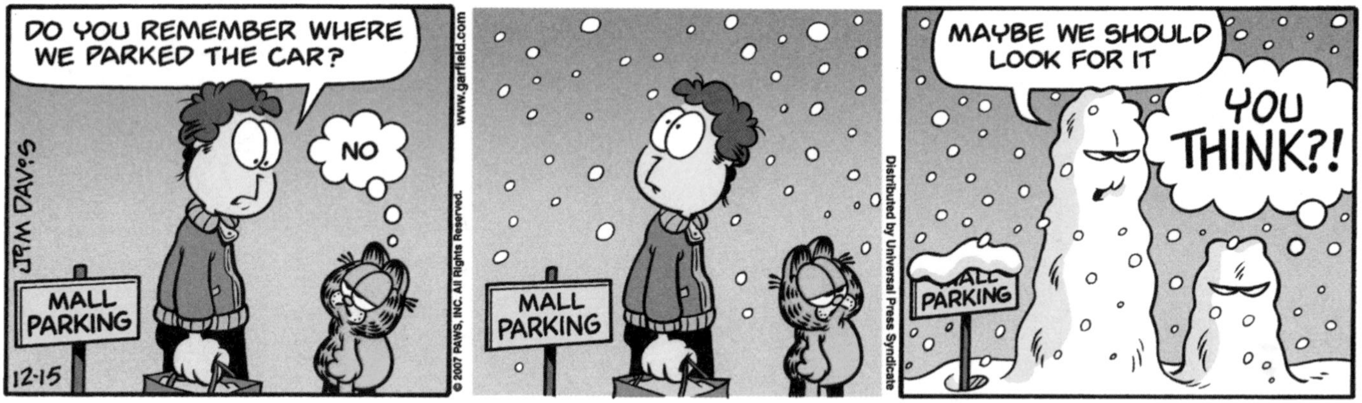
DO YOU REMEMBER WHERE WE PARKED THE CAR?
NO
JIM DAVIS
MALL PARKING
12-15
www.garfield.com
© 2007 PAWS, INC. All Rights Reserved.
MALL PARKING
Distributed by Universal Press Syndicate
MAYBE WE SHOULD LOOK FOR IT
YOU THINK?!
PARKING

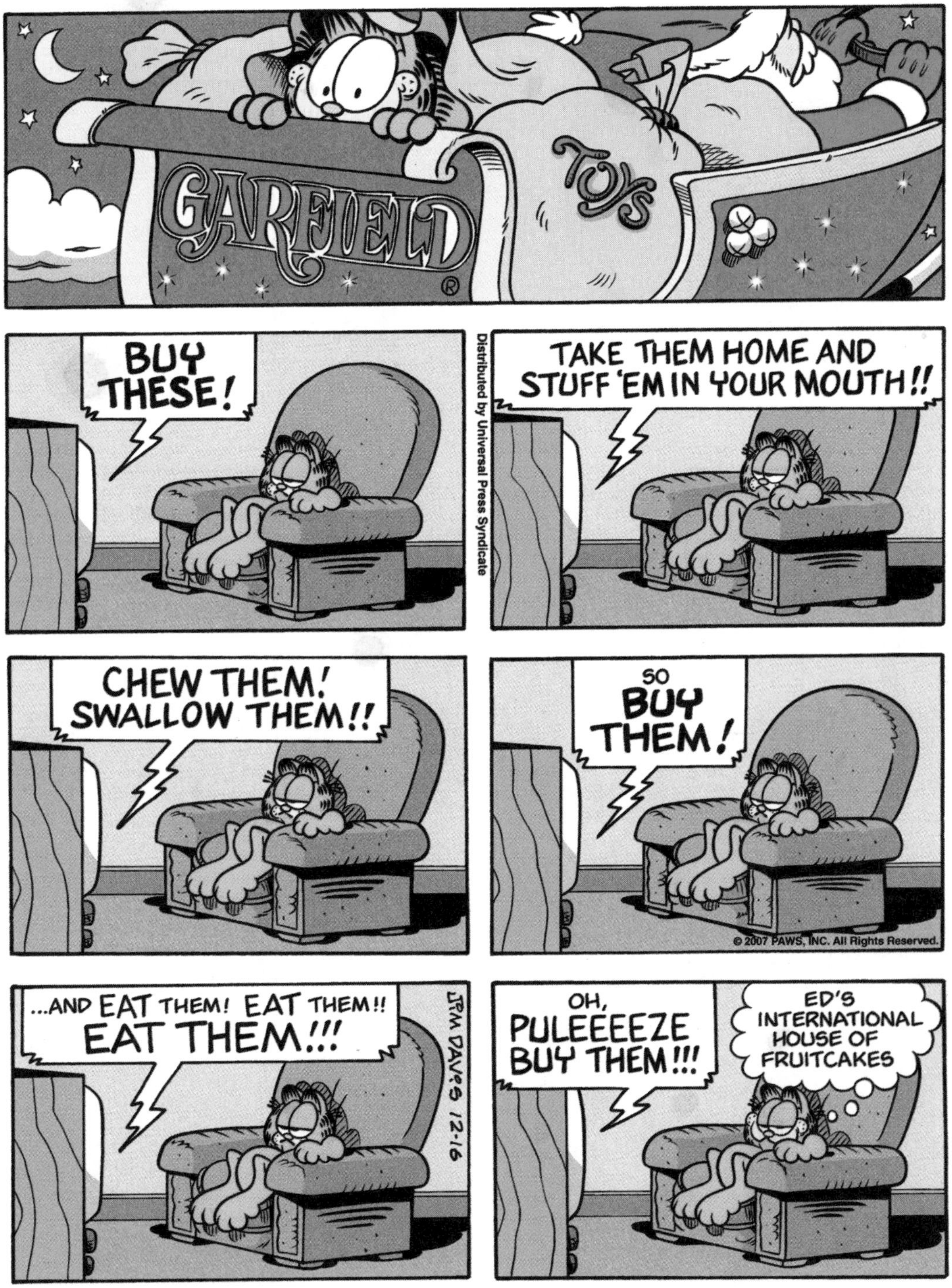
GARFIELD ®
TOYS
BUY THESE!
TAKE THEM HOME AND STUFF 'EM IN YOUR MOUTH!!
CHEW THEM! SWALLOW THEM!!
SO BUY THEM!
...AND EAT THEM! EAT THEM!! EAT THEM!!!
JPM DAVPS 12-16
OH, PULEEEEZE BUY THEM!!!
ED'S INTERNATIONAL HOUSE OF FRUITCAKES

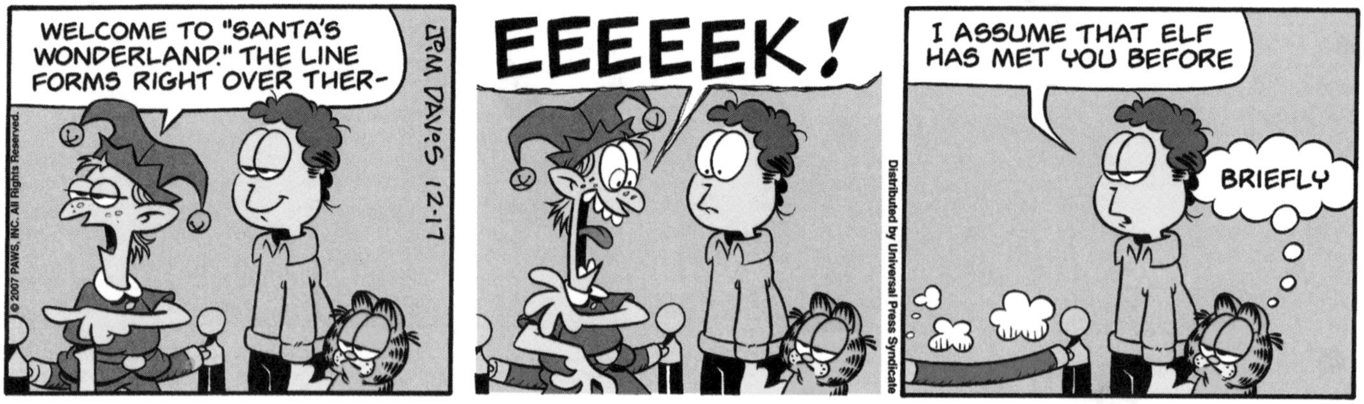
WELCOME TO "SANTA'S WONDERLAND." THE LINE FORMS RIGHT OVER THER-
JPM DAVPS 12-17
EEEEEK!
I ASSUME THAT ELF HAS MET YOU BEFORE
BRIEFLY

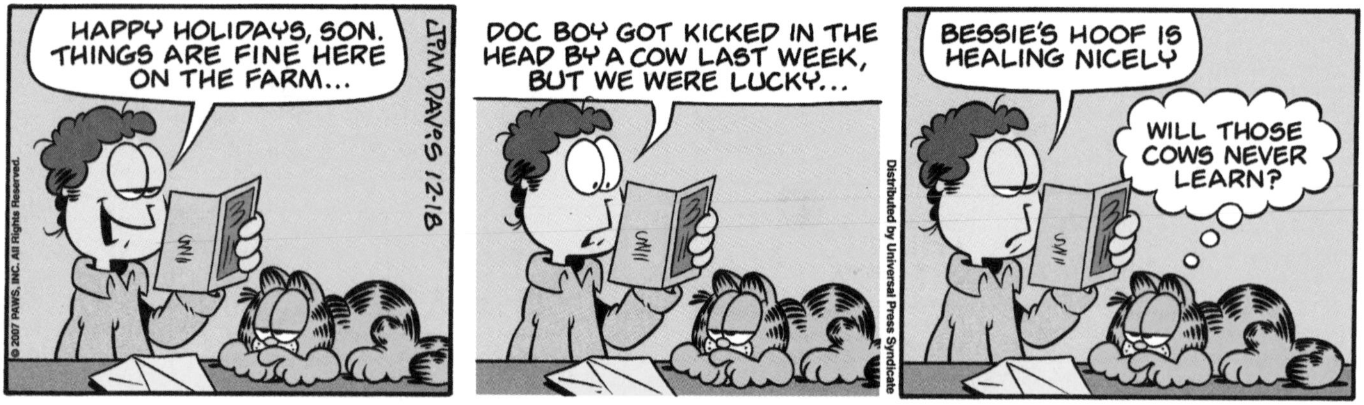
HAPPY HOLIDAYS, SON. THINGS ARE FINE HERE ON THE FARM...
JPM DAVPS 12-18
DOC BOY GOT KICKED IN THE HEAD BY A COW LAST WEEK, BUT WE WERE LUCKY...
BESSIE'S HOOF IS HEALING NICELY
WILL THOSE COWS NEVER LEARN?

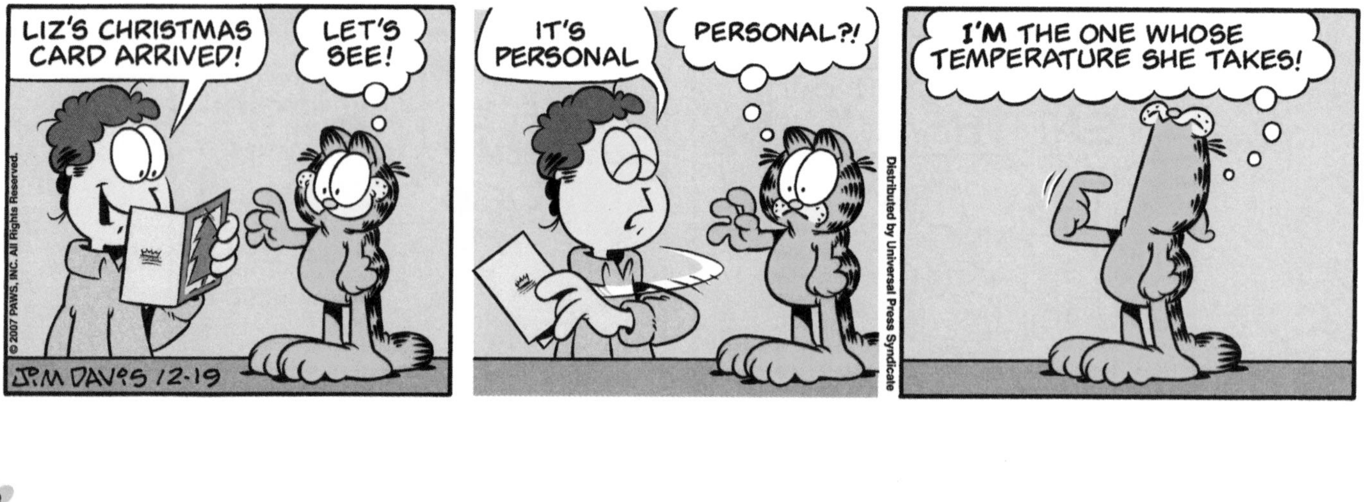
LIZ'S CHRISTMAS CARD ARRIVED!
LET'S SEE!
JPM DAVPS 12-19
IT'S PERSONAL
PERSONAL?!
I'M THE ONE WHOSE TEMPERATURE SHE TAKES!

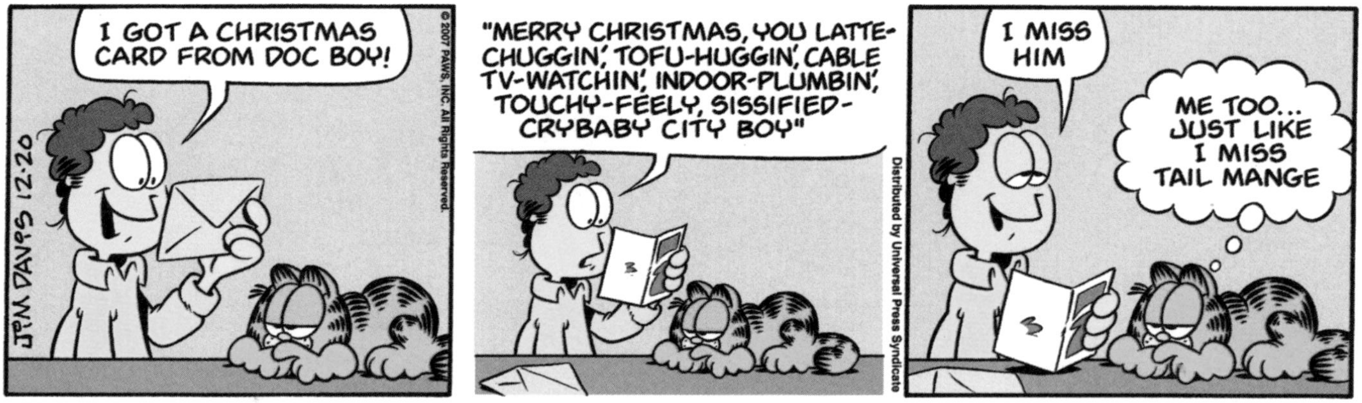
I GOT A CHRISTMAS CARD FROM DOC BOY!
"MERRY CHRISTMAS, YOU LATTE-CHUGGIN', TOFU-HUGGIN', CABLE TV-WATCHIN', INDOOR-PLUMBIN', TOUCHY-FEELY, SISSIFIED-CRYBABY CITY BOY"
I MISS HIM
ME TOO... JUST LIKE I MISS TAIL MANGE
JIM DAVIS 12·20
© 2007 PAWS, INC. All Rights Reserved.
Distributed by Universal Press Syndicate

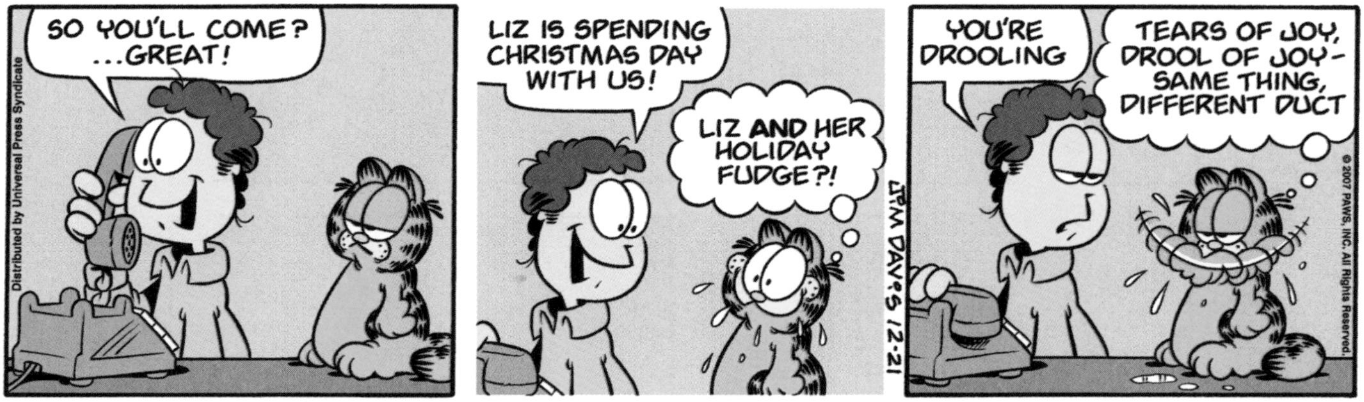
SO YOU'LL COME? ...GREAT!
LIZ IS SPENDING CHRISTMAS DAY WITH US!
LIZ AND HER HOLIDAY FUDGE?!
YOU'RE DROOLING
TEARS OF JOY, DROOL OF JOY-SAME THING, DIFFERENT DUCT
JIM DAVIS 12·21
Distributed by Universal Press Syndicate
© 2007 PAWS, INC. All Rights Reserved.

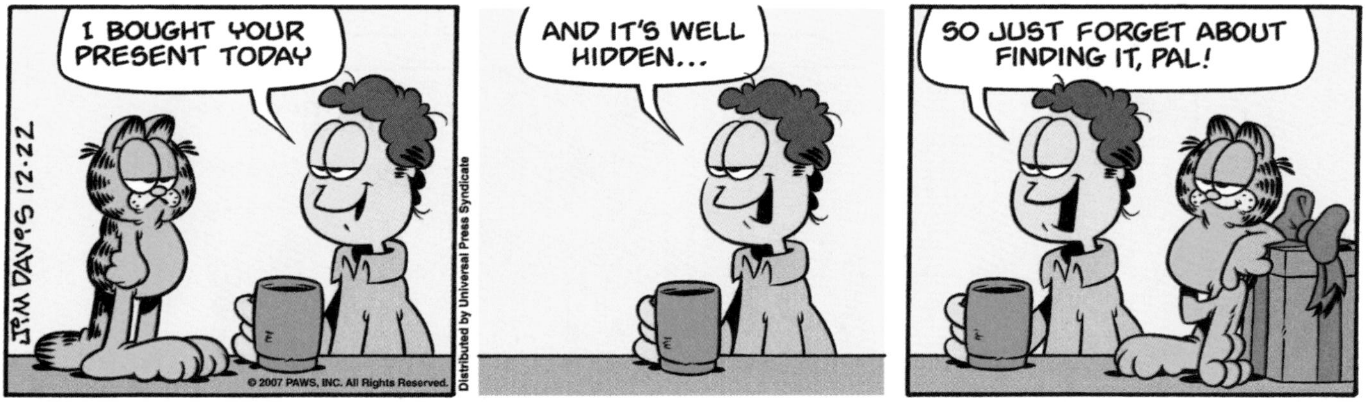
I BOUGHT YOUR PRESENT TODAY
AND IT'S WELL HIDDEN...
SO JUST FORGET ABOUT FINDING IT, PAL!
JIM DAVIS 12·22
© 2007 PAWS, INC. All Rights Reserved.
Distributed by Universal Press Syndicate

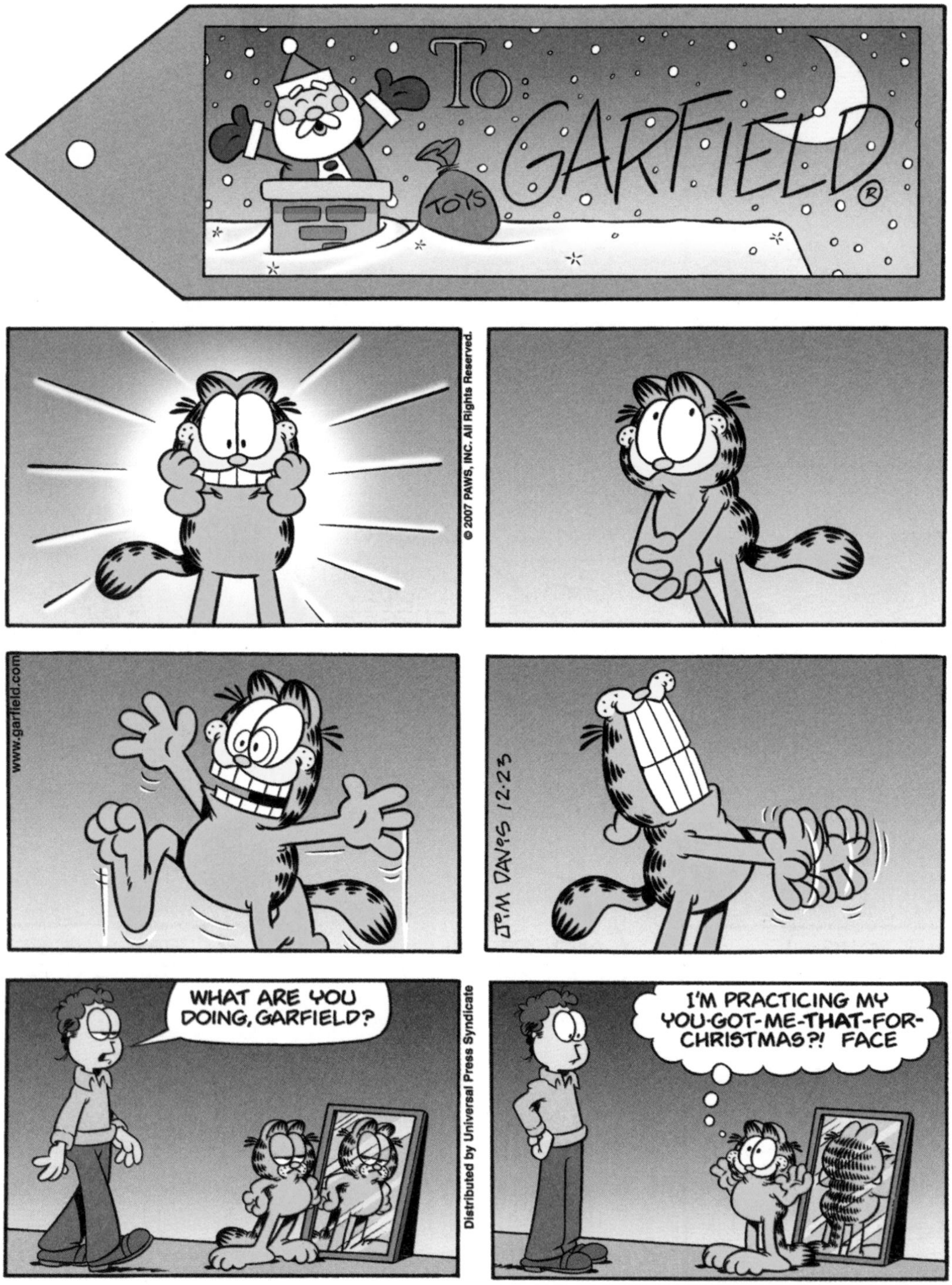
TO GARFIELD®
TOYS
© 2007 PAWS, INC. All Rights Reserved.
www.garfield.com
JPM DAVIS 12-23
Distributed by Universal Press Syndicate
WHAT ARE YOU DOING, GARFIELD?
I'M PRACTICING MY YOU-GOT-ME-THAT-FOR-CHRISTMAS?! FACE

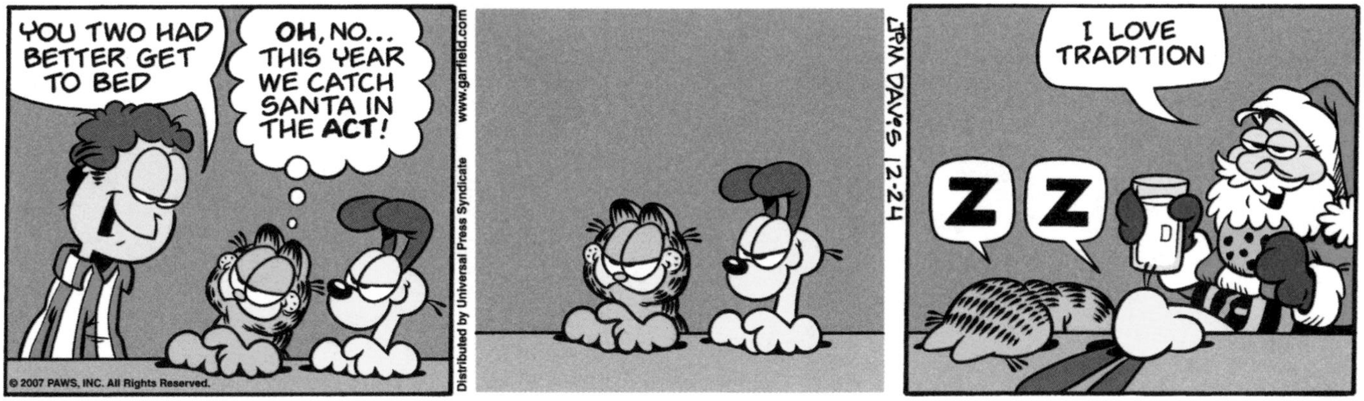
YOU TWO HAD BETTER GET TO BED
OH, NO... THIS YEAR WE CATCH SANTA IN THE ACT!
© 2007 PAWS, INC. All Rights Reserved.
www.garfield.com
Distributed by Universal Press Syndicate
JIM DAVIS 12-24
Z
Z
I LOVE TRADITION

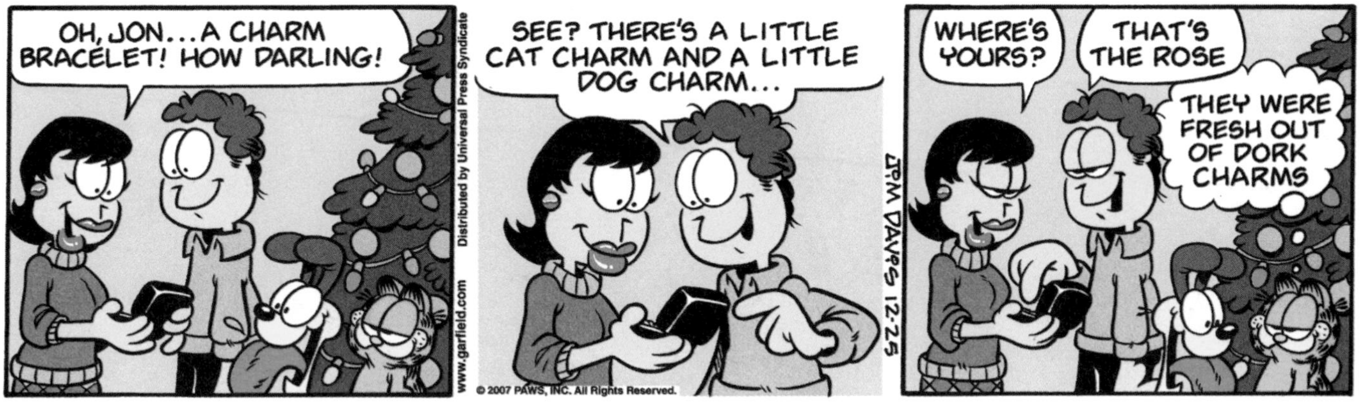
OH, JON... A CHARM BRACELET! HOW DARLING!
Distributed by Universal Press Syndicate
www.garfield.com
SEE? THERE'S A LITTLE CAT CHARM AND A LITTLE DOG CHARM...
© 2007 PAWS, INC. All Rights Reserved.
JIM DAVIS 12-25
WHERE'S YOURS?
THAT'S THE ROSE
THEY WERE FRESH OUT OF DORK CHARMS

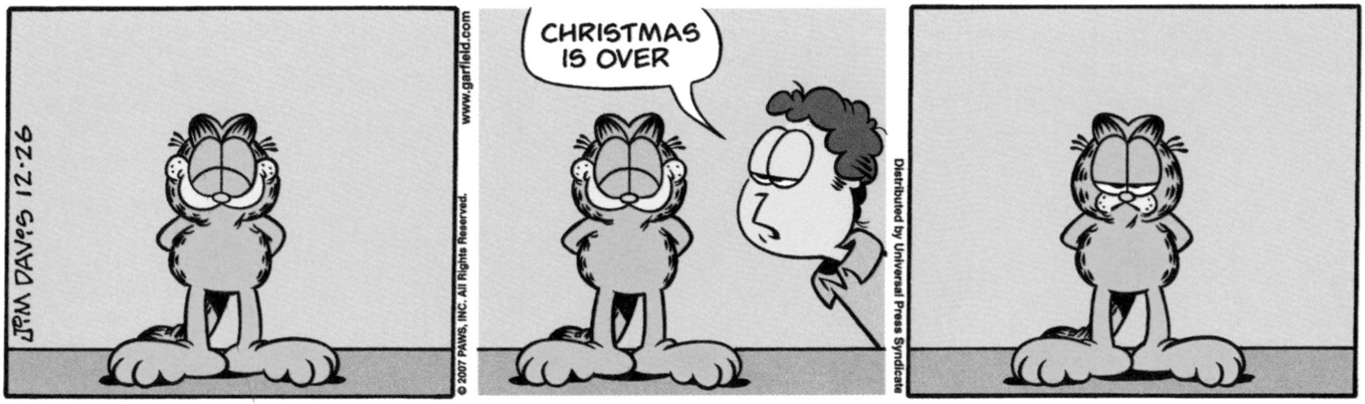
JIM DAVIS 12-26
www.garfield.com
© 2007 PAWS, INC. All Rights Reserved.
CHRISTMAS IS OVER
Distributed by Universal Press Syndicate

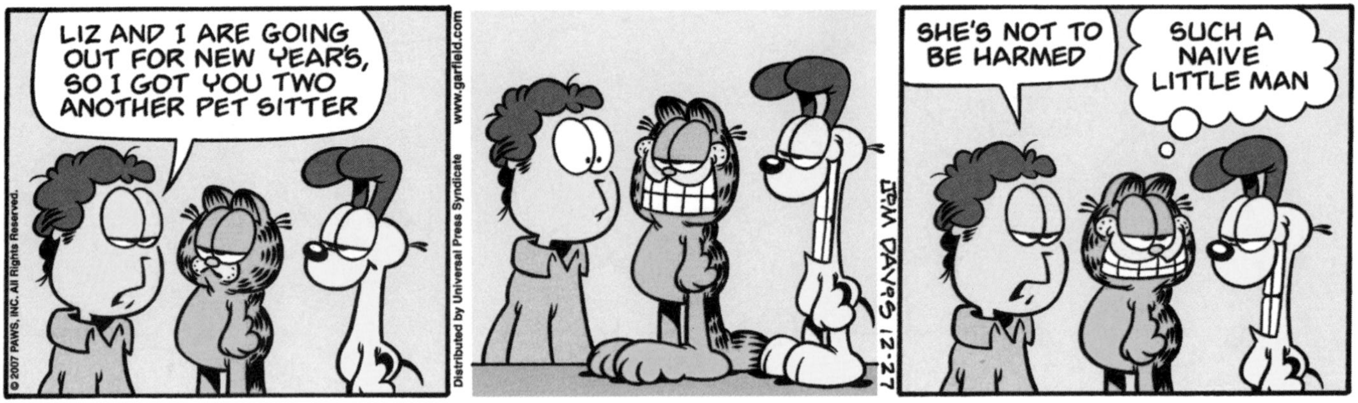
LIZ AND I ARE GOING OUT FOR NEW YEAR'S, SO I GOT YOU TWO ANOTHER PET SITTER
SHE'S NOT TO BE HARMED
SUCH A NAIVE LITTLE MAN
© 2007 PAWS, INC. All Rights Reserved.
Distributed by Universal Press Syndicate
www.garfield.com
JIM DAVIS 12-27

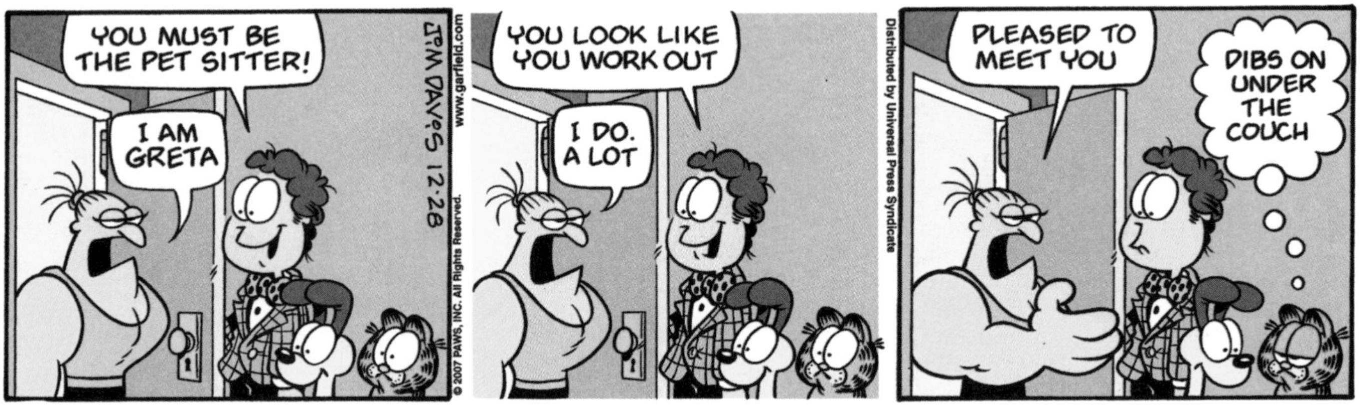
YOU MUST BE THE PET SITTER!
I AM GRETA
YOU LOOK LIKE YOU WORK OUT
I DO. A LOT
PLEASED TO MEET YOU
DIBS ON UNDER THE COUCH
JIM DAVIS 12-28
www.garfield.com
© 2007 PAWS, INC. All Rights Reserved.
Distributed by Universal Press Syndicate

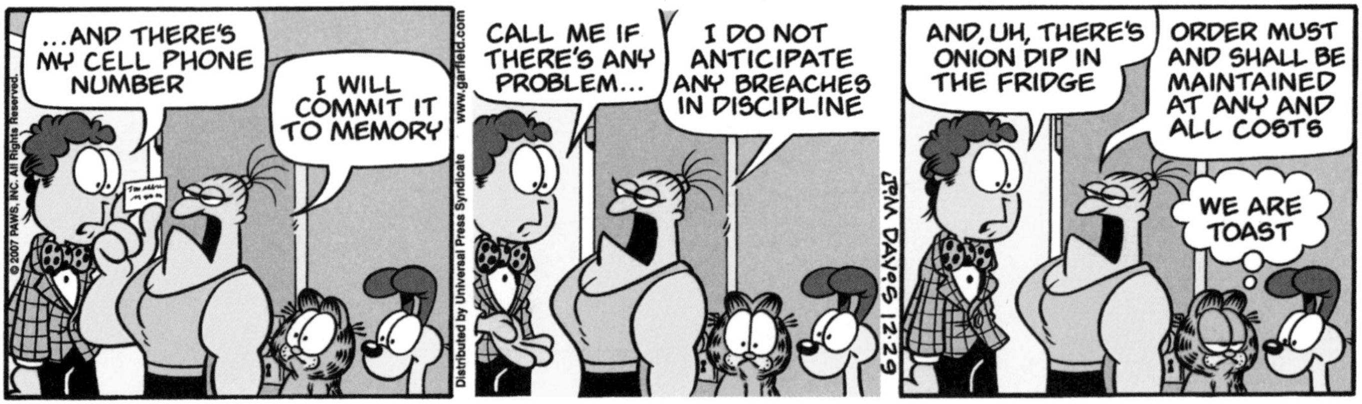
...AND THERE'S MY CELL PHONE NUMBER
I WILL COMMIT IT TO MEMORY
CALL ME IF THERE'S ANY PROBLEM...
I DO NOT ANTICIPATE ANY BREACHES IN DISCIPLINE
AND, UH, THERE'S ONION DIP IN THE FRIDGE
ORDER MUST AND SHALL BE MAINTAINED AT ANY AND ALL COSTS
WE ARE TOAST
© 2007 PAWS, INC. All Rights Reserved.
Distributed by Universal Press Syndicate
www.garfield.com
JIM DAVIS 12-29

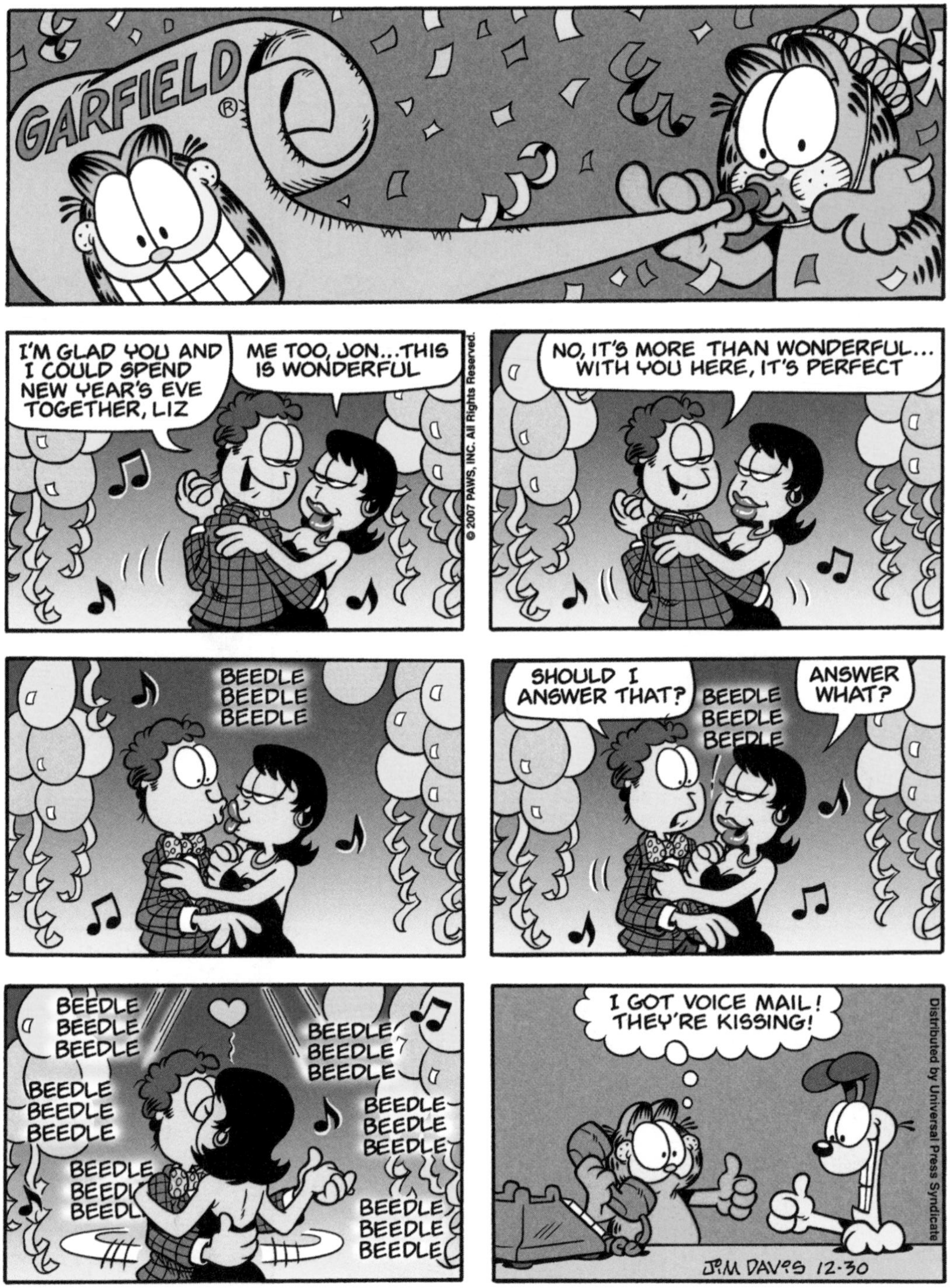
GARFIELD®
© 2007 PAWS, INC. All Rights Reserved.
I'M GLAD YOU AND I COULD SPEND NEW YEAR'S EVE TOGETHER, LIZ
ME TOO, JON...THIS IS WONDERFUL
NO, IT'S MORE THAN WONDERFUL... WITH YOU HERE, IT'S PERFECT
BEEDLE BEEDLE BEEDLE
SHOULD I ANSWER THAT?
BEEDLE BEEDLE BEEDLE
ANSWER WHAT?
BEEDLE BEEDLE BEEDLE
BEEDLE BEEDLE BEEDLE
BEEDLE BEEDLE BEEDLE
BEEDLE BEEDLE BEEDLE
BEEDLE BEEDLE BEEDLE
I GOT VOICE MAIL! THEY'RE KISSING!
JIM DAVIS 12-30
Distributed by Universal Press Syndicate

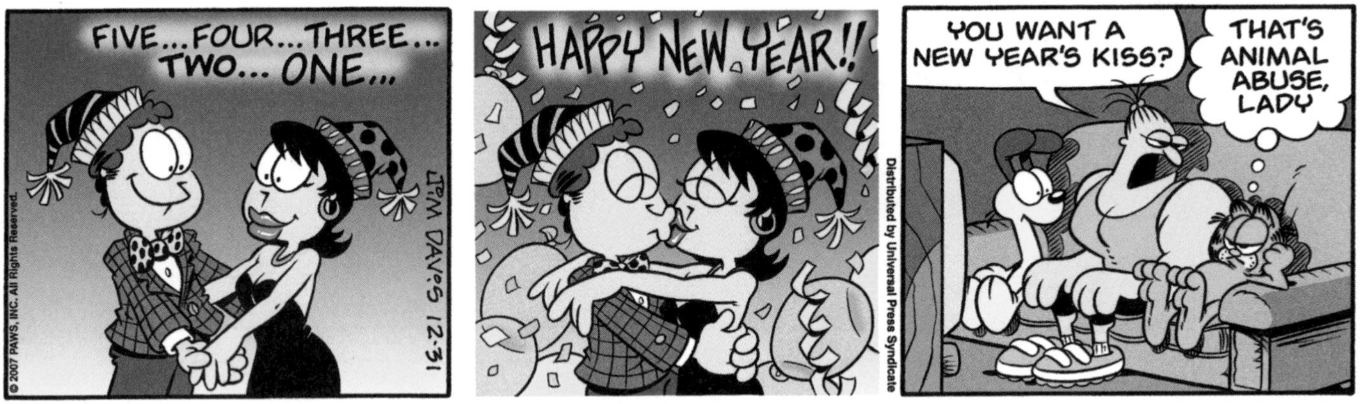
FIVE... FOUR... THREE... TWO... ONE...
JIM DAVIS 12-31
© 2007 PAWS, INC. All Rights Reserved.
HAPPY NEW YEAR!!
Distributed by Universal Press Syndicate
YOU WANT A NEW YEAR'S KISS?
THAT'S ANIMAL ABUSE, LADY

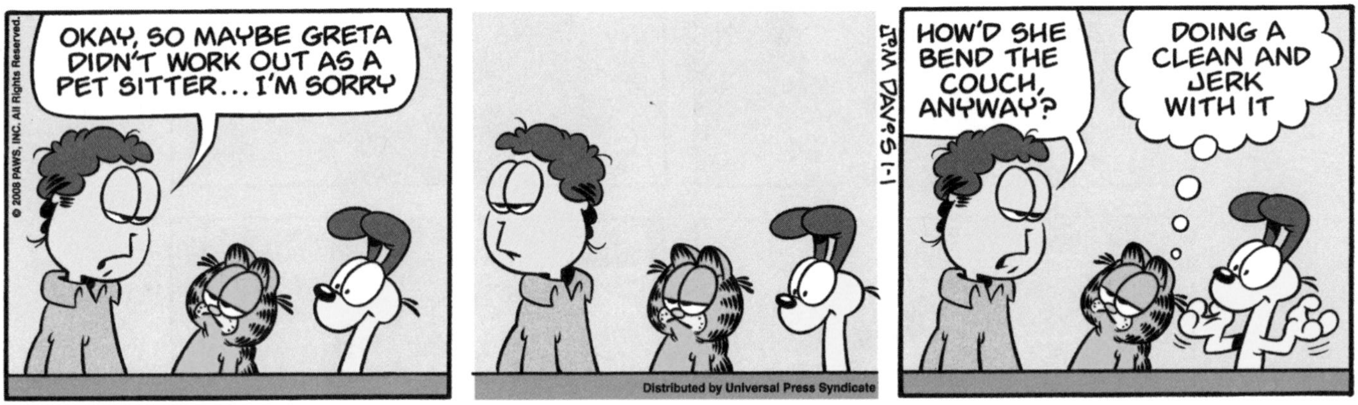
© 2008 PAWS, INC. All Rights Reserved.
OKAY, SO MAYBE GRETA DIDN'T WORK OUT AS A PET SITTER... I'M SORRY
Distributed by Universal Press Syndicate
JIM DAVIS 1-1
HOW'D SHE BEND THE COUCH, ANYWAY?
DOING A CLEAN AND JERK WITH IT

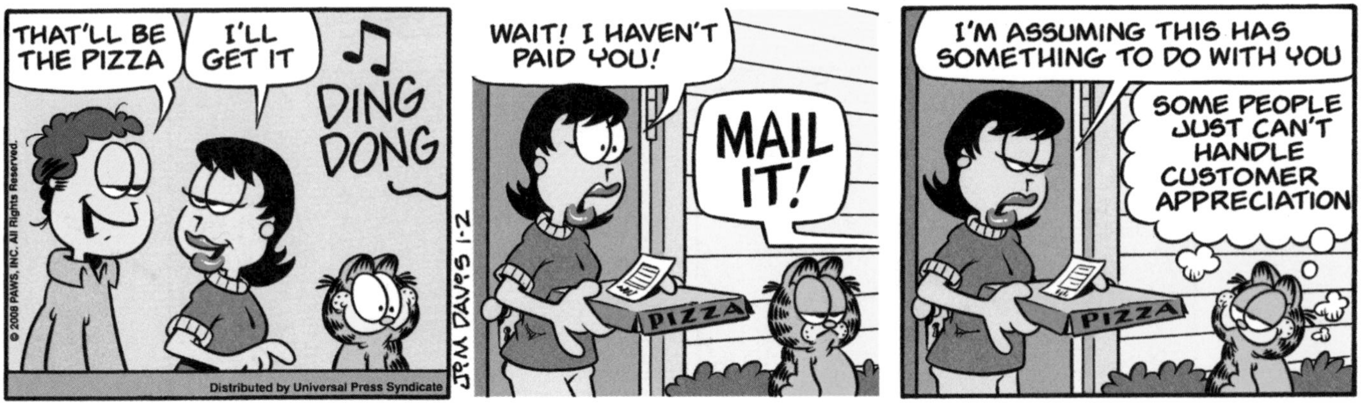
© 2008 PAWS, INC. All Rights Reserved.
THAT'LL BE THE PIZZA
I'LL GET IT
DING DONG
Distributed by Universal Press Syndicate
JIM DAVIS 1-2
WAIT! I HAVEN'T PAID YOU!
MAIL IT!
PIZZA
I'M ASSUMING THIS HAS SOMETHING TO DO WITH YOU
SOME PEOPLE JUST CAN'T HANDLE CUSTOMER APPRECIATION
PIZZA

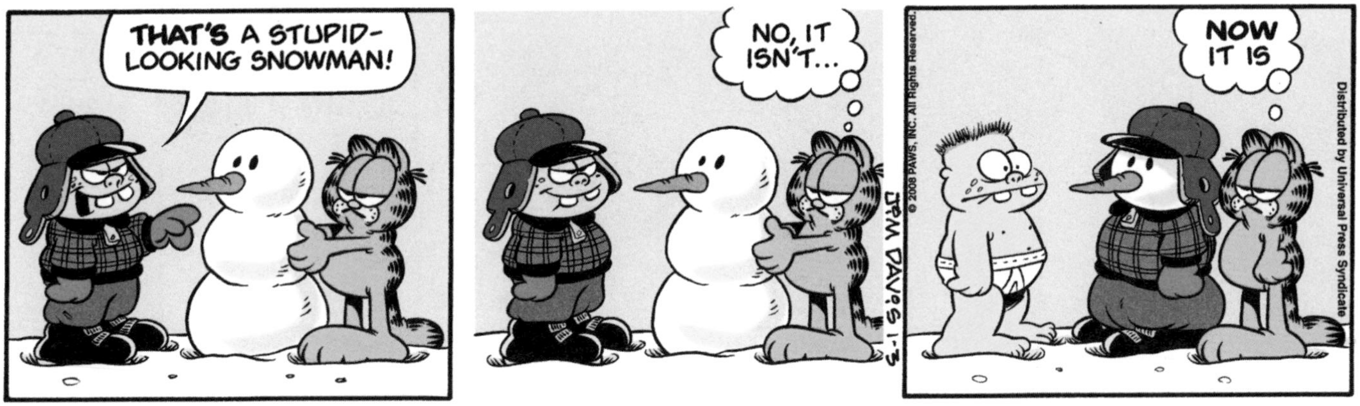
THAT'S A STUPID-LOOKING SNOWMAN!
NO, IT ISN'T...
NOW IT IS
© 2008 PAWS, INC. All Rights Reserved.
Distributed by Universal Press Syndicate

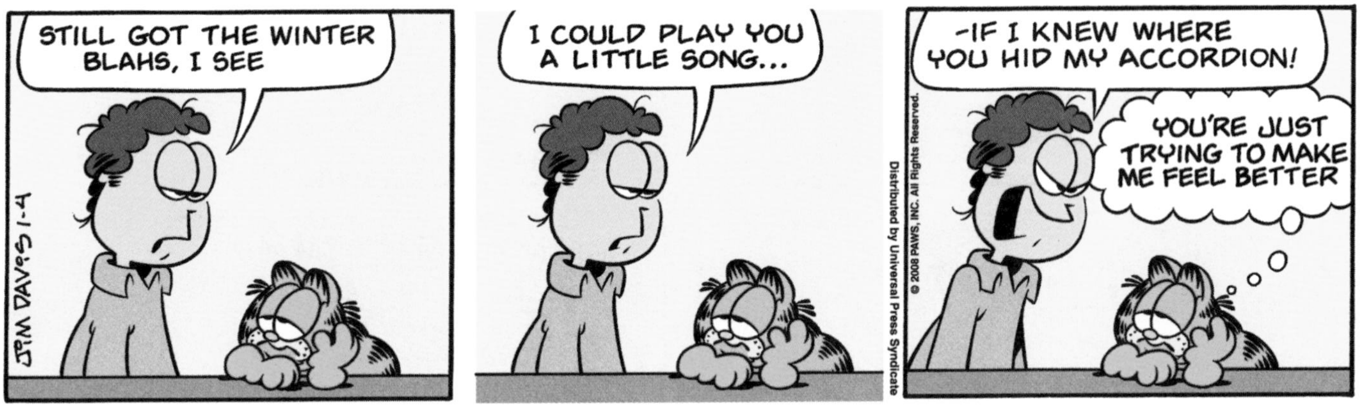
STILL GOT THE WINTER BLAHS, I SEE
I COULD PLAY YOU A LITTLE SONG...
-IF I KNEW WHERE YOU HID MY ACCORDION!
YOU'RE JUST TRYING TO MAKE ME FEEL BETTER
© 2008 PAWS, INC. All Rights Reserved.
Distributed by Universal Press Syndicate

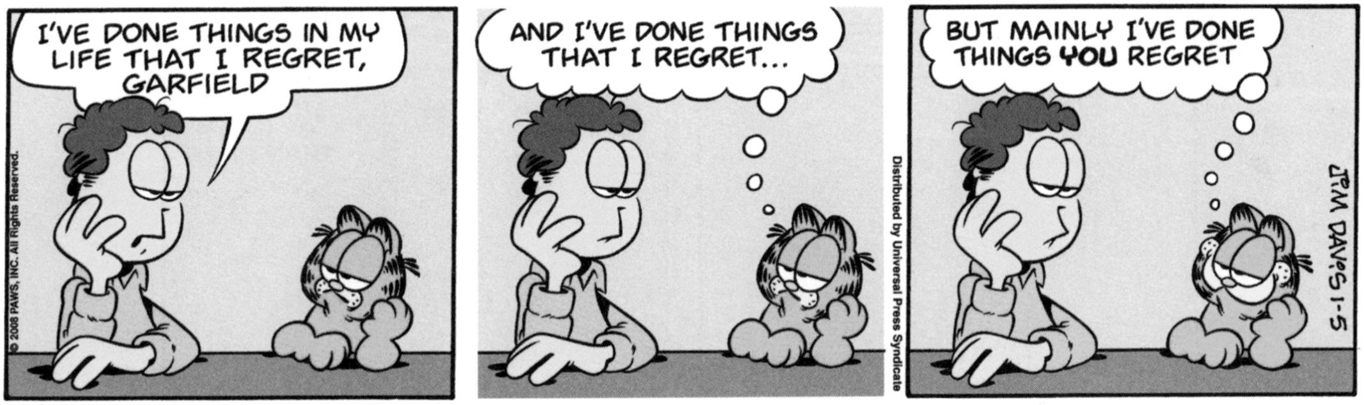
I'VE DONE THINGS IN MY LIFE THAT I REGRET, GARFIELD
AND I'VE DONE THINGS THAT I REGRET...
BUT MAINLY I'VE DONE THINGS YOU REGRET
© 2008 PAWS, INC. All Rights Reserved.
Distributed by Universal Press Syndicate

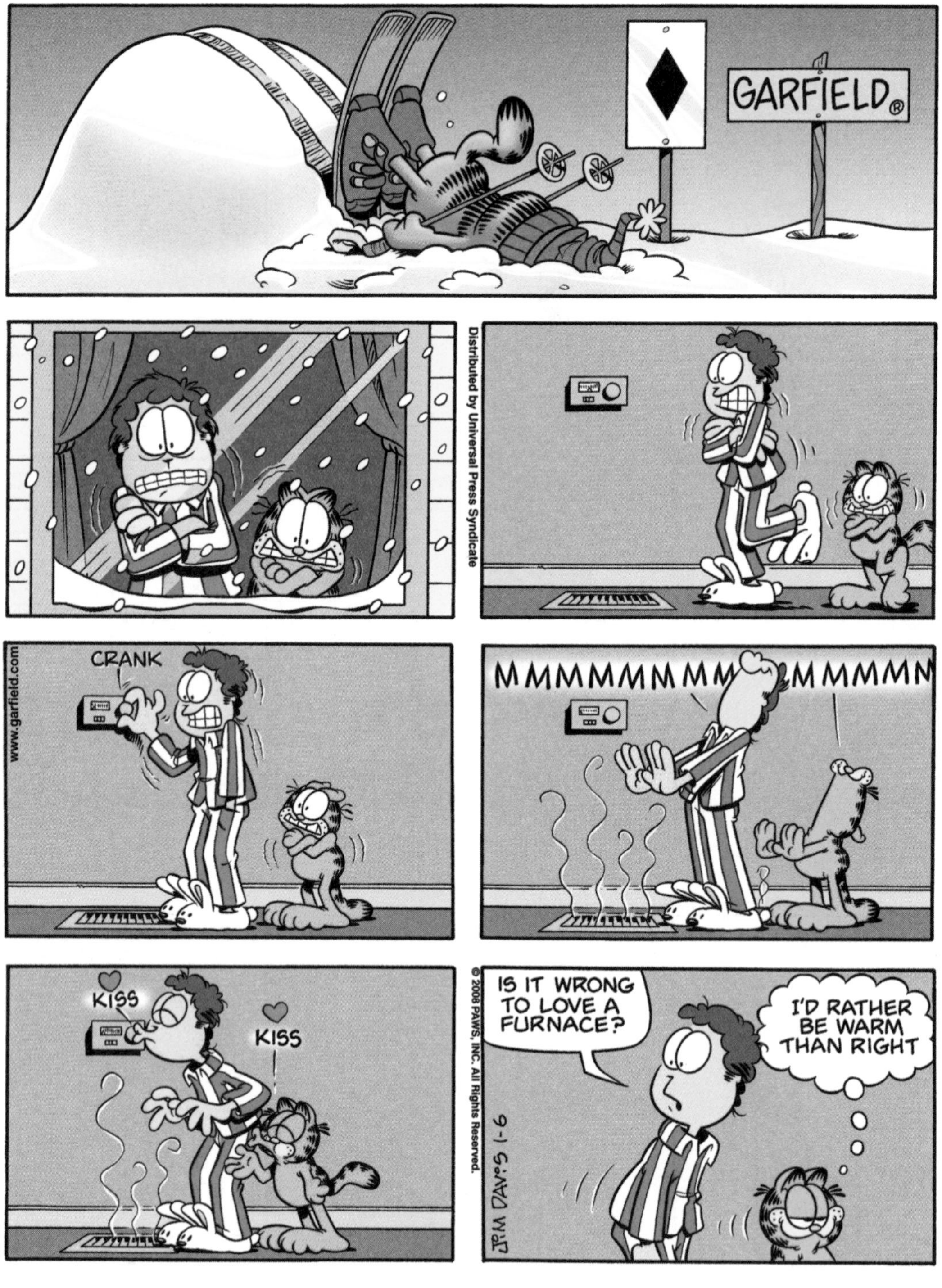
GARFIELD®
CRANK
MMMMMMMMMMMMMMMN
KISS
KISS
IS IT WRONG TO LOVE A FURNACE?
I'D RATHER BE WARM THAN RIGHT
JIM DAVIS 1-6
Distributed by Universal Press Syndicate
www.garfield.com

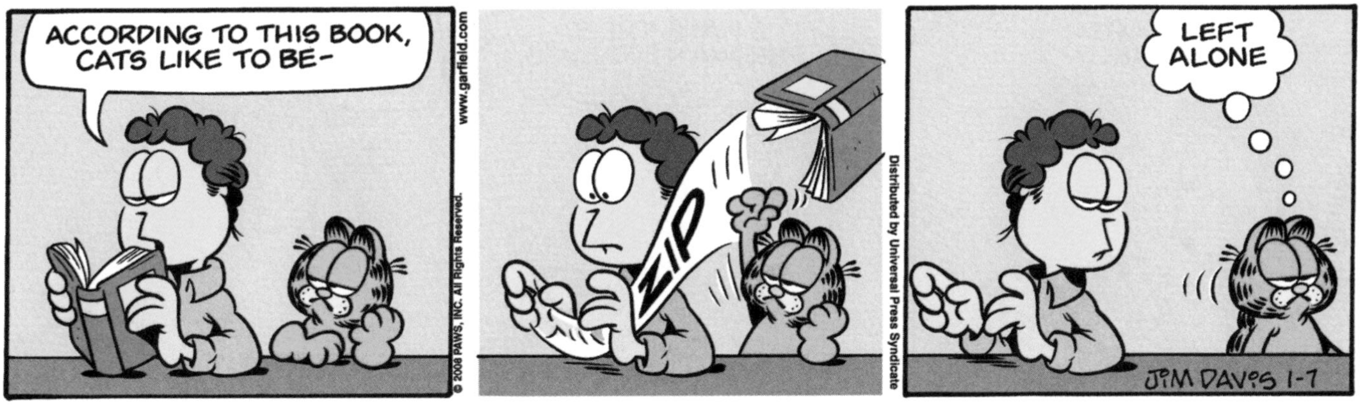
ACCORDING TO THIS BOOK, CATS LIKE TO BE-
© 2008 PAWS, INC. All Rights Reserved. www.garfield.com
ZIP
Distributed by Universal Press Syndicate
LEFT ALONE
JIM DAVIS 1-7

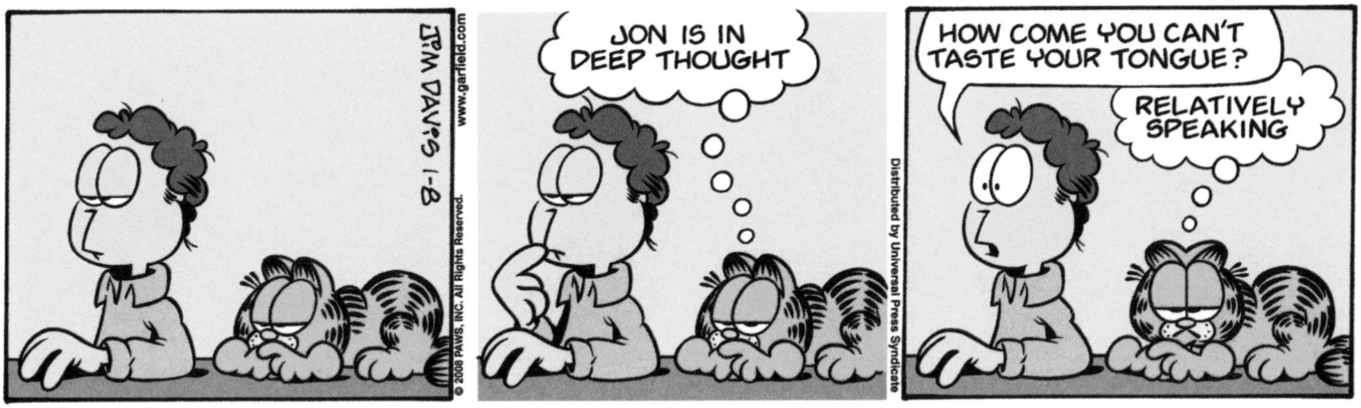
JIM DAVIS 1-8
© 2008 PAWS, INC. All Rights Reserved. www.garfield.com
JON IS IN DEEP THOUGHT
Distributed by Universal Press Syndicate
HOW COME YOU CAN'T TASTE YOUR TONGUE?
RELATIVELY SPEAKING

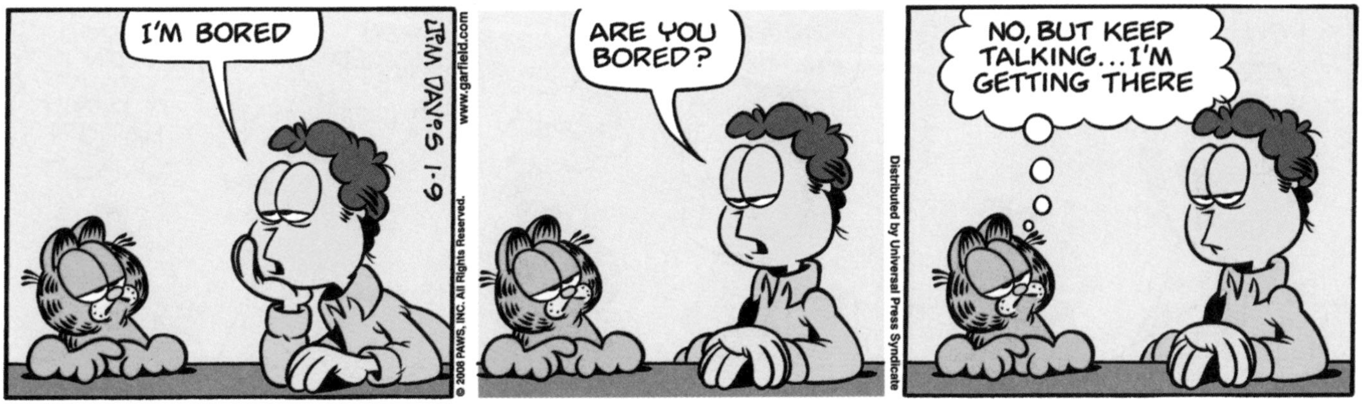
I'M BORED
JIM DAVIS 1-9
© 2008 PAWS, INC. All Rights Reserved. www.garfield.com
ARE YOU BORED?
Distributed by Universal Press Syndicate
NO, BUT KEEP TALKING... I'M GETTING THERE

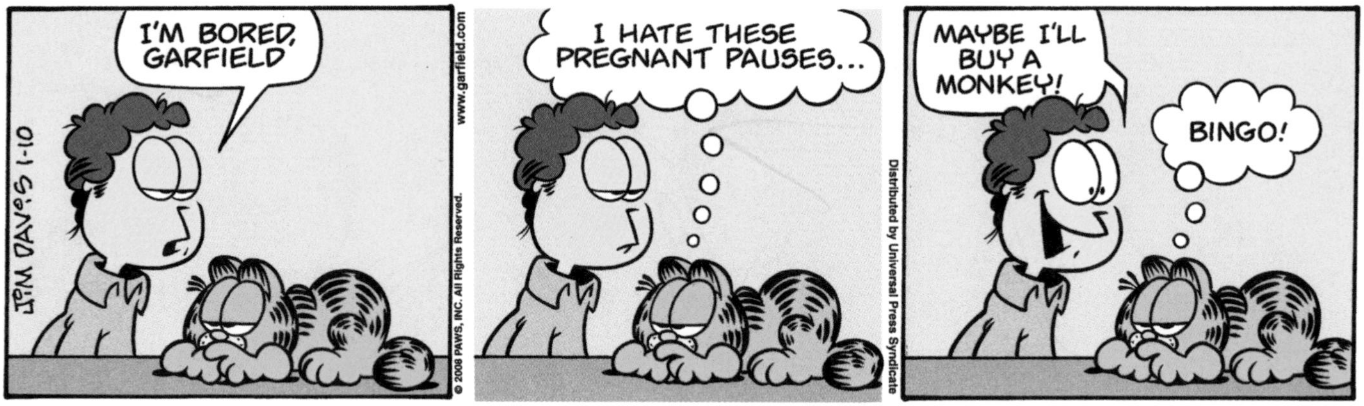
I'M BORED, GARFIELD
JIM DAVIS 1-10
© 2008 PAWS, INC. All Rights Reserved.
www.garfield.com
I HATE THESE PREGNANT PAUSES...
Distributed by Universal Press Syndicate
MAYBE I'LL BUY A MONKEY!
BINGO!

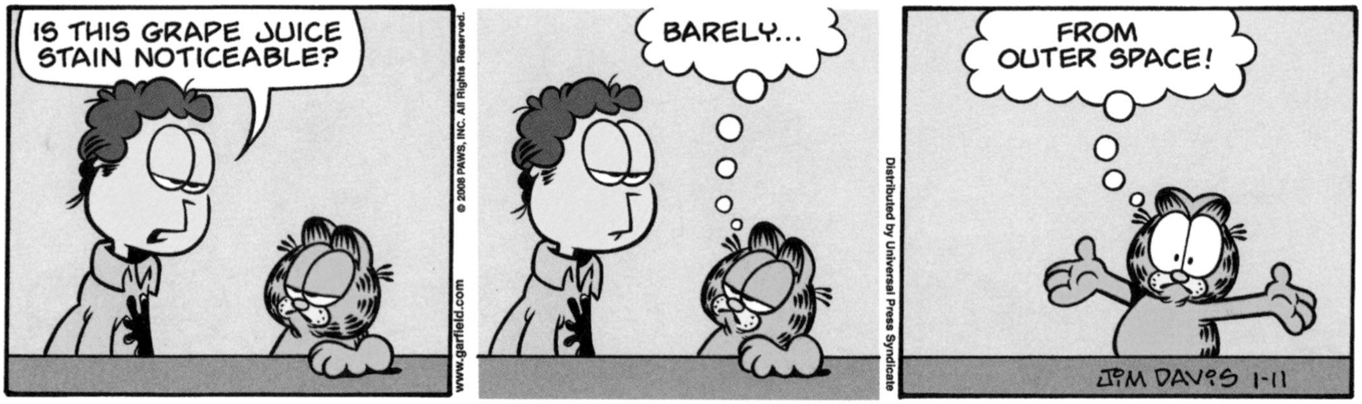
IS THIS GRAPE JUICE STAIN NOTICEABLE?
www.garfield.com
© 2008 PAWS, INC. All Rights Reserved.
BARELY...
Distributed by Universal Press Syndicate
FROM OUTER SPACE!
JIM DAVIS 1-11

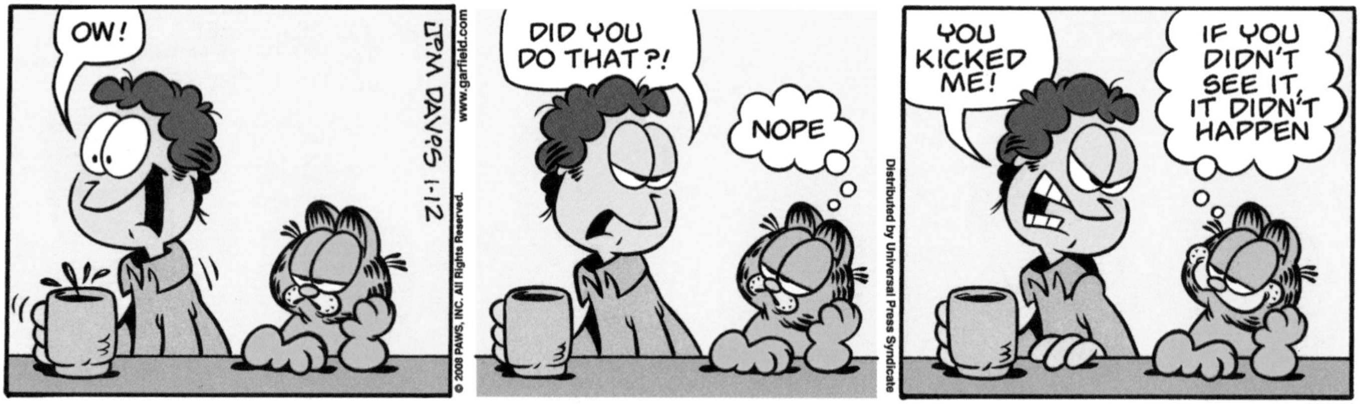
OW!
JIM DAVIS 1-12
www.garfield.com
© 2008 PAWS, INC. All Rights Reserved.
DID YOU DO THAT?!
NOPE
Distributed by Universal Press Syndicate
YOU KICKED ME!
IF YOU DIDN'T SEE IT, IT DIDN'T HAPPEN

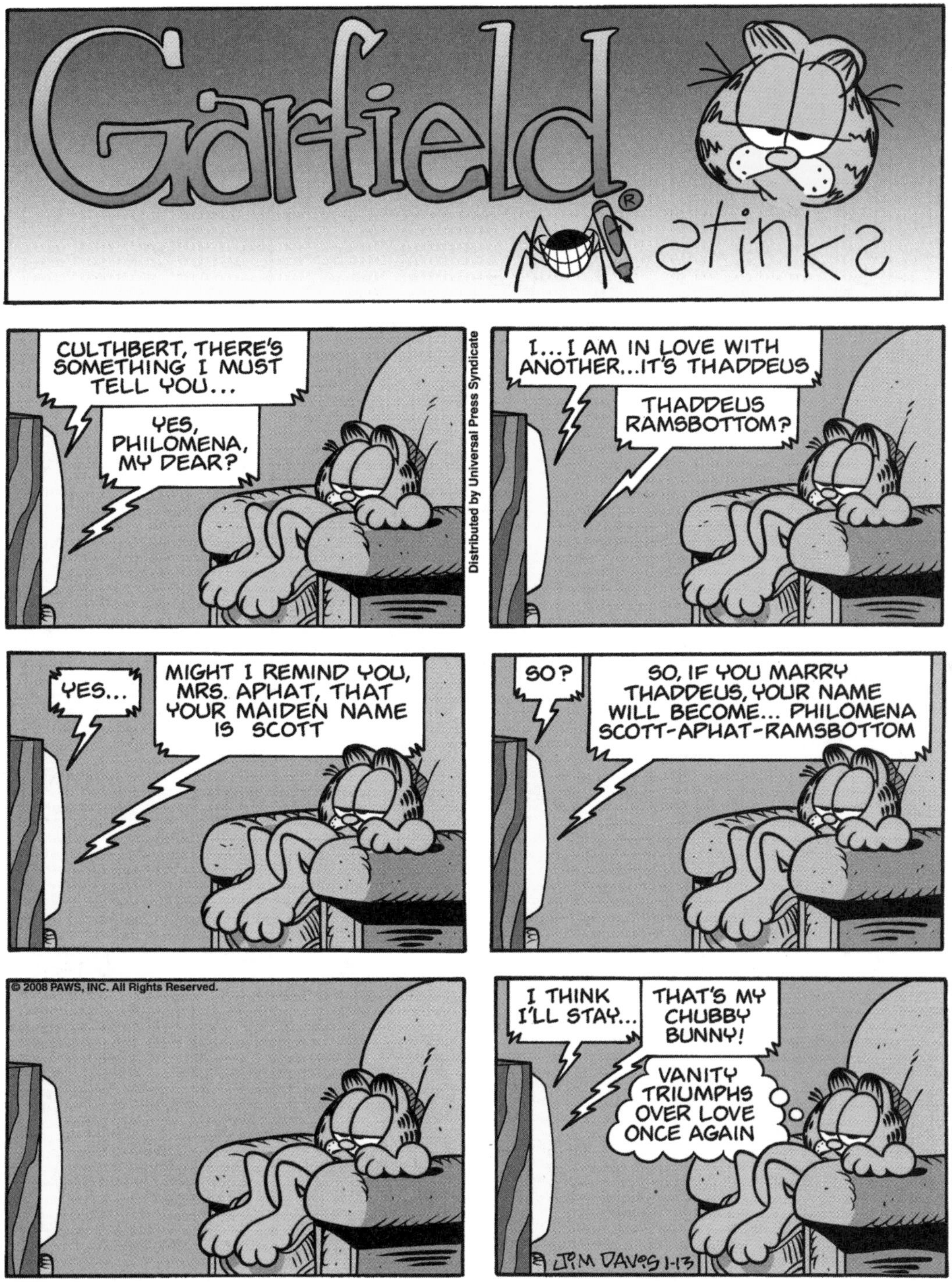
Garfield
stinks
Distributed by Universal Press Syndicate
CULTHBERT, THERE'S SOMETHING I MUST TELL YOU...
YES, PHILOMENA, MY DEAR?
I... I AM IN LOVE WITH ANOTHER...IT'S THADDEUS
THADDEUS RAMSBOTTOM?
YES...
MIGHT I REMIND YOU, MRS. APHAT, THAT YOUR MAIDEN NAME IS SCOTT
SO?
SO, IF YOU MARRY THADDEUS, YOUR NAME WILL BECOME... PHILOMENA SCOTT-APHAT-RAMSBOTTOM
© 2008 PAWS, INC. All Rights Reserved.
I THINK I'LL STAY...
THAT'S MY CHUBBY BUNNY!
VANITY TRIUMPHS OVER LOVE ONCE AGAIN
JIM DAVIS 1-13

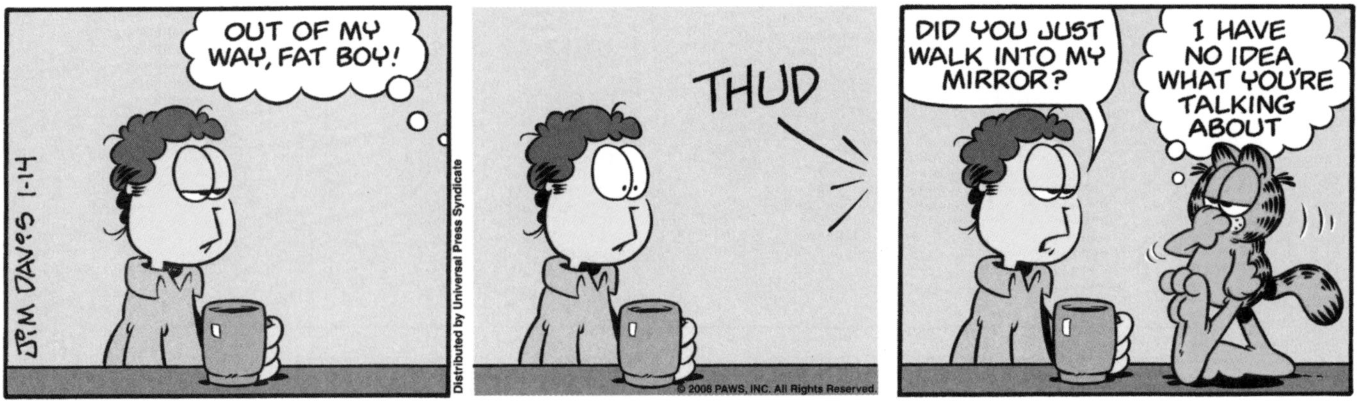
OUT OF MY WAY, FAT BOY!
JIM DAVIS 1-14
THUD
Distributed by Universal Press Syndicate
© 2008 PAWS, INC. All Rights Reserved.
DID YOU JUST WALK INTO MY MIRROR?
I HAVE NO IDEA WHAT YOU'RE TALKING ABOUT

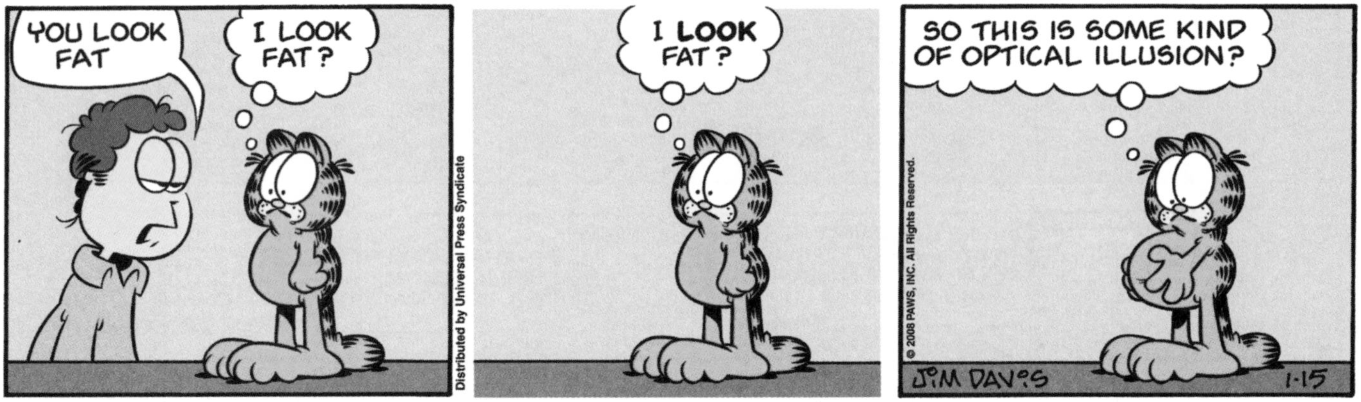
YOU LOOK FAT
I LOOK FAT?
Distributed by Universal Press Syndicate
I **LOOK** FAT?
SO THIS IS SOME KIND OF OPTICAL ILLUSION?
© 2008 PAWS, INC. All Rights Reserved.
JIM DAVIS 1-15

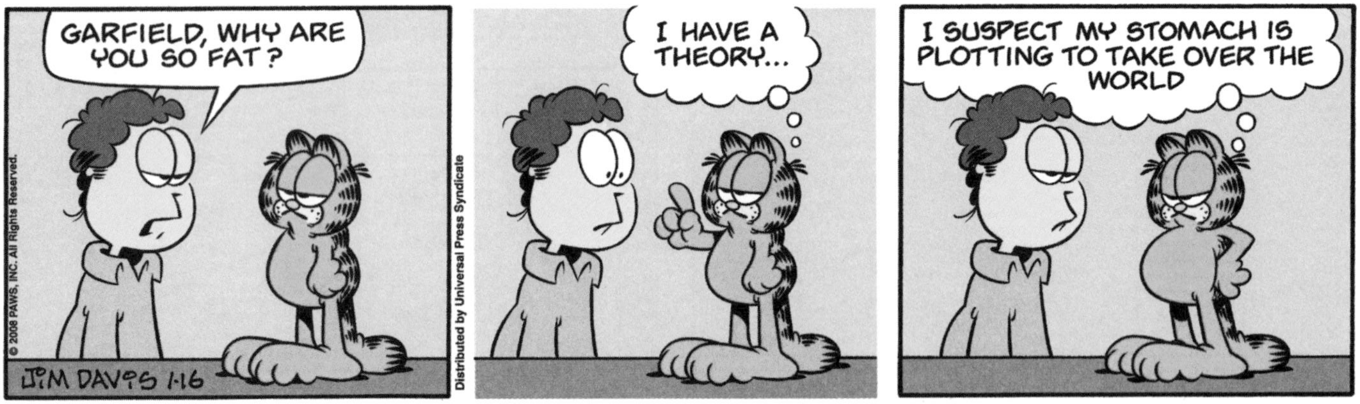
GARFIELD, WHY ARE YOU SO FAT?
© 2008 PAWS, INC. All Rights Reserved.
JIM DAVIS 1-16
Distributed by Universal Press Syndicate
I HAVE A THEORY...
I SUSPECT MY STOMACH IS PLOTTING TO TAKE OVER THE WORLD

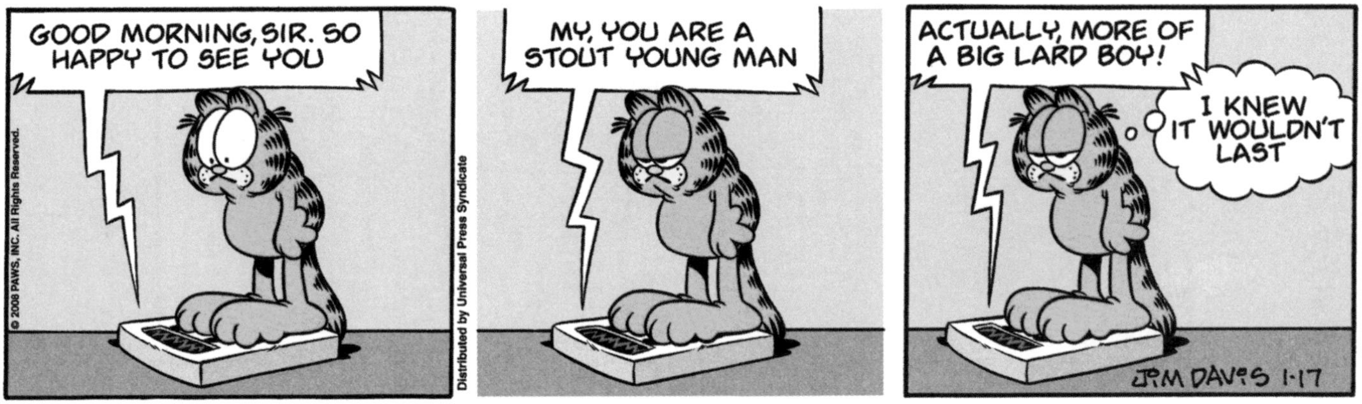
GOOD MORNING, SIR. SO HAPPY TO SEE YOU
MY, YOU ARE A STOUT YOUNG MAN
ACTUALLY, MORE OF A BIG LARD BOY!
I KNEW IT WOULDN'T LAST
JIM DAVIS 1-17
© 2008 PAWS, INC. All Rights Reserved.
Distributed by Universal Press Syndicate

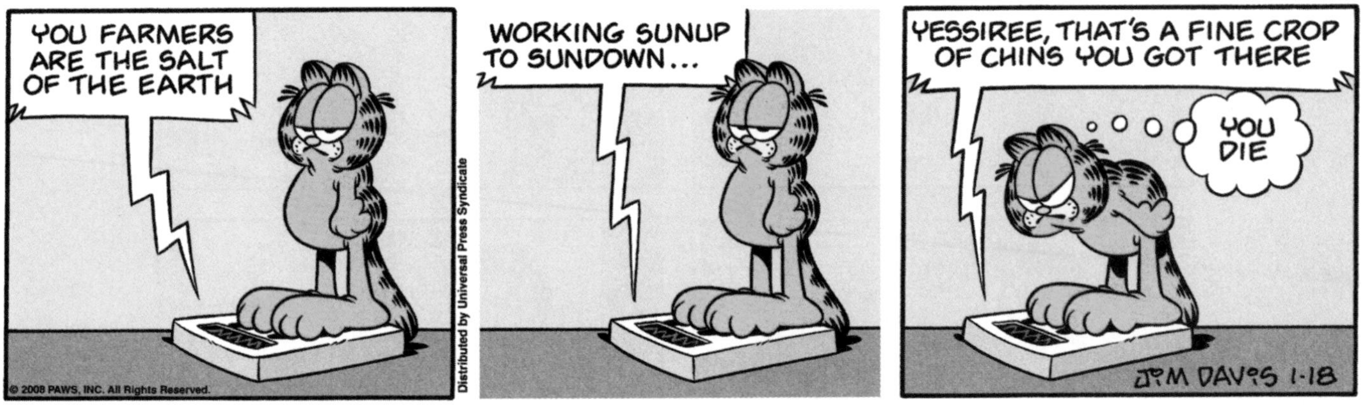
YOU FARMERS ARE THE SALT OF THE EARTH
WORKING SUNUP TO SUNDOWN...
YESSIREE, THAT'S A FINE CROP OF CHINS YOU GOT THERE
YOU DIE
JIM DAVIS 1-18
© 2008 PAWS, INC. All Rights Reserved.
Distributed by Universal Press Syndicate

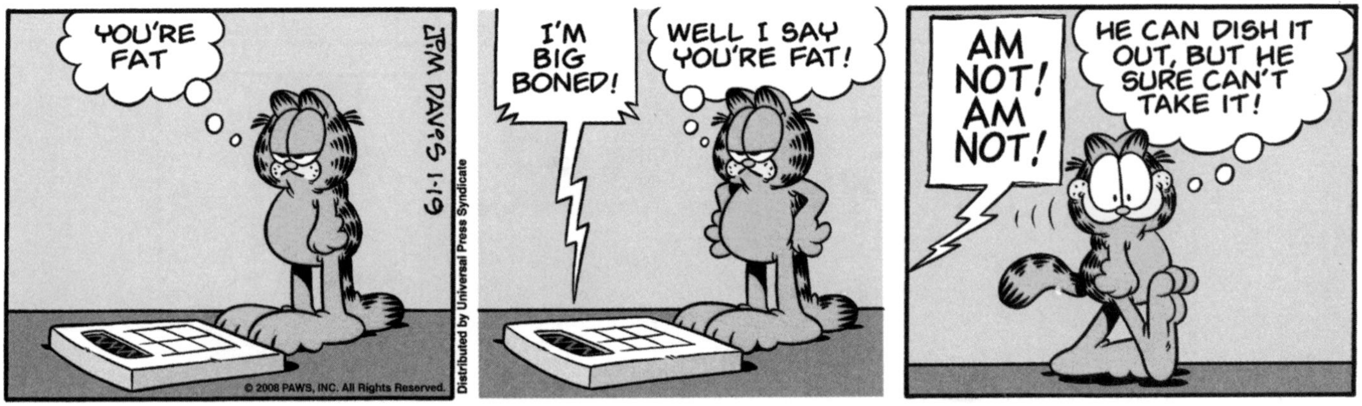
YOU'RE FAT
JIM DAVIS 1-19
I'M BIG BONED!
WELL I SAY YOU'RE FAT!
AM NOT! AM NOT!
HE CAN DISH IT OUT, BUT HE SURE CAN'T TAKE IT!
© 2008 PAWS, INC. All Rights Reserved.
Distributed by Universal Press Syndicate

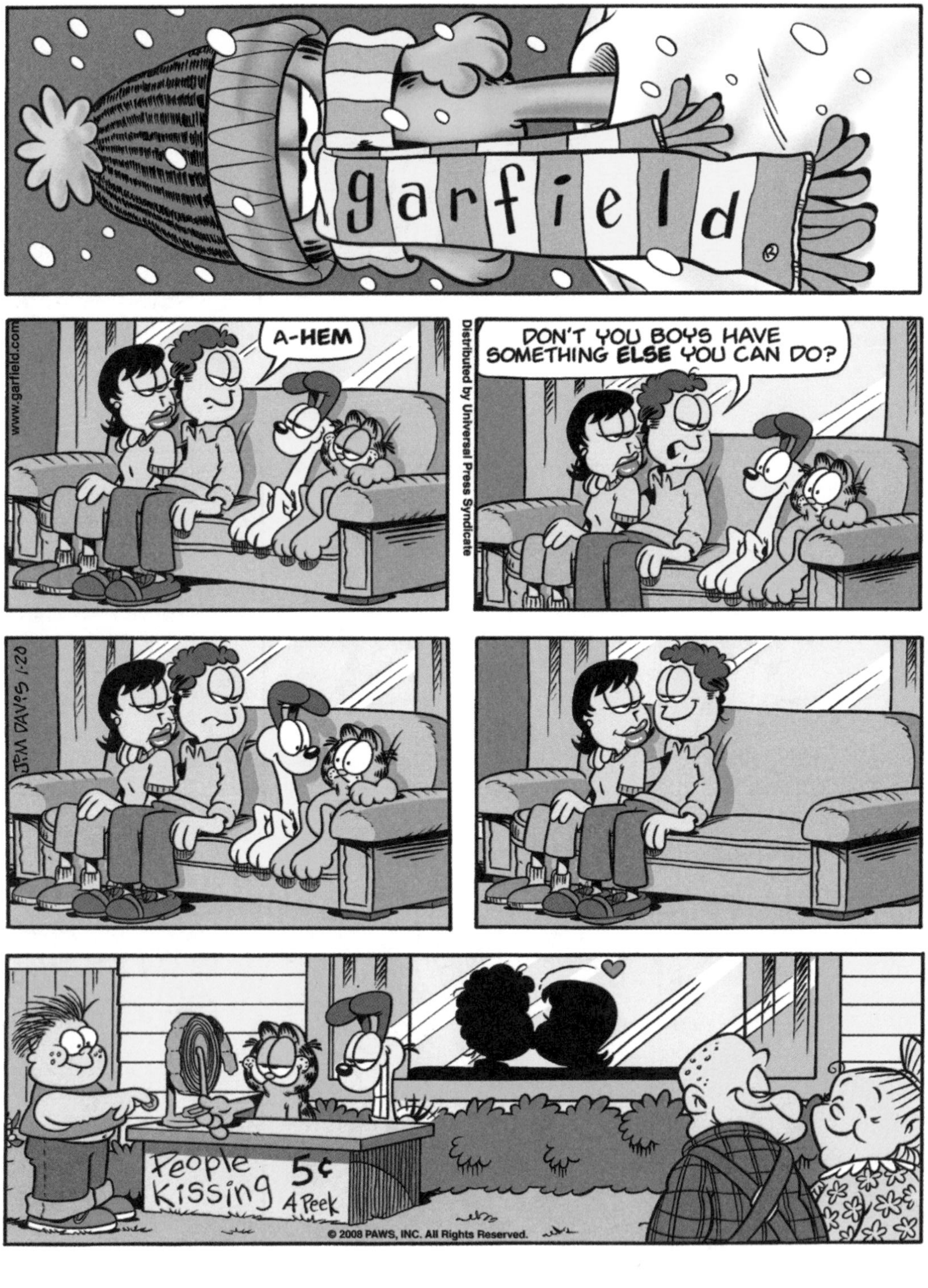
garfield
www.garfield.com
Distributed by Universal Press Syndicate
A-HEM
DON'T YOU BOYS HAVE SOMETHING ELSE YOU CAN DO?
JIM DAVIS 1-20
People Kissing 5¢ A Peek
© 2008 PAWS, INC. All Rights Reserved.

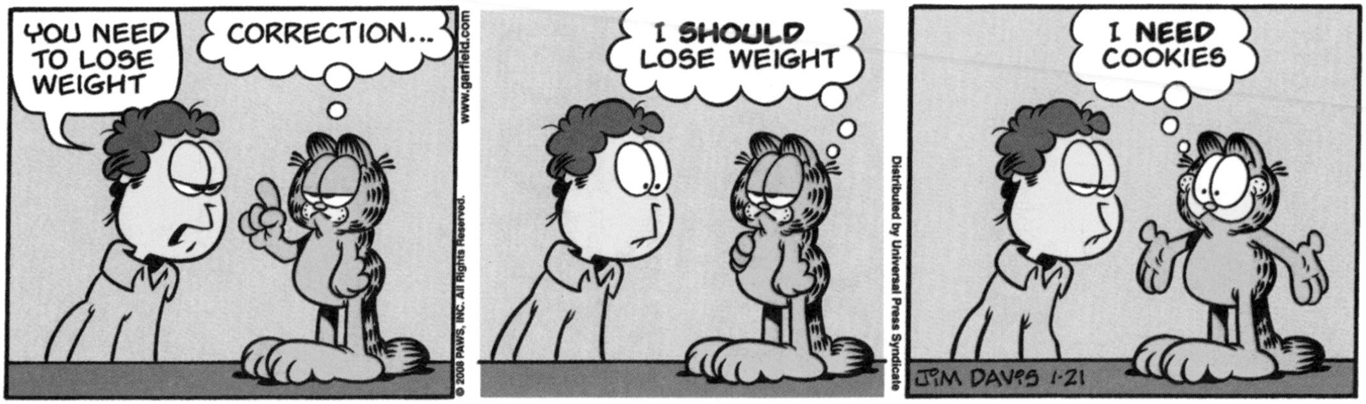
YOU NEED TO LOSE WEIGHT
CORRECTION...
I SHOULD LOSE WEIGHT
I NEED COOKIES
© 2008 PAWS, INC. All Rights Reserved. www.garfield.com
Distributed by Universal Press Syndicate
JIM DAVIS 1-21

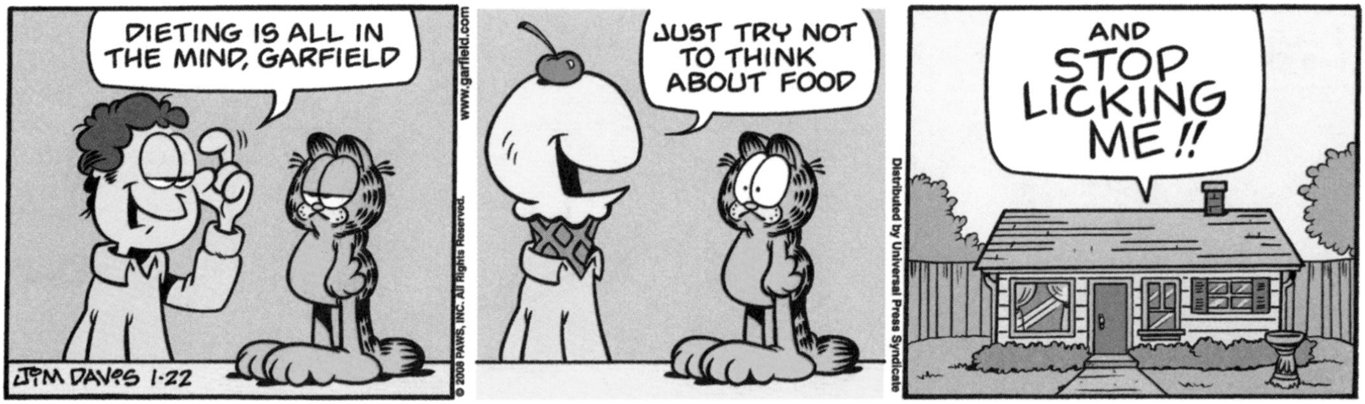
DIETING IS ALL IN THE MIND, GARFIELD
JUST TRY NOT TO THINK ABOUT FOOD
AND STOP LICKING ME!!
JIM DAVIS 1-22
© 2008 PAWS, INC. All Rights Reserved. www.garfield.com
Distributed by Universal Press Syndicate

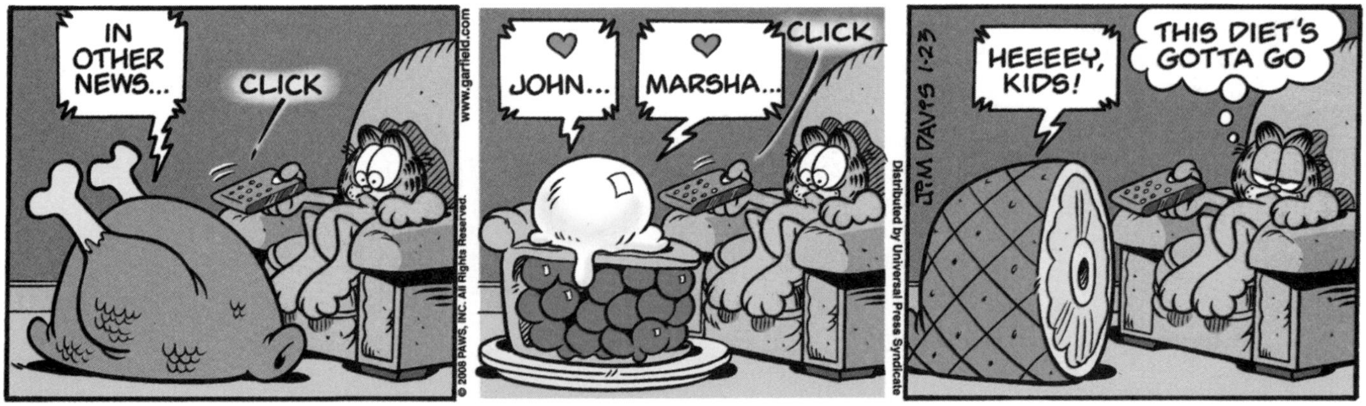
IN OTHER NEWS...
CLICK
JOHN...
MARSHA...
CLICK
HEEEEY, KIDS!
THIS DIET'S GOTTA GO
© 2008 PAWS, INC. All Rights Reserved. www.garfield.com
Distributed by Universal Press Syndicate
JIM DAVIS 1-23

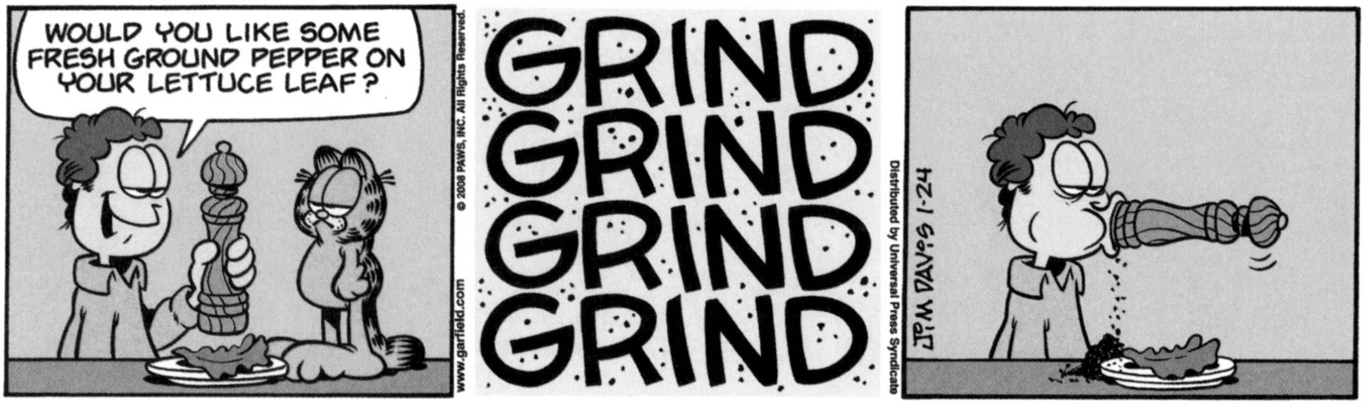
WOULD YOU LIKE SOME FRESH GROUND PEPPER ON YOUR LETTUCE LEAF?
GRIND GRIND GRIND GRIND

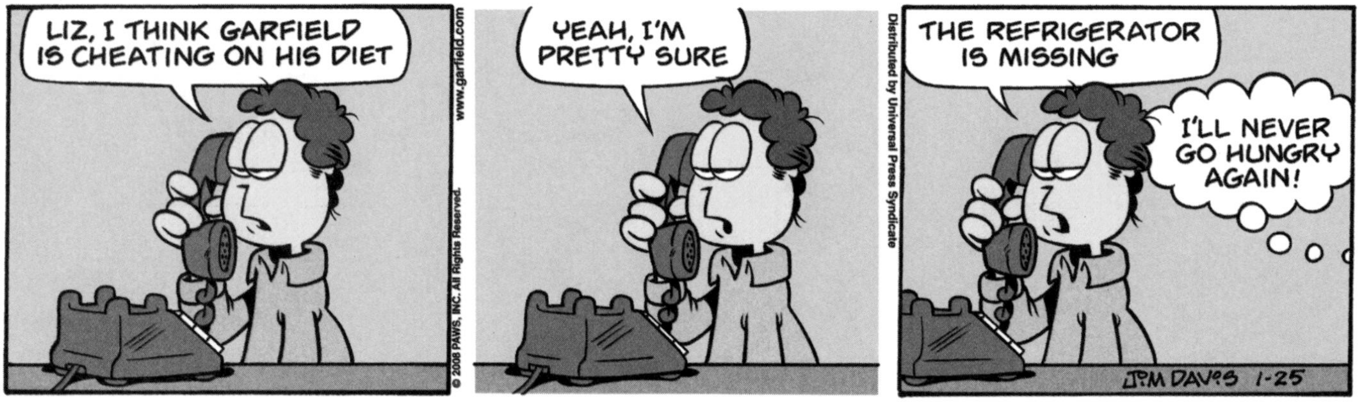
LIZ, I THINK GARFIELD IS CHEATING ON HIS DIET
YEAH, I'M PRETTY SURE
THE REFRIGERATOR IS MISSING
I'LL NEVER GO HUNGRY AGAIN!

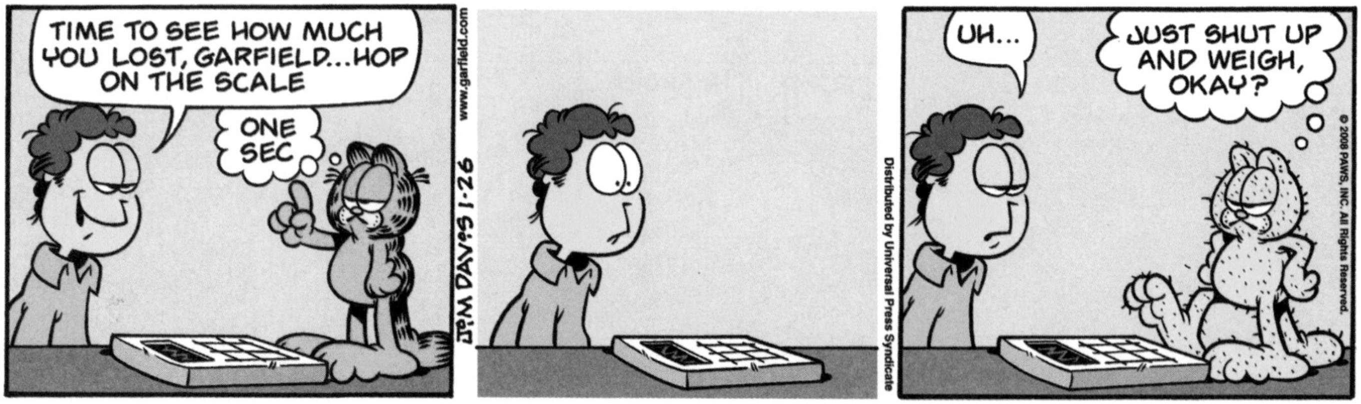
TIME TO SEE HOW MUCH YOU LOST, GARFIELD...HOP ON THE SCALE
ONE SEC
UH...
JUST SHUT UP AND WEIGH, OKAY?

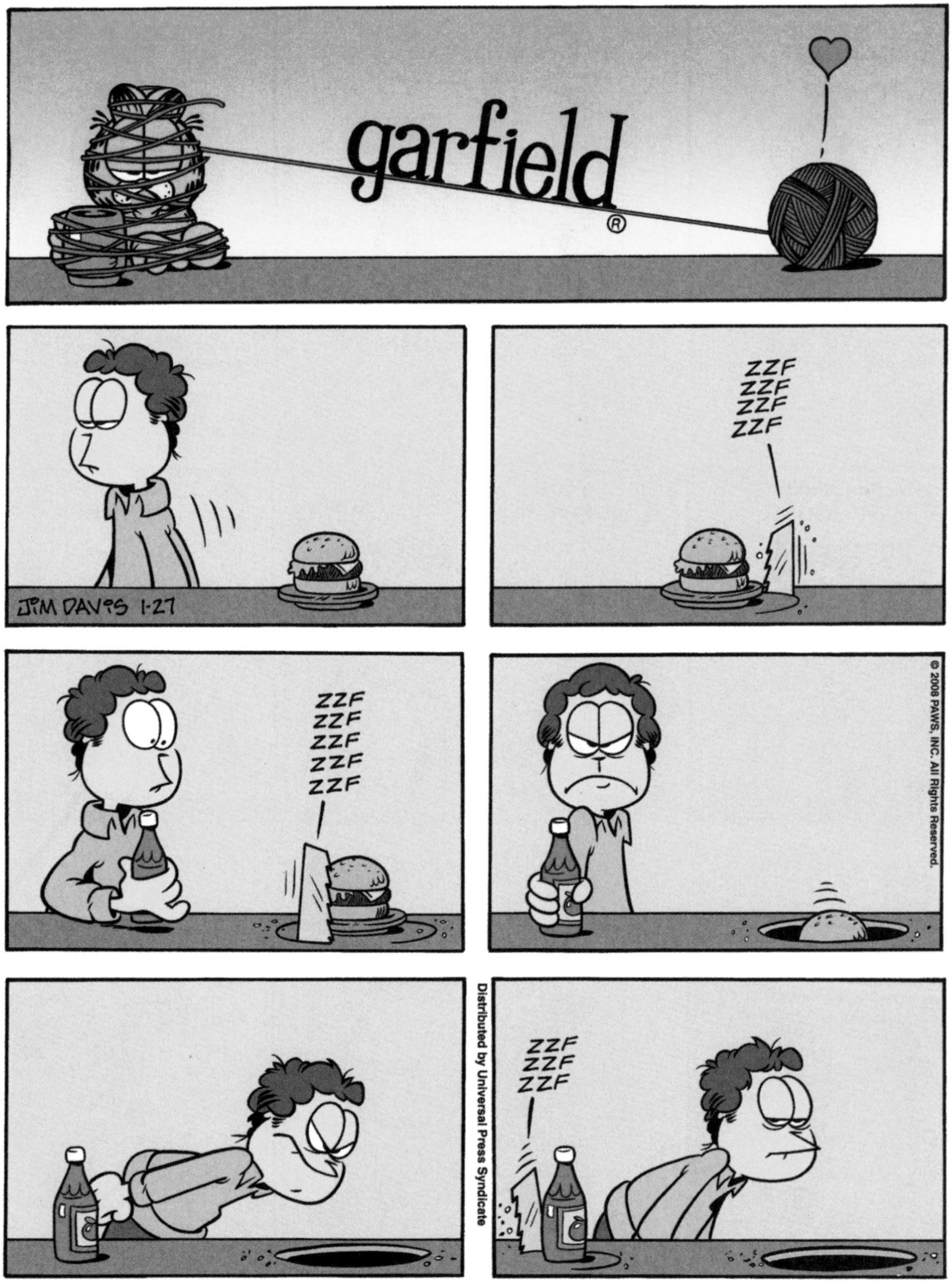
garfield
JIM DAVIS 1-27
ZZF
ZZF
ZZF
ZZF
ZZF
ZZF
ZZF
ZZF
ZZF
© 2008 PAWS, INC. All Rights Reserved.
Distributed by Universal Press Syndicate
ZZF
ZZF
ZZF

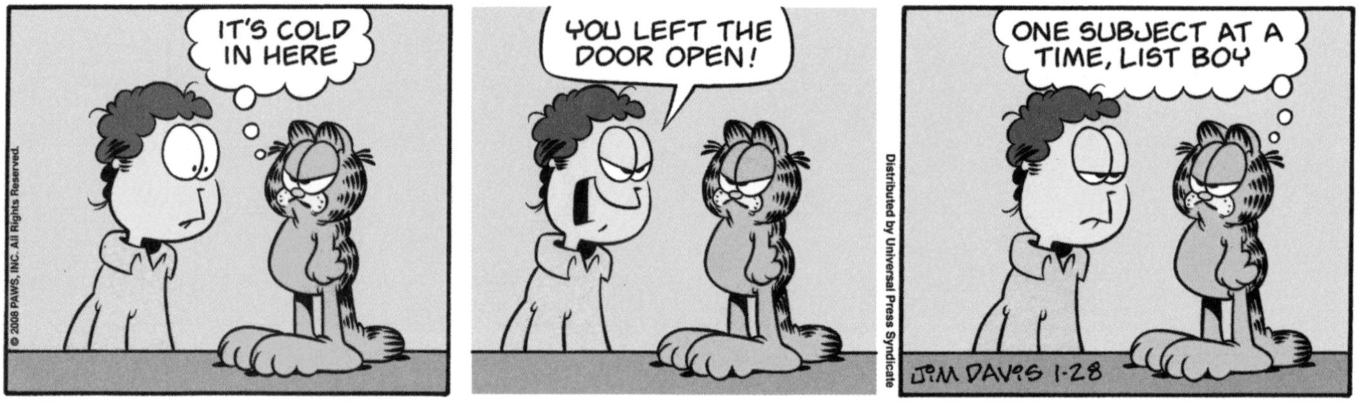
© 2008 PAWS, INC. All Rights Reserved.
IT'S COLD IN HERE
YOU LEFT THE DOOR OPEN!
Distributed by Universal Press Syndicate
ONE SUBJECT AT A TIME, LIST BOY
JIM DAVIS 1-28

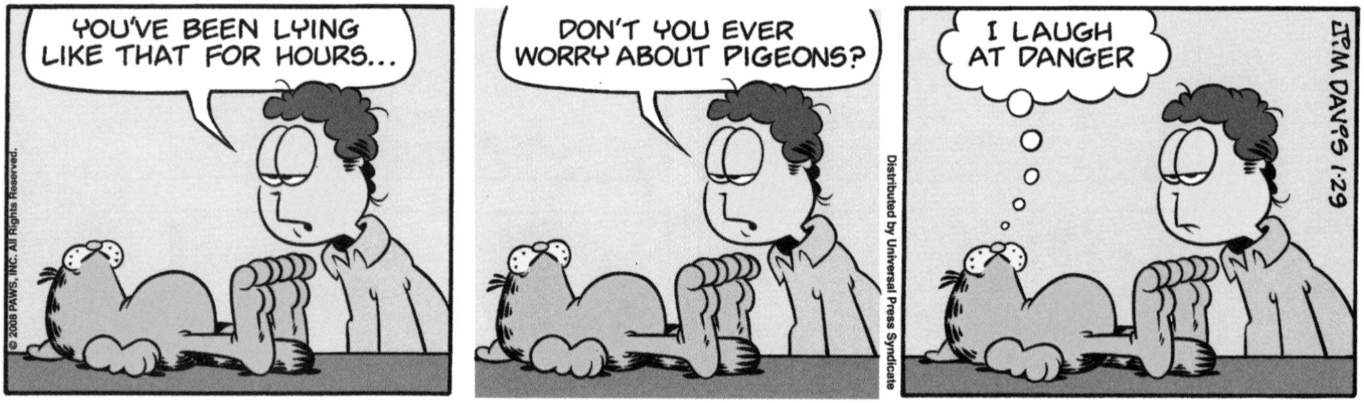
© 2008 PAWS, INC. All Rights Reserved.
YOU'VE BEEN LYING LIKE THAT FOR HOURS...
DON'T YOU EVER WORRY ABOUT PIGEONS?
Distributed by Universal Press Syndicate
I LAUGH AT DANGER
JIM DAVIS 1-29

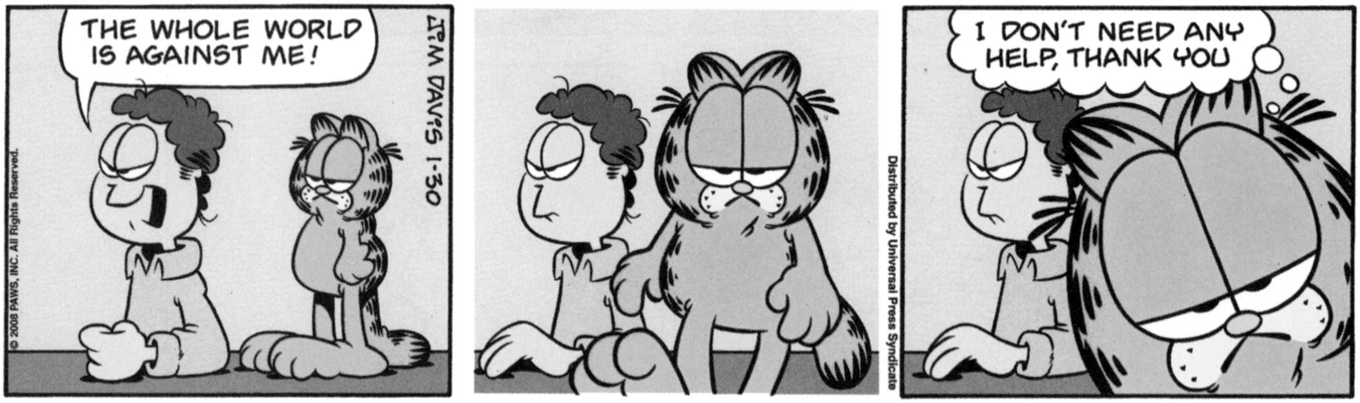
© 2008 PAWS, INC. All Rights Reserved.
THE WHOLE WORLD IS AGAINST ME!
JIM DAVIS 1-30
Distributed by Universal Press Syndicate
I DON'T NEED ANY HELP, THANK YOU

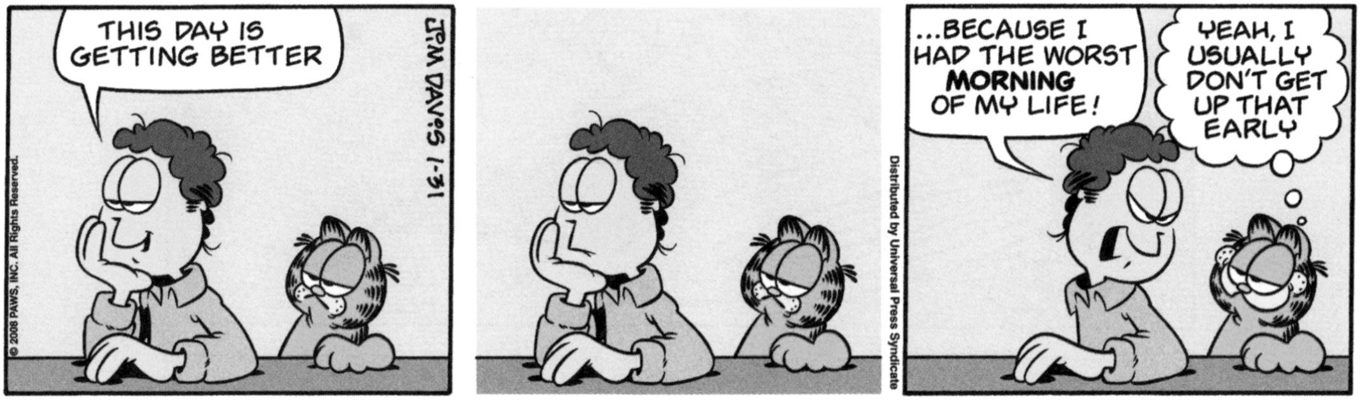
THIS DAY IS GETTING BETTER
JPM DAVPS 1-31
© 2008 PAWS, INC. All Rights Reserved.
...BECAUSE I HAD THE WORST **MORNING** OF MY LIFE!
YEAH, I USUALLY DON'T GET UP THAT EARLY
Distributed by Universal Press Syndicate

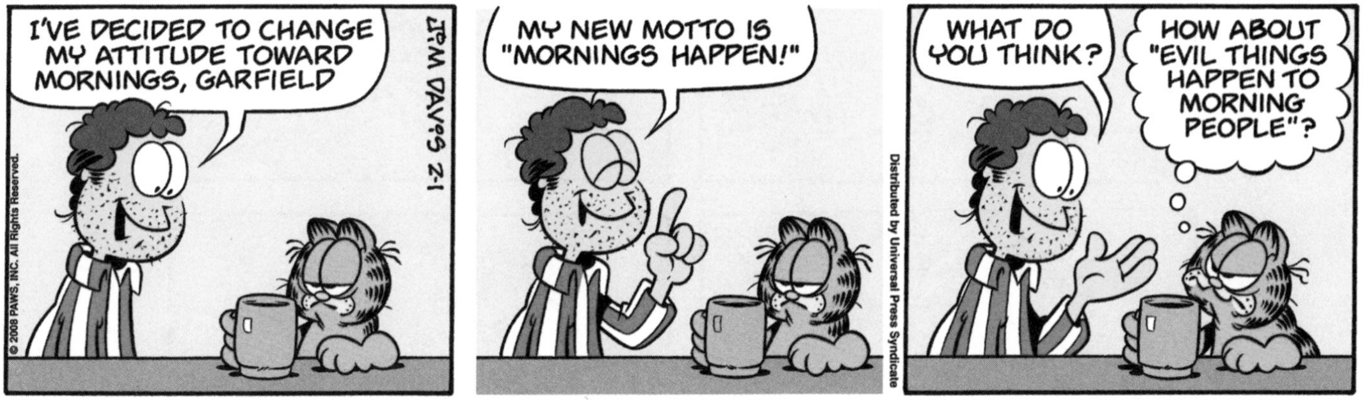
I'VE DECIDED TO CHANGE MY ATTITUDE TOWARD MORNINGS, GARFIELD
JPM DAVPS 2-1
© 2008 PAWS, INC. All Rights Reserved.
MY NEW MOTTO IS "MORNINGS HAPPEN!"
WHAT DO YOU THINK?
HOW ABOUT "EVIL THINGS HAPPEN TO MORNING PEOPLE"?
Distributed by Universal Press Syndicate

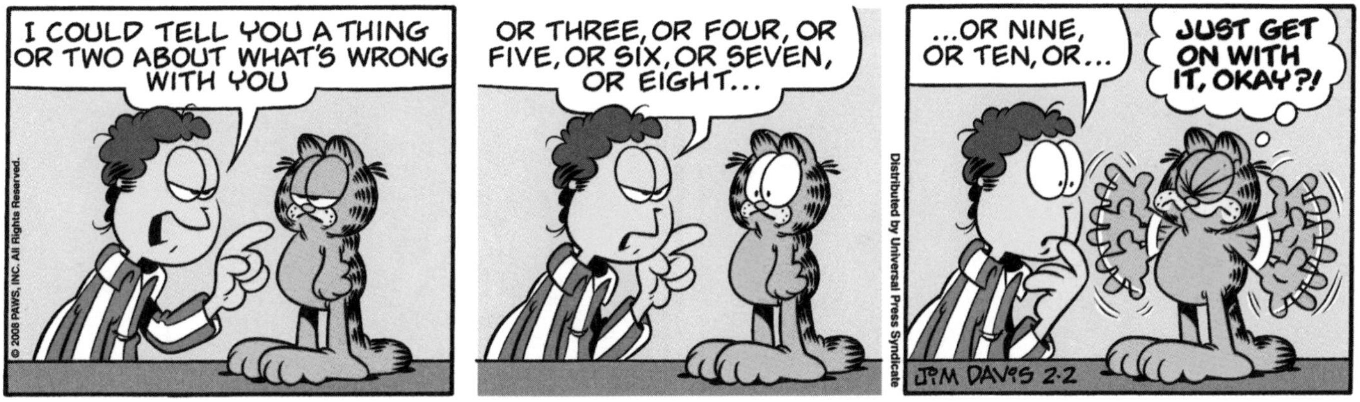
I COULD TELL YOU A THING OR TWO ABOUT WHAT'S WRONG WITH YOU
© 2008 PAWS, INC. All Rights Reserved.
OR THREE, OR FOUR, OR FIVE, OR SIX, OR SEVEN, OR EIGHT...
...OR NINE, OR TEN, OR...
JUST GET ON WITH IT, OKAY?!
JPM DAVPS 2-2
Distributed by Universal Press Syndicate

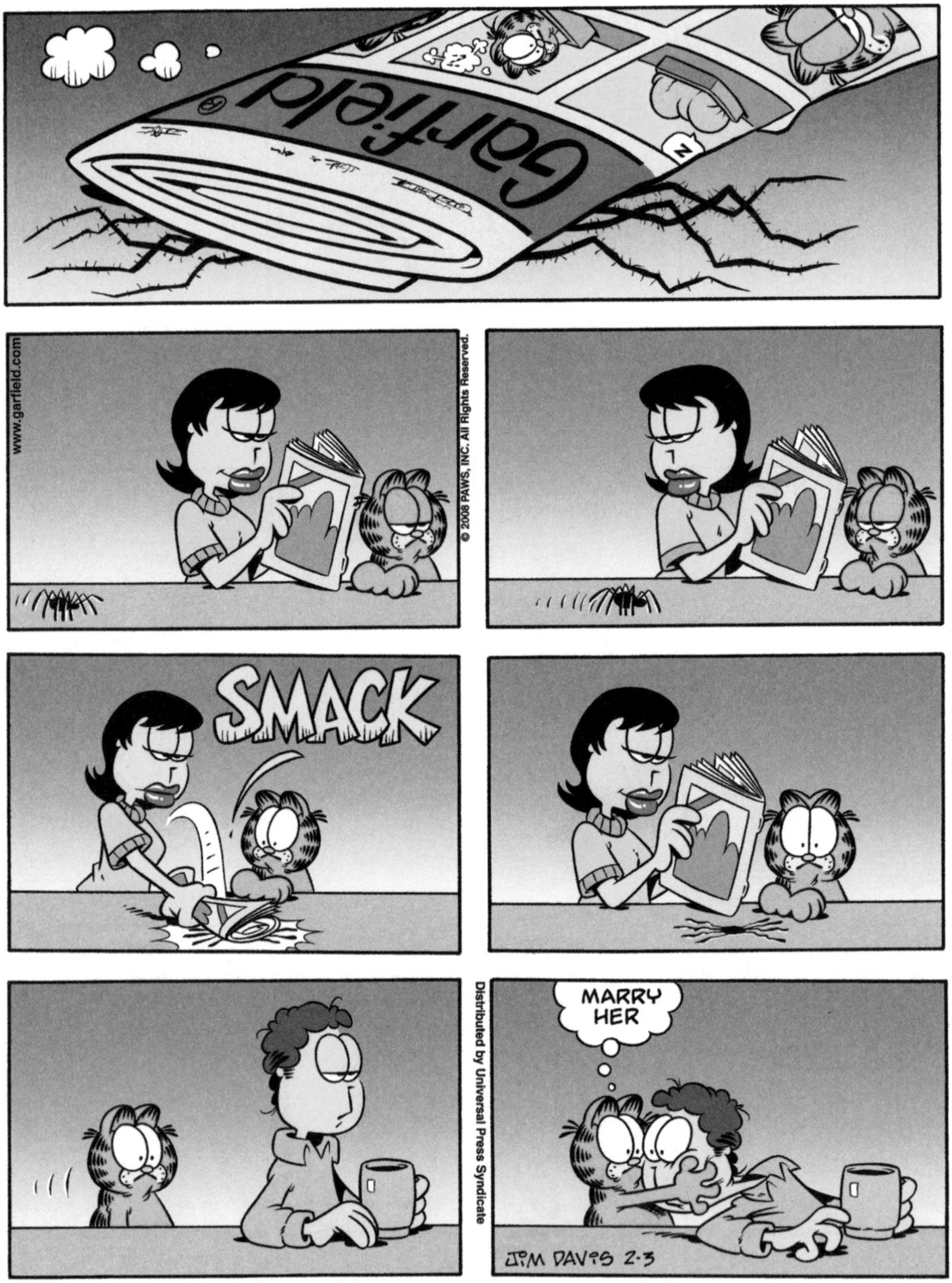
Garfield
www.garfield.com
© 2008 PAWS, INC. All Rights Reserved.
SMACK
Distributed by Universal Press Syndicate
MARRY HER
JIM DAVIS 2-3

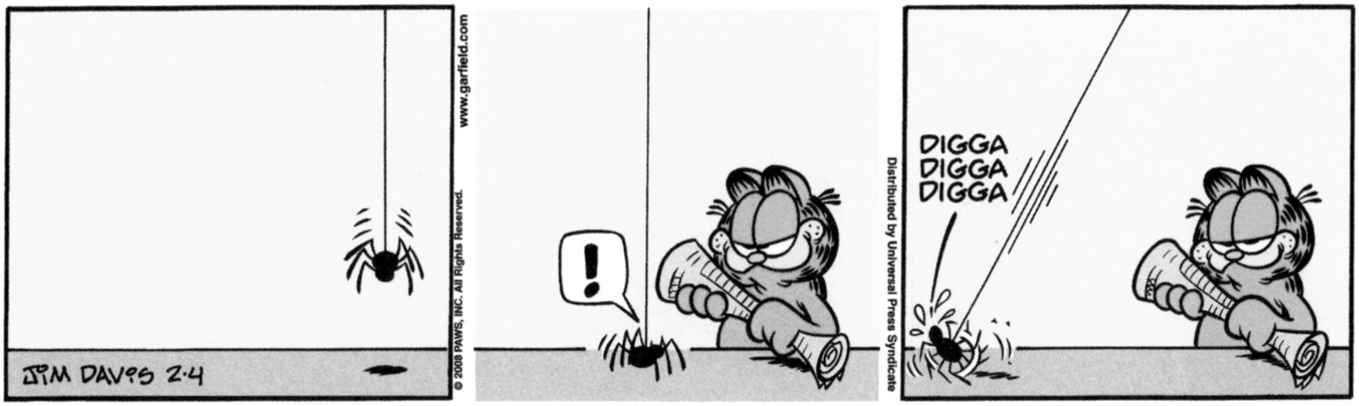
JIM DAVIS 2·4
© 2008 PAWS, INC. All Rights Reserved. www.garfield.com
!
Distributed by Universal Press Syndicate
DIGGA DIGGA DIGGA

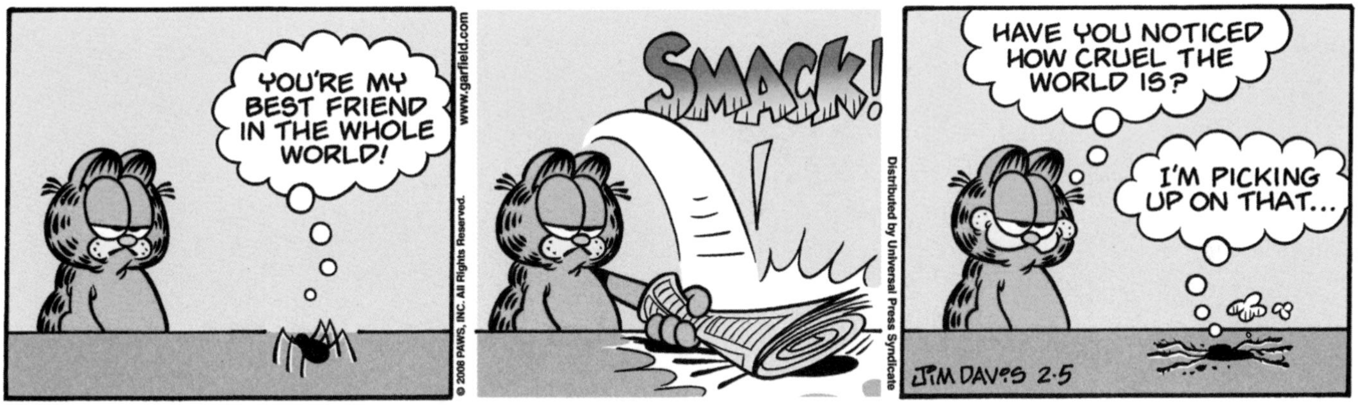
YOU'RE MY BEST FRIEND IN THE WHOLE WORLD!
© 2008 PAWS, INC. All Rights Reserved. www.garfield.com
SMACK!
Distributed by Universal Press Syndicate
HAVE YOU NOTICED HOW CRUEL THE WORLD IS?
I'M PICKING UP ON THAT...
JIM DAVIS 2·5

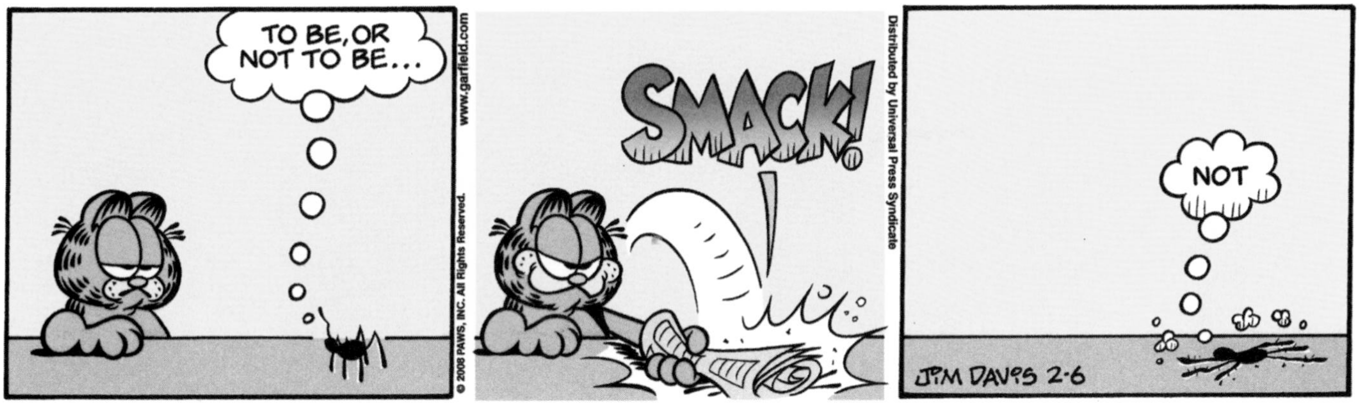
TO BE, OR NOT TO BE...
© 2008 PAWS, INC. All Rights Reserved. www.garfield.com
SMACK!
Distributed by Universal Press Syndicate
NOT
JIM DAVIS 2·6

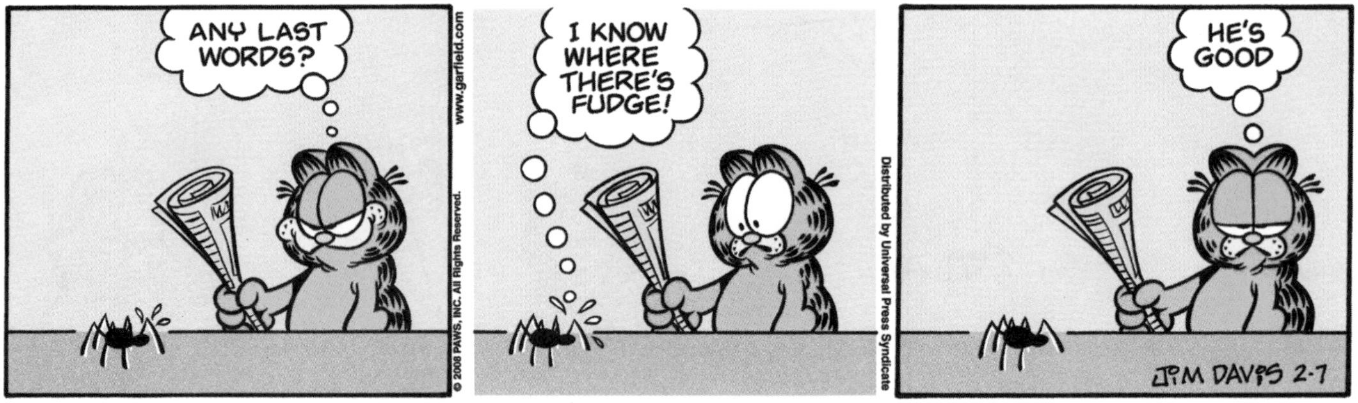
ANY LAST WORDS?
I KNOW WHERE THERE'S FUDGE!
HE'S GOOD
JIM DAVIS 2-7
© 2008 PAWS, INC. All Rights Reserved.
www.garfield.com
Distributed by Universal Press Syndicate

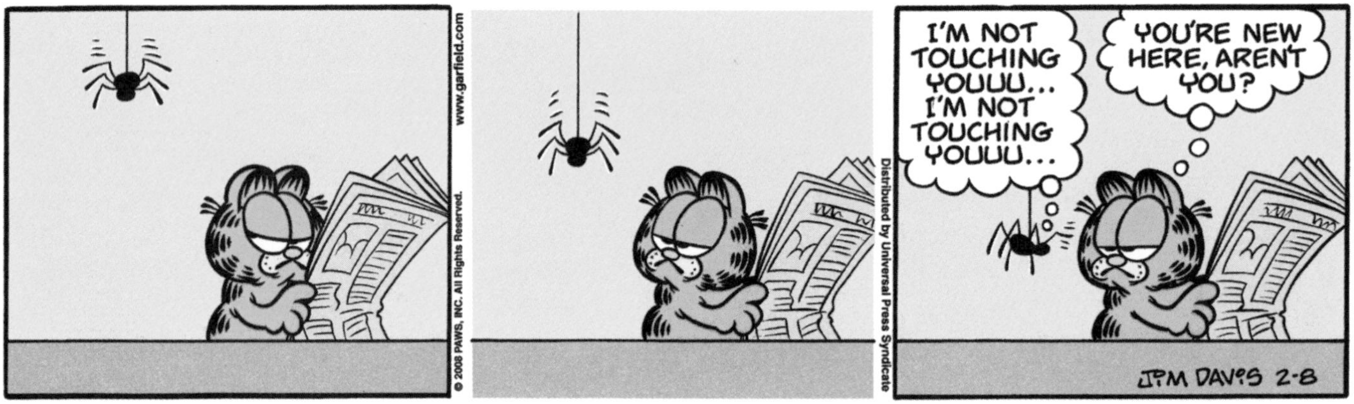
I'M NOT TOUCHING YOUUU... I'M NOT TOUCHING YOUUU...
YOU'RE NEW HERE, AREN'T YOU?
JIM DAVIS 2-8
© 2008 PAWS, INC. All Rights Reserved.
www.garfield.com
Distributed by Universal Press Syndicate

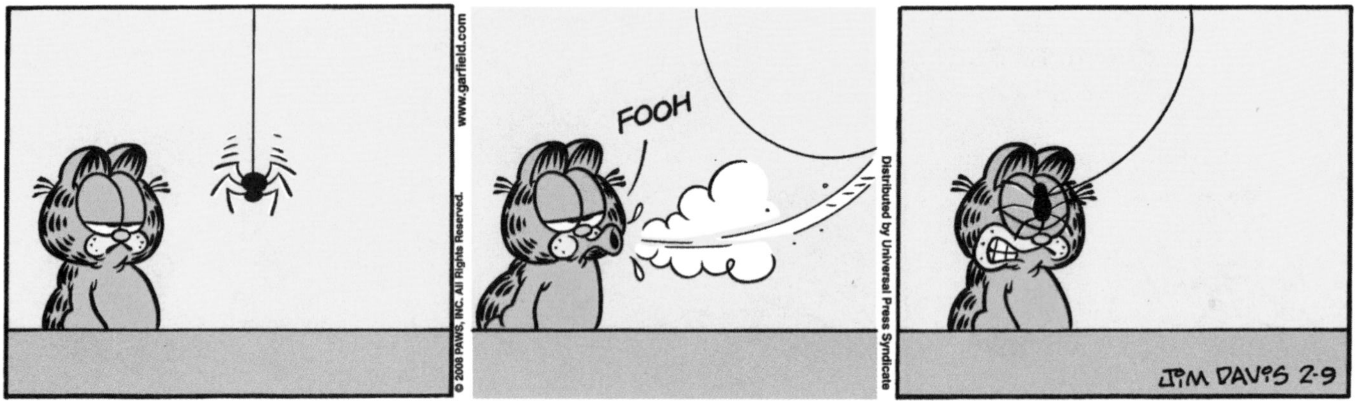
FOOH
JIM DAVIS 2-9
© 2008 PAWS, INC. All Rights Reserved.
www.garfield.com
Distributed by Universal Press Syndicate

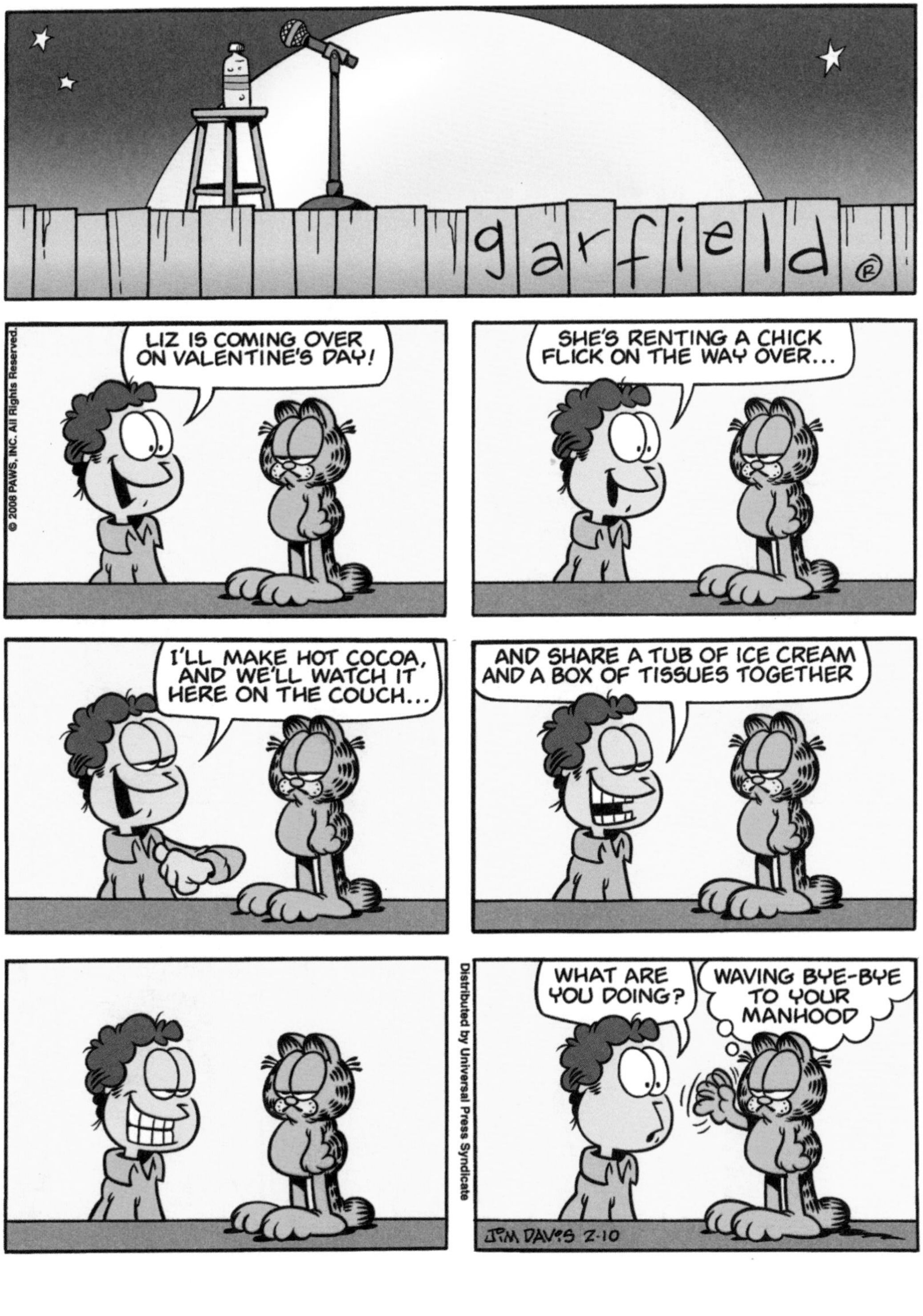
garfield®
© 2008 PAWS, INC. All Rights Reserved.
LIZ IS COMING OVER ON VALENTINE'S DAY!
SHE'S RENTING A CHICK FLICK ON THE WAY OVER...
I'LL MAKE HOT COCOA, AND WE'LL WATCH IT HERE ON THE COUCH...
AND SHARE A TUB OF ICE CREAM AND A BOX OF TISSUES TOGETHER
Distributed by Universal Press Syndicate
WHAT ARE YOU DOING?
WAVING BYE-BYE TO YOUR MANHOOD
JIM DAVIS 2-10

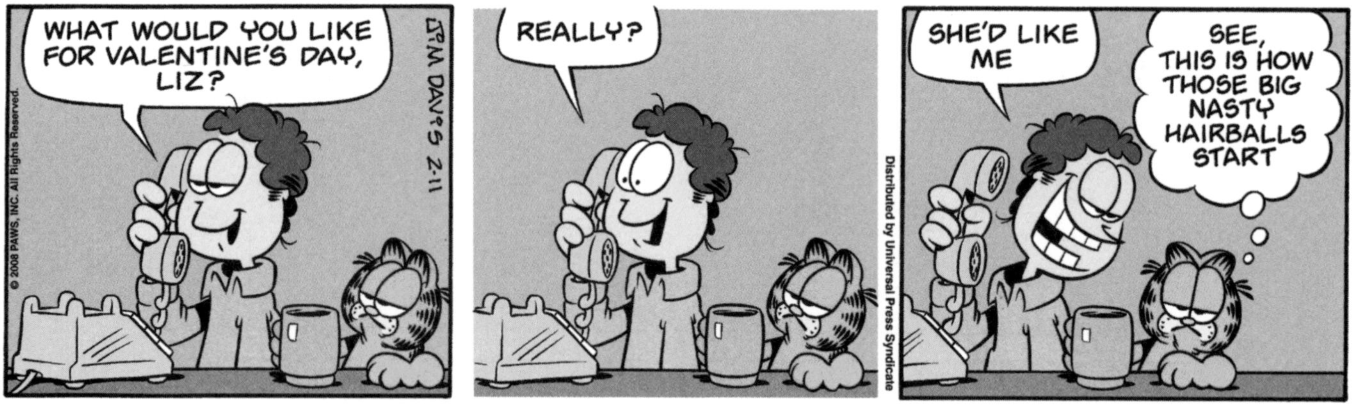
WHAT WOULD YOU LIKE FOR VALENTINE'S DAY, LIZ?
JPM DAVIS 2-11
© 2008 PAWS, INC. All Rights Reserved.
REALLY?
SHE'D LIKE ME
SEE, THIS IS HOW THOSE BIG NASTY HAIRBALLS START
Distributed by Universal Press Syndicate

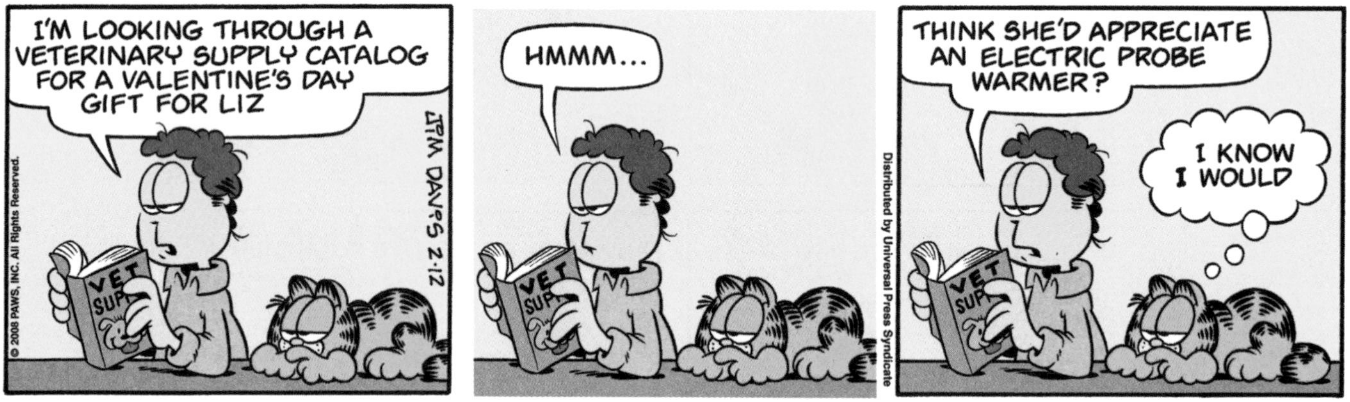
I'M LOOKING THROUGH A VETERINARY SUPPLY CATALOG FOR A VALENTINE'S DAY GIFT FOR LIZ
JPM DAVIS 2-12
© 2008 PAWS, INC. All Rights Reserved.
VET SUP
HMMM...
THINK SHE'D APPRECIATE AN ELECTRIC PROBE WARMER?
I KNOW I WOULD
Distributed by Universal Press Syndicate

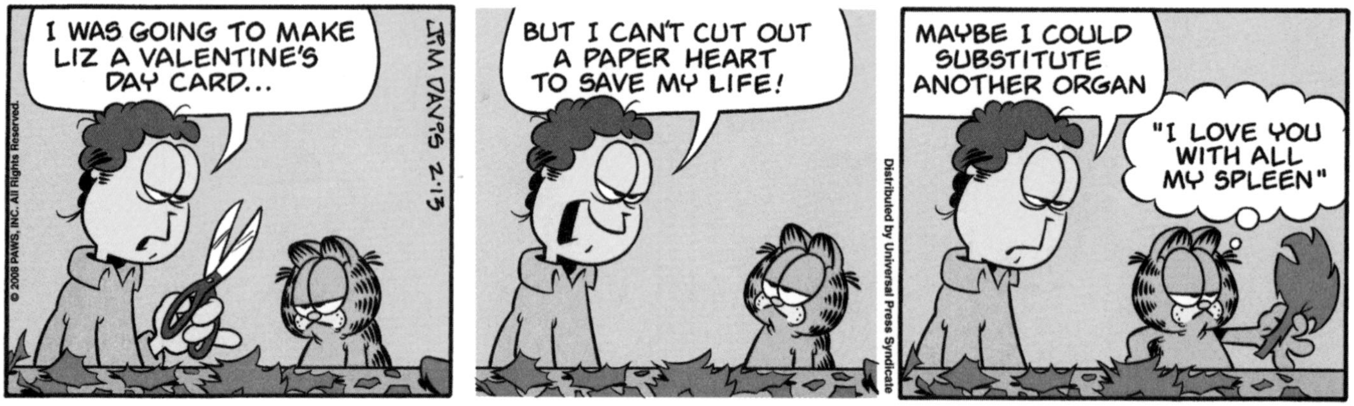
I WAS GOING TO MAKE LIZ A VALENTINE'S DAY CARD...
JPM DAVIS 2-13
© 2008 PAWS, INC. All Rights Reserved.
BUT I CAN'T CUT OUT A PAPER HEART TO SAVE MY LIFE!
MAYBE I COULD SUBSTITUTE ANOTHER ORGAN
"I LOVE YOU WITH ALL MY SPLEEN"
Distributed by Universal Press Syndicate

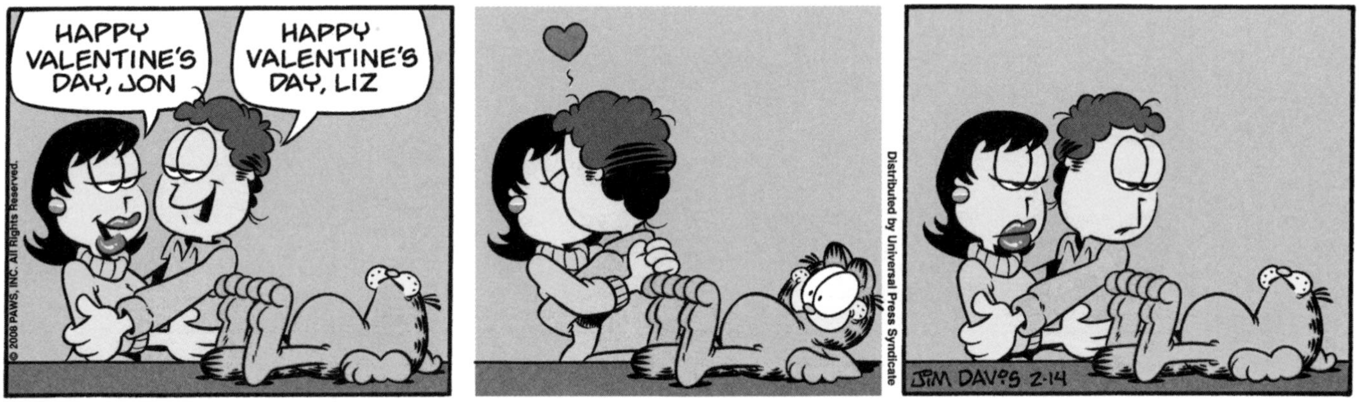
HAPPY VALENTINE'S DAY, JON
HAPPY VALENTINE'S DAY, LIZ
© 2008 PAWS, INC. All Rights Reserved.
Distributed by Universal Press Syndicate
JIM DAVIS 2-14

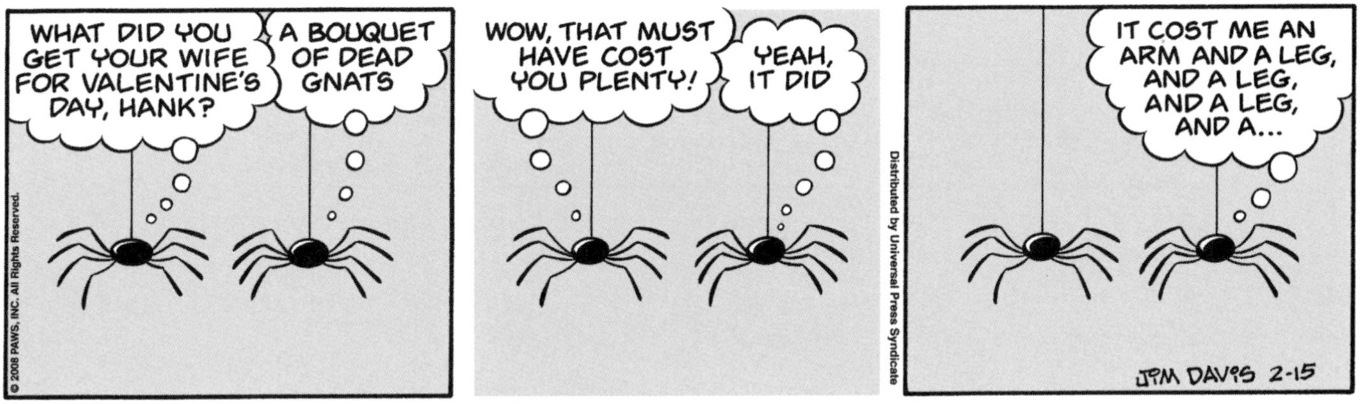
WHAT DID YOU GET YOUR WIFE FOR VALENTINE'S DAY, HANK?
A BOUQUET OF DEAD GNATS
WOW, THAT MUST HAVE COST YOU PLENTY!
YEAH, IT DID
IT COST ME AN ARM AND A LEG, AND A LEG, AND A LEG, AND A...
© 2008 PAWS, INC. All Rights Reserved.
Distributed by Universal Press Syndicate
JIM DAVIS 2-15

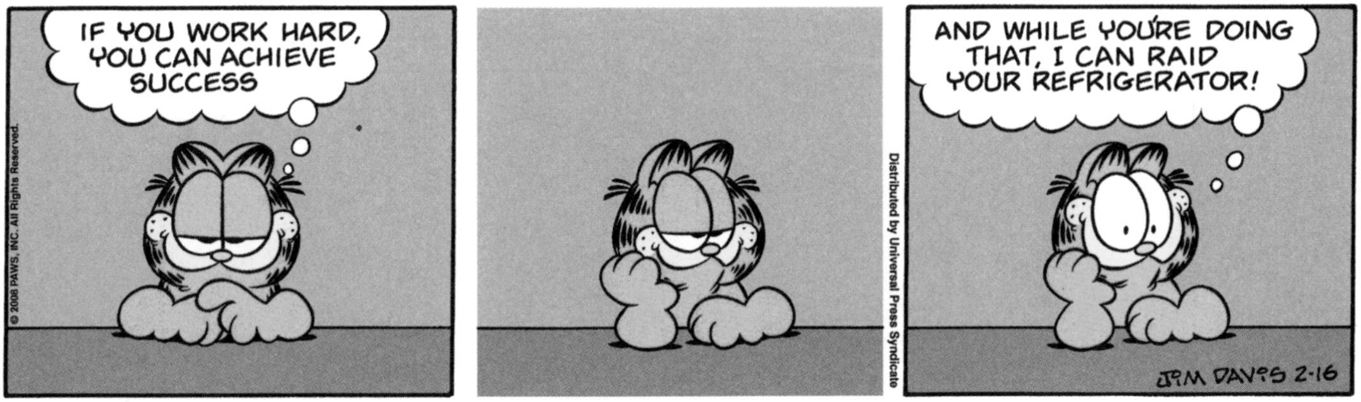
IF YOU WORK HARD, YOU CAN ACHIEVE SUCCESS
AND WHILE YOU'RE DOING THAT, I CAN RAID YOUR REFRIGERATOR!
© 2008 PAWS, INC. All Rights Reserved.
Distributed by Universal Press Syndicate
JIM DAVIS 2-16

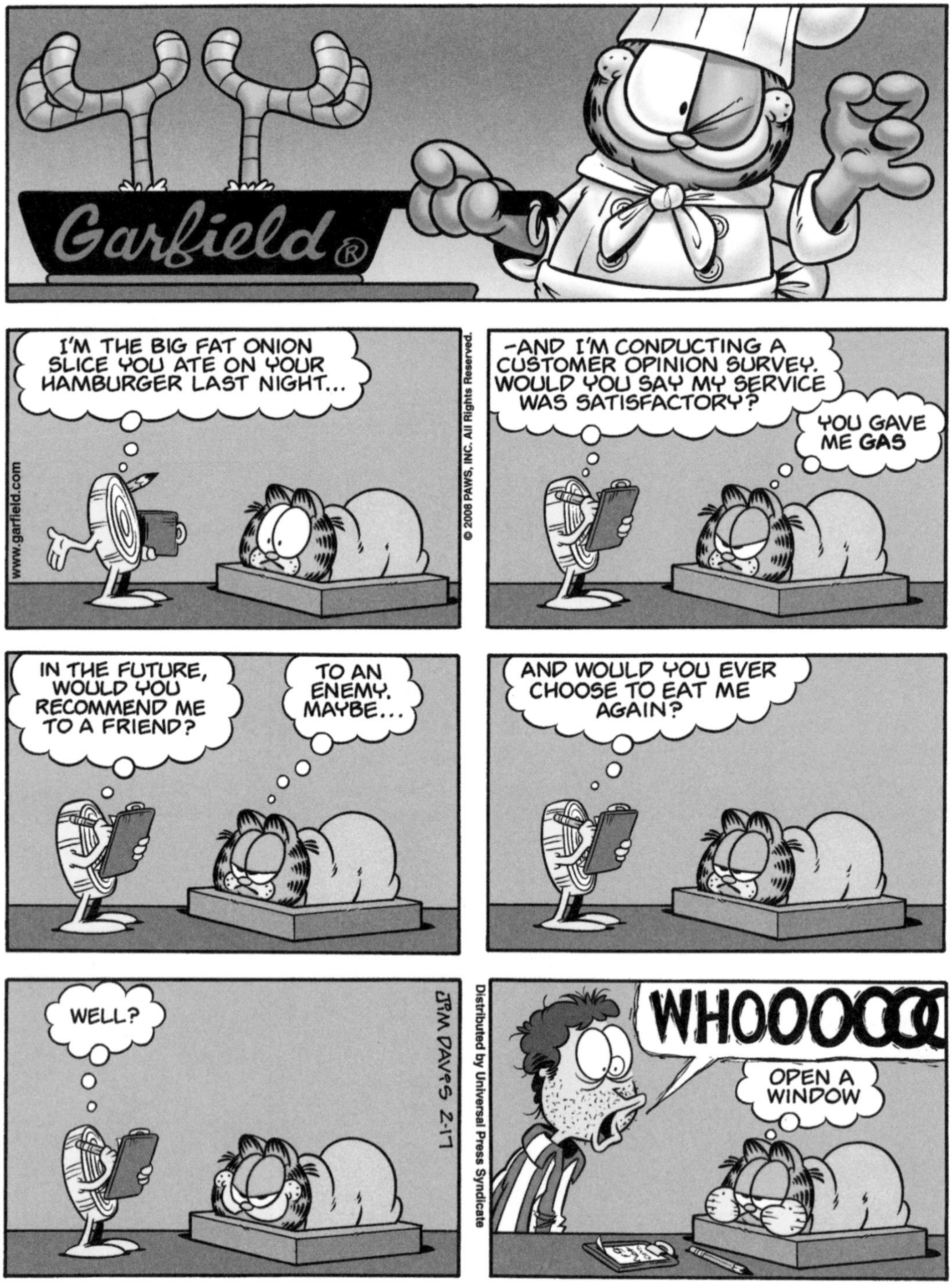
Garfield®
I'M THE BIG FAT ONION SLICE YOU ATE ON YOUR HAMBURGER LAST NIGHT...
www.garfield.com
© 2008 PAWS, INC. All Rights Reserved.
-AND I'M CONDUCTING A CUSTOMER OPINION SURVEY. WOULD YOU SAY MY SERVICE WAS SATISFACTORY?
YOU GAVE ME **GAS**
IN THE FUTURE, WOULD YOU RECOMMEND ME TO A FRIEND?
TO AN ENEMY. MAYBE...
AND WOULD YOU EVER CHOOSE TO EAT ME AGAIN?
WELL?
JIM DAVIS 2-17
Distributed by Universal Press Syndicate
WHOOOOOO
OPEN A WINDOW

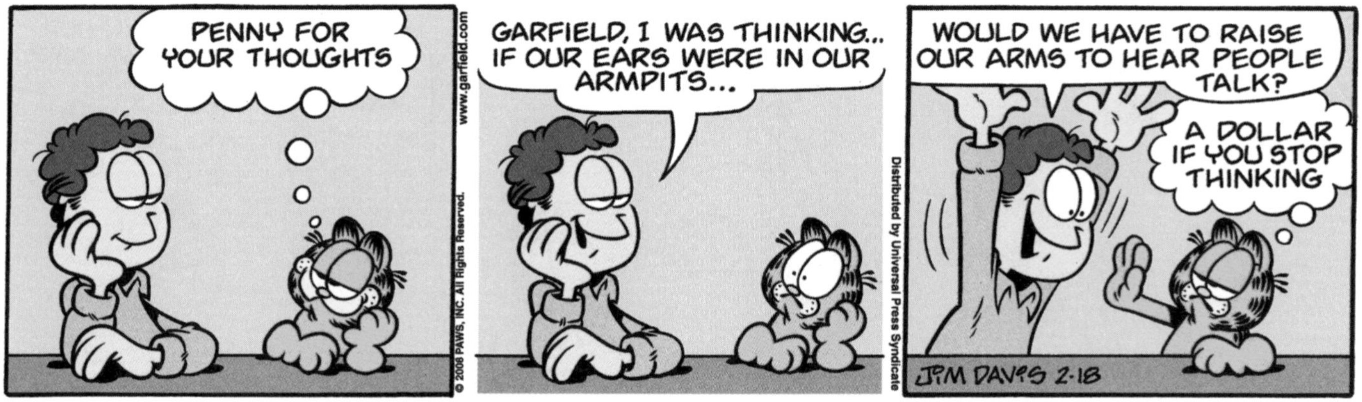
PENNY FOR YOUR THOUGHTS
GARFIELD, I WAS THINKING... IF OUR EARS WERE IN OUR ARMPITS...
WOULD WE HAVE TO RAISE OUR ARMS TO HEAR PEOPLE TALK?
A DOLLAR IF YOU STOP THINKING
JIM DAVIS 2·18
© 2008 PAWS, INC. All Rights Reserved. www.garfield.com
Distributed by Universal Press Syndicate

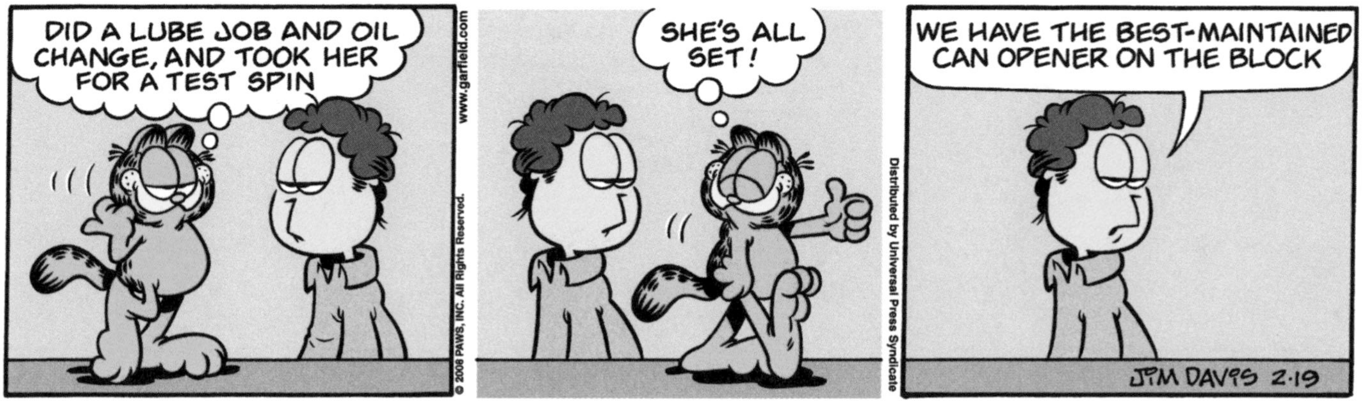
DID A LUBE JOB AND OIL CHANGE, AND TOOK HER FOR A TEST SPIN
SHE'S ALL SET!
WE HAVE THE BEST-MAINTAINED CAN OPENER ON THE BLOCK
JIM DAVIS 2·19
© 2008 PAWS, INC. All Rights Reserved. www.garfield.com
Distributed by Universal Press Syndicate

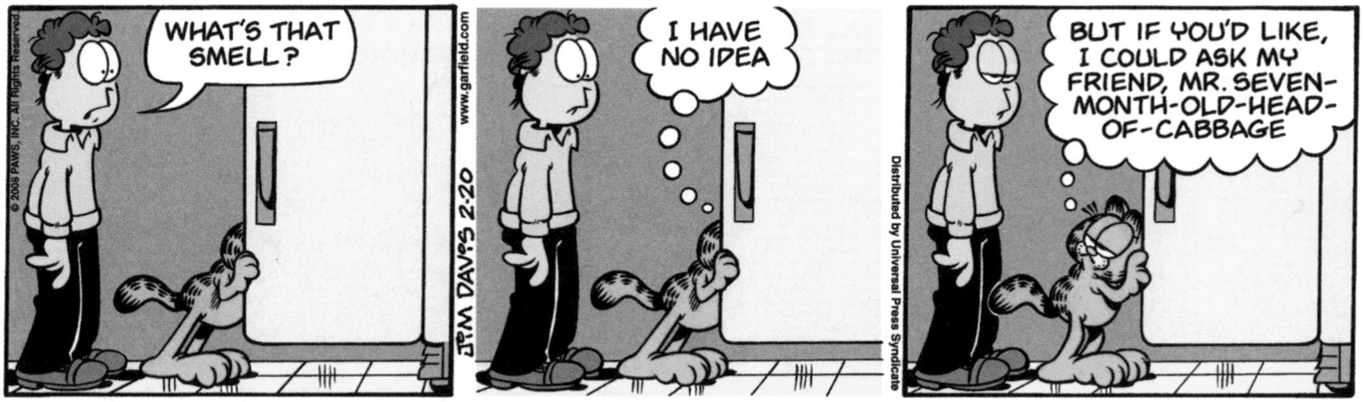
WHAT'S THAT SMELL?
I HAVE NO IDEA
BUT IF YOU'D LIKE, I COULD ASK MY FRIEND, MR. SEVEN-MONTH-OLD-HEAD-OF-CABBAGE
JIM DAVIS 2·20
© 2008 PAWS, INC. All Rights Reserved www.garfield.com
Distributed by Universal Press Syndicate

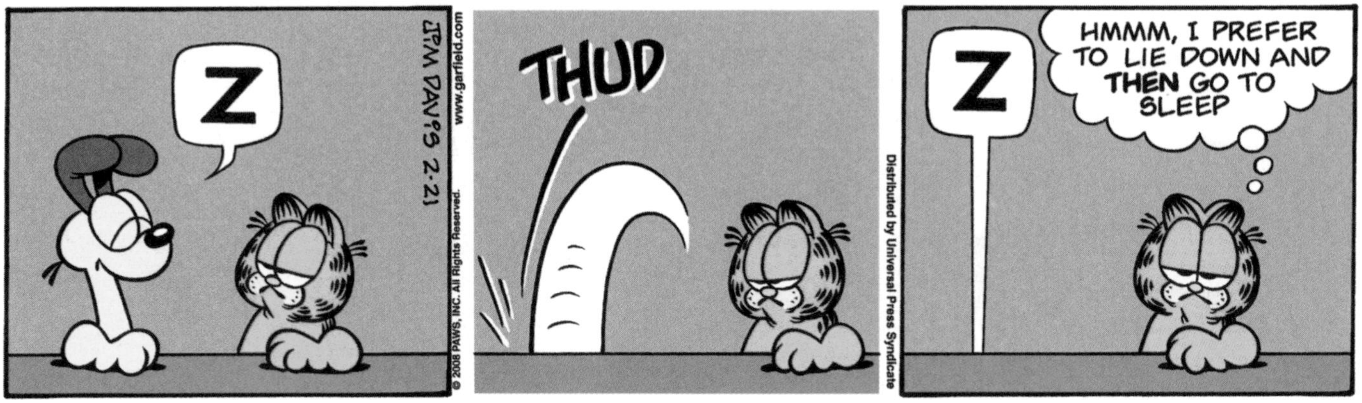
Z
JIM DAVIS 2·21
© 2008 PAWS, INC. All Rights Reserved. www.garfield.com
THUD
Distributed by Universal Press Syndicate
Z
HMMM, I PREFER TO LIE DOWN AND THEN GO TO SLEEP

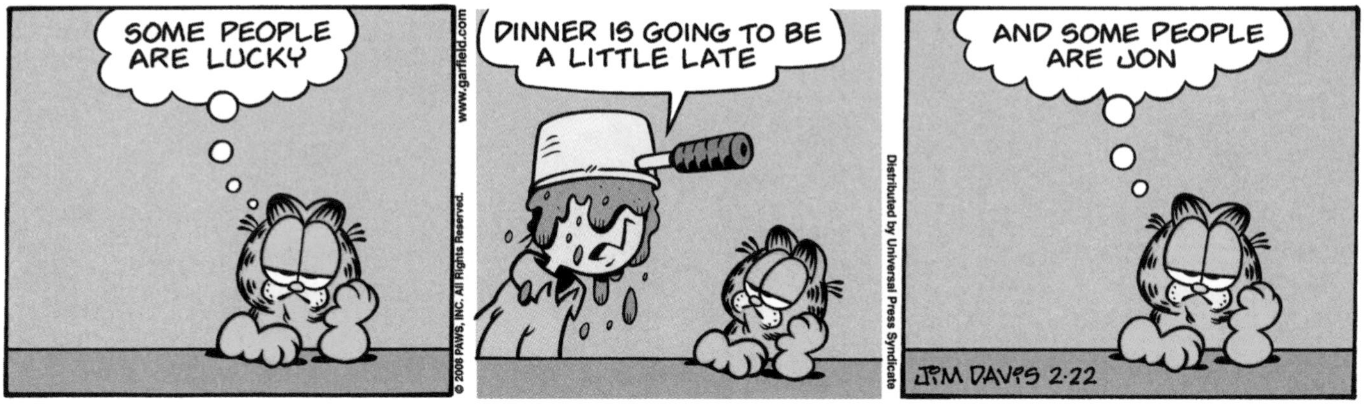
SOME PEOPLE ARE LUCKY
© 2008 PAWS, INC. All Rights Reserved. www.garfield.com
DINNER IS GOING TO BE A LITTLE LATE
Distributed by Universal Press Syndicate
AND SOME PEOPLE ARE JON
JIM DAVIS 2·22

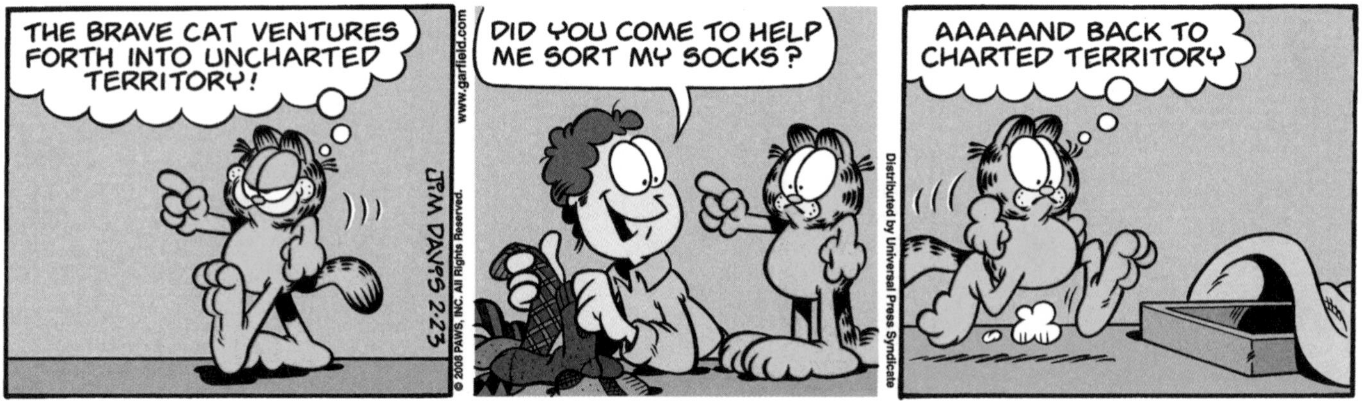
THE BRAVE CAT VENTURES FORTH INTO UNCHARTED TERRITORY!
JIM DAVIS 2·23
© 2008 PAWS, INC. All Rights Reserved. www.garfield.com
DID YOU COME TO HELP ME SORT MY SOCKS?
Distributed by Universal Press Syndicate
AAAAAND BACK TO CHARTED TERRITORY

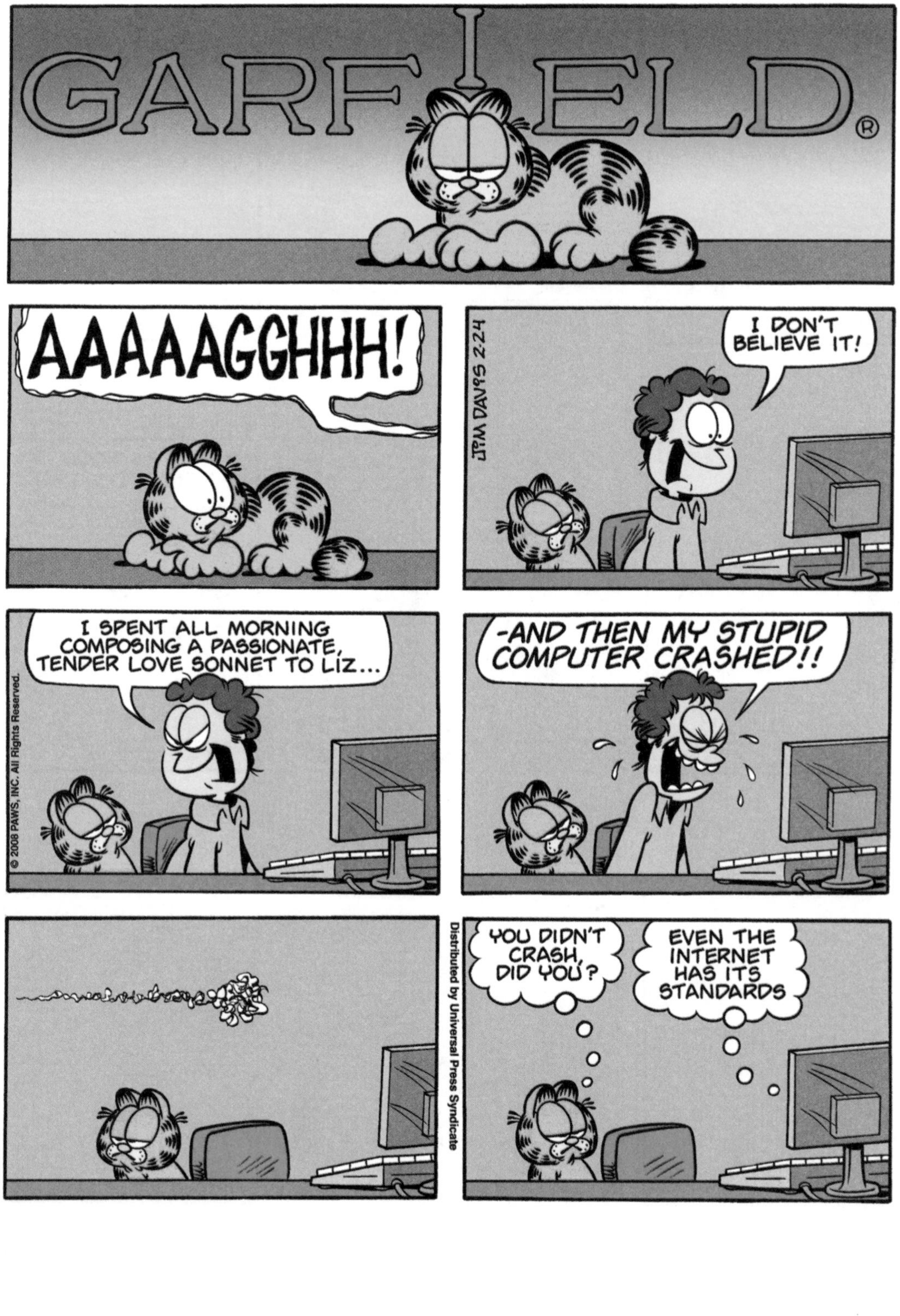
GARFIELD®
AAAAAGGHHH!
JIM DAVIS 2·24
I DON'T BELIEVE IT!
I SPENT ALL MORNING COMPOSING A PASSIONATE, TENDER LOVE SONNET TO LIZ...
© 2008 PAWS, INC. All Rights Reserved.
-AND THEN MY STUPID COMPUTER CRASHED!!
Distributed by Universal Press Syndicate
YOU DIDN'T CRASH, DID YOU?
EVEN THE INTERNET HAS ITS STANDARDS

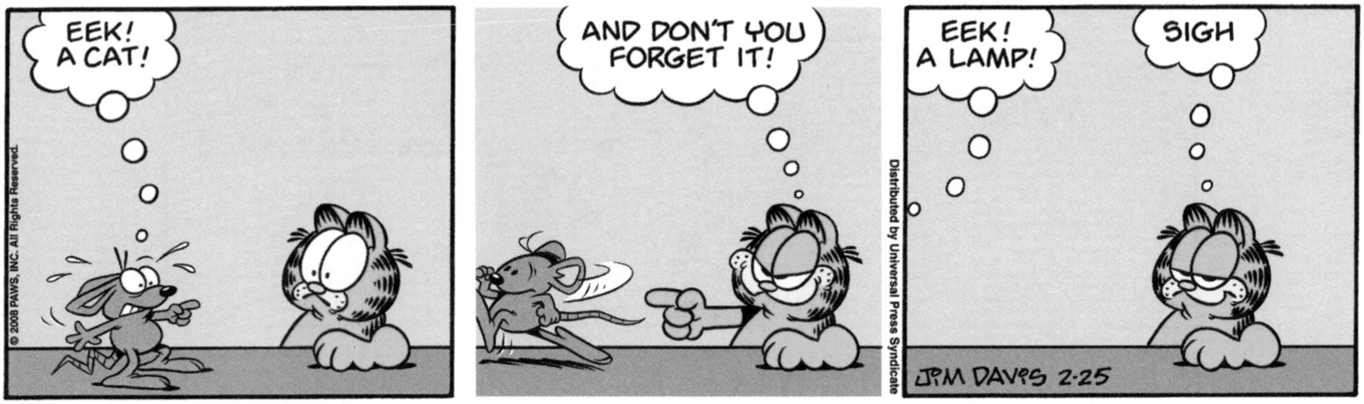
EEK! A CAT!
AND DON'T YOU FORGET IT!
EEK! A LAMP!
SIGH
JIM DAVIS 2·25
© 2008 PAWS, INC. All Rights Reserved.
Distributed by Universal Press Syndicate

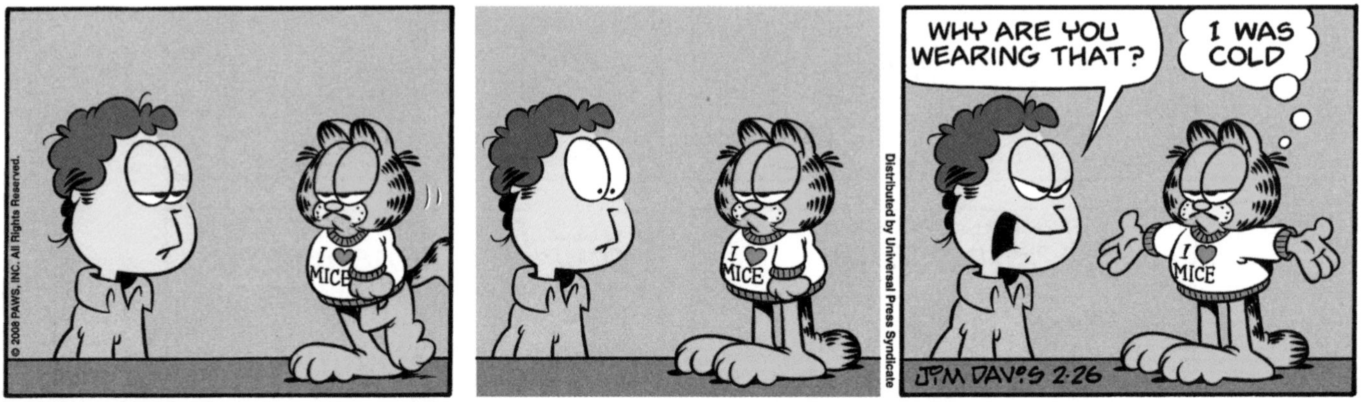
I ♥ MICE
WHY ARE YOU WEARING THAT?
I WAS COLD
JIM DAVIS 2·26
© 2008 PAWS, INC. All Rights Reserved.
Distributed by Universal Press Syndicate

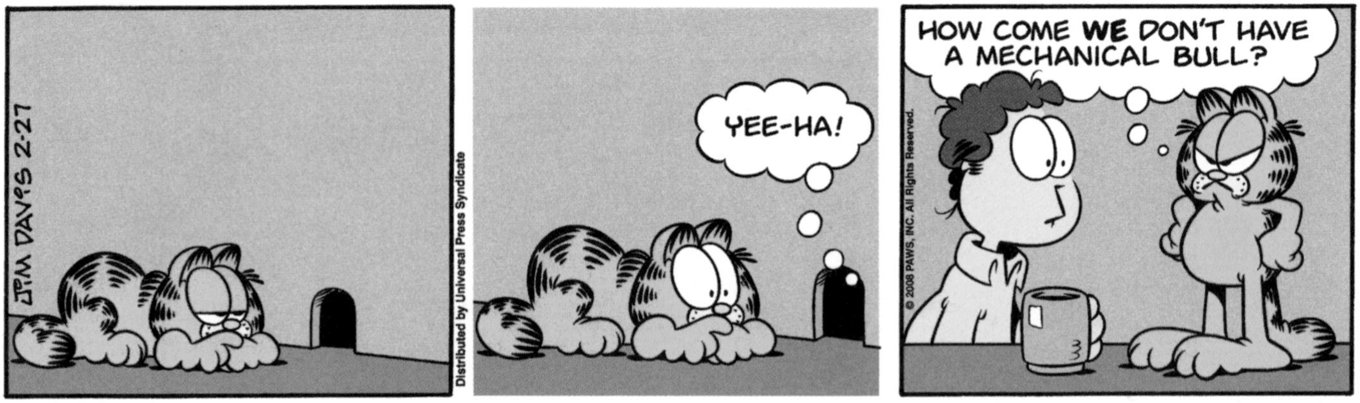
JIM DAVIS 2·27
YEE-HA!
HOW COME WE DON'T HAVE A MECHANICAL BULL?
Distributed by Universal Press Syndicate
© 2008 PAWS, INC. All Rights Reserved.

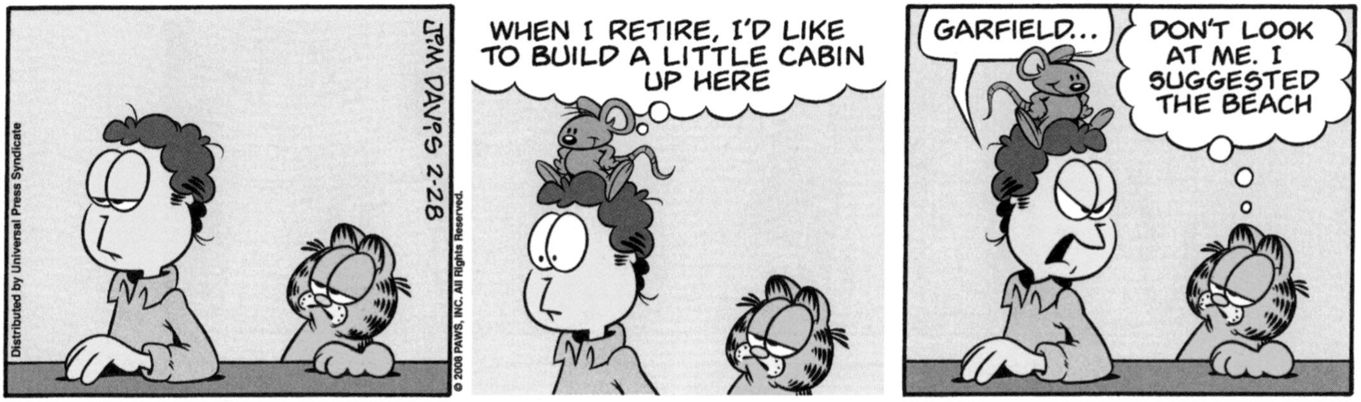
JIM DAVIS 2-28
Distributed by Universal Press Syndicate
© 2008 PAWS, INC. All Rights Reserved.
WHEN I RETIRE, I'D LIKE TO BUILD A LITTLE CABIN UP HERE
GARFIELD...
DON'T LOOK AT ME. I SUGGESTED THE BEACH

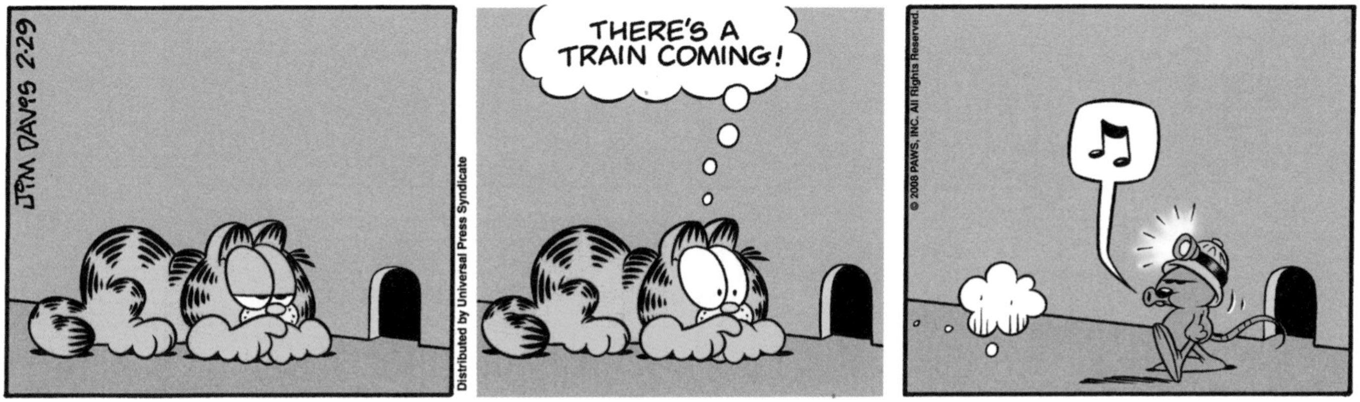
JIM DAVIS 2-29
Distributed by Universal Press Syndicate
THERE'S A TRAIN COMING!
© 2008 PAWS, INC. All Rights Reserved.

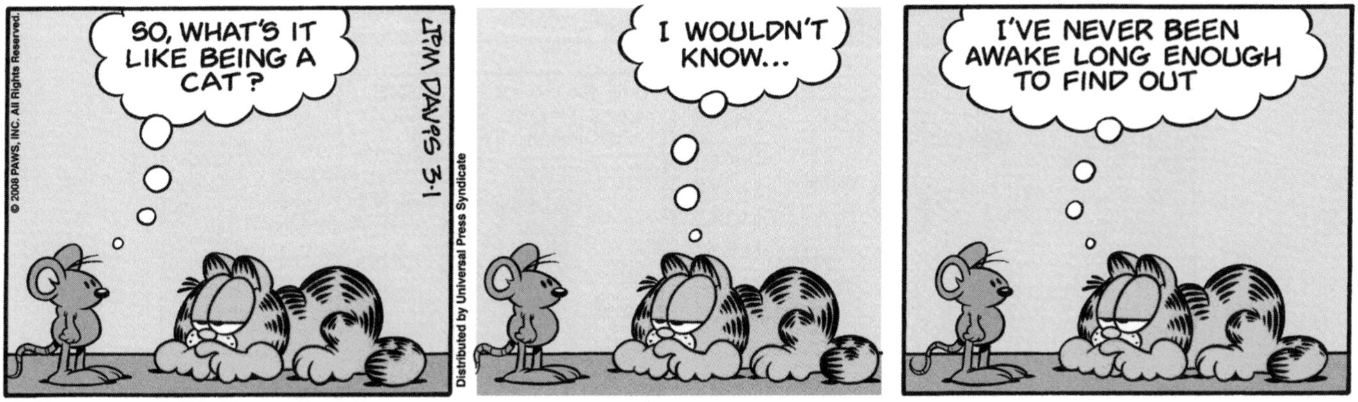
© 2008 PAWS, INC. All Rights Reserved.
SO, WHAT'S IT LIKE BEING A CAT?
JIM DAVIS 3-1
Distributed by Universal Press Syndicate
I WOULDN'T KNOW...
I'VE NEVER BEEN AWAKE LONG ENOUGH TO FIND OUT

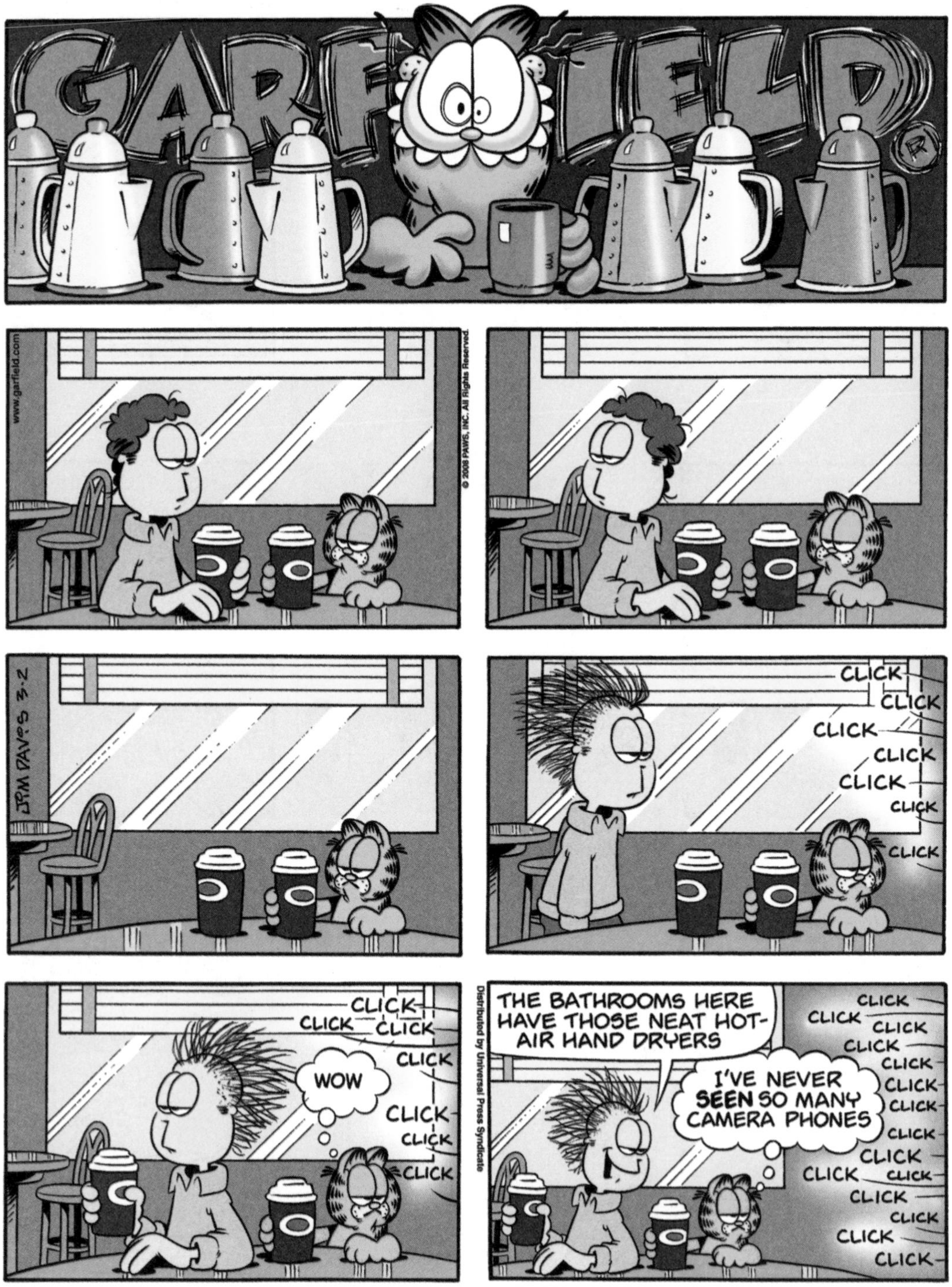
GARFIELD
www.garfield.com
© 2008 PAWS, INC. All Rights Reserved.
JIM DAVIS 3-2
CLICK CLICK CLICK CLICK CLICK CLICK CLICK
CLICK CLICK CLICK CLICK CLICK CLICK CLICK
WOW
Distributed by Universal Press Syndicate
THE BATHROOMS HERE HAVE THOSE NEAT HOT-AIR HAND DRYERS
I'VE NEVER SEEN SO MANY CAMERA PHONES
CLICK CLICK CLICK CLICK CLICK CLICK CLICK CLICK CLICK CLICK CLICK CLICK CLICK CLICK CLICK CLICK

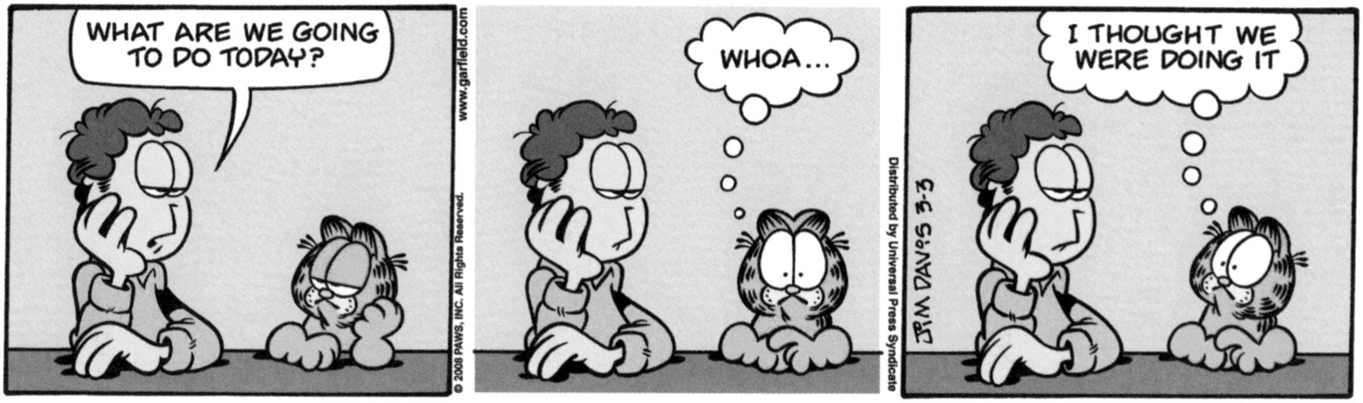
WHAT ARE WE GOING TO DO TODAY?
WHOA...
I THOUGHT WE WERE DOING IT
JIM DAVIS 3-3
© 2008 PAWS, INC. All Rights Reserved.
www.garfield.com
Distributed by Universal Press Syndicate

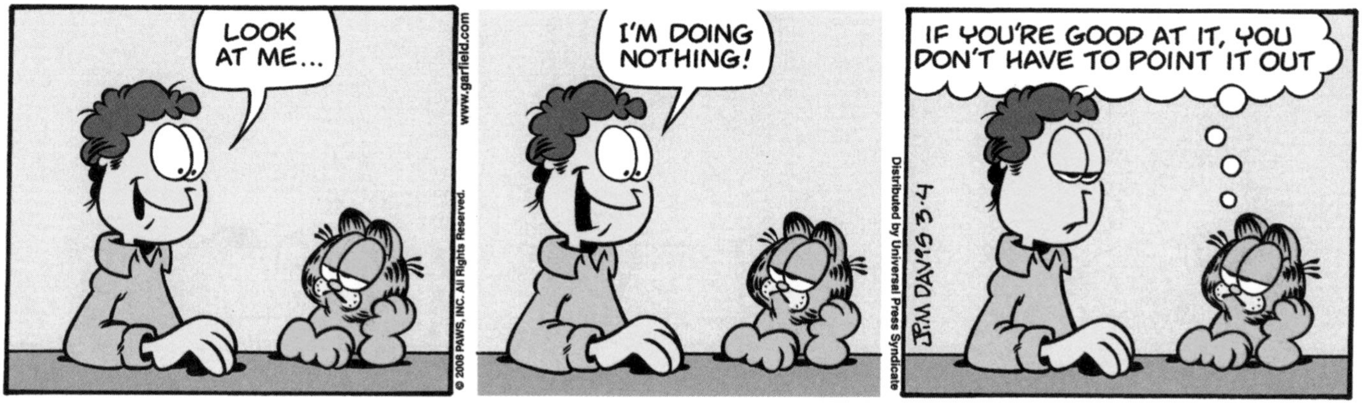
LOOK AT ME...
I'M DOING NOTHING!
IF YOU'RE GOOD AT IT, YOU DON'T HAVE TO POINT IT OUT
JIM DAVIS 3-4
© 2008 PAWS, INC. All Rights Reserved.
www.garfield.com
Distributed by Universal Press Syndicate

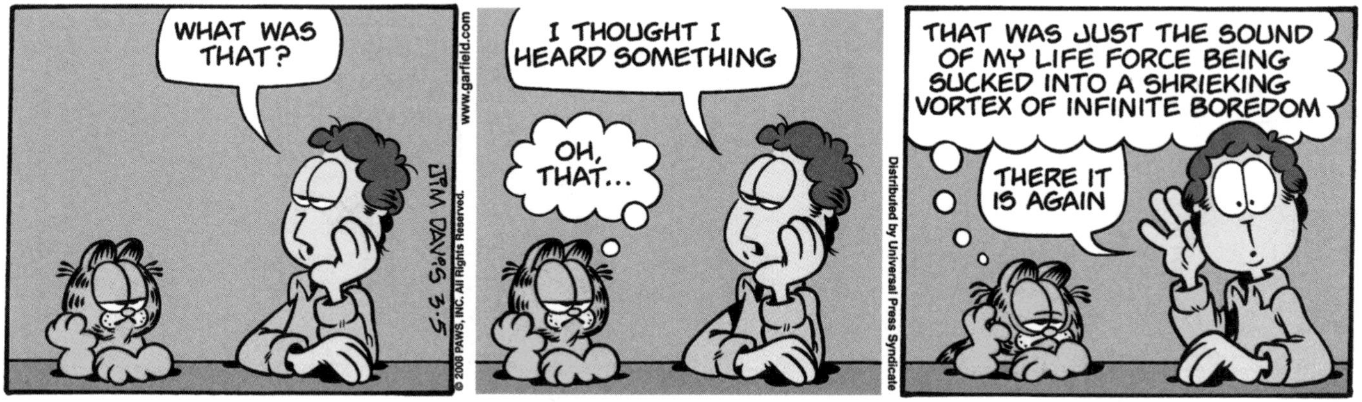
WHAT WAS THAT?
I THOUGHT I HEARD SOMETHING
OH, THAT...
THAT WAS JUST THE SOUND OF MY LIFE FORCE BEING SUCKED INTO A SHRIEKING VORTEX OF INFINITE BOREDOM
THERE IT IS AGAIN
JIM DAVIS 3-5
© 2008 PAWS, INC. All Rights Reserved.
www.garfield.com
Distributed by Universal Press Syndicate

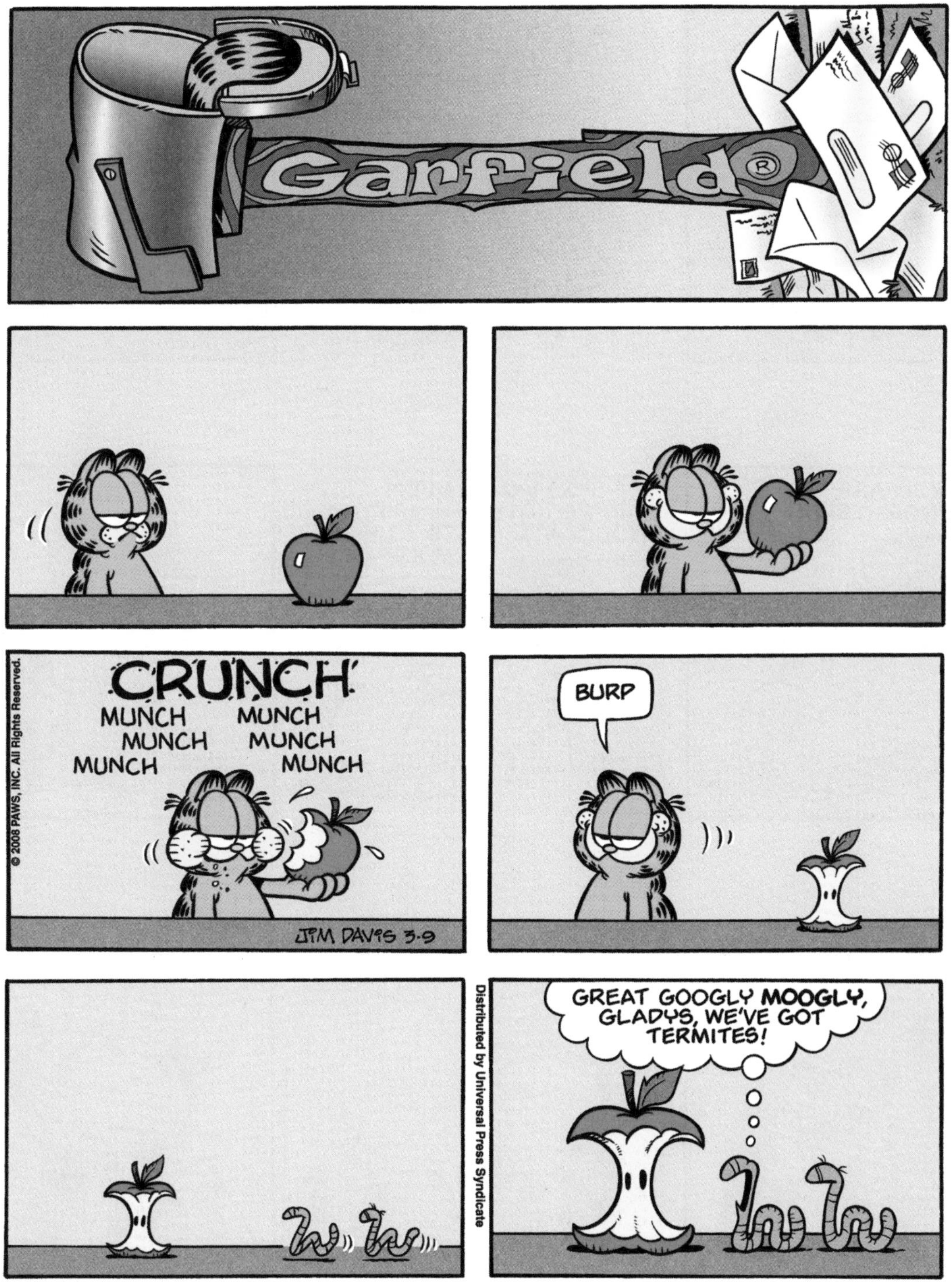
Garfield®
CRUNCH
MUNCH
MUNCH
MUNCH
MUNCH
MUNCH
MUNCH
JIM DAVIS 3-9
BURP
GREAT GOOGLY MOOGLY, GLADYS, WE'VE GOT TERMITES!

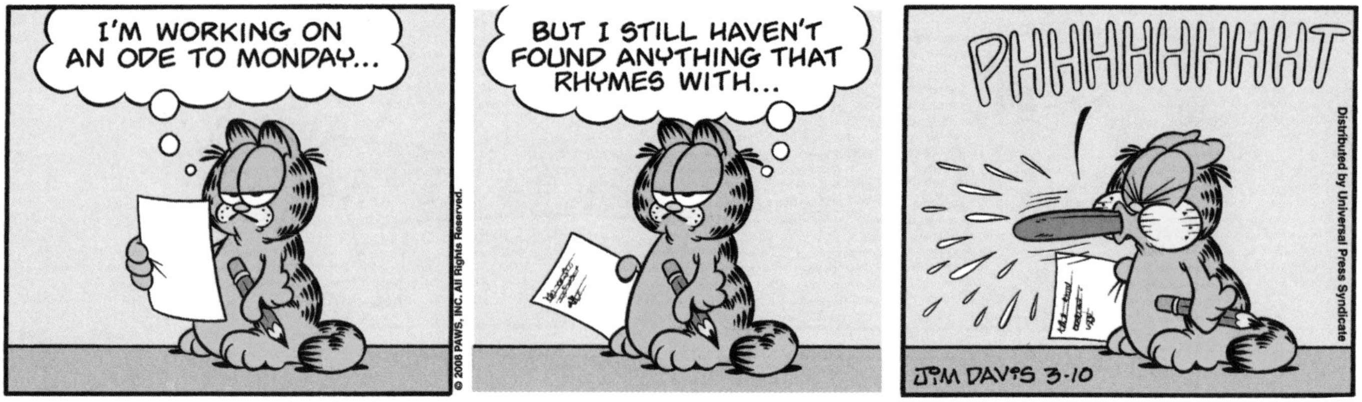
I'M WORKING ON AN ODE TO MONDAY...
BUT I STILL HAVEN'T FOUND ANYTHING THAT RHYMES WITH...
PHHHHHHHHT
© 2008 PAWS, INC. All Rights Reserved.
JIM DAVIS 3-10
Distributed by Universal Press Syndicate

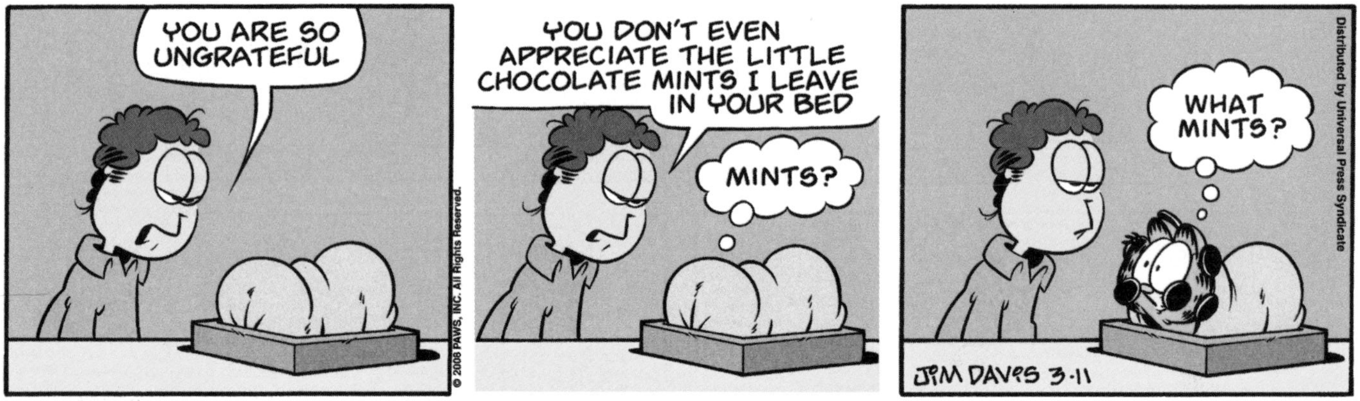
YOU ARE SO UNGRATEFUL
YOU DON'T EVEN APPRECIATE THE LITTLE CHOCOLATE MINTS I LEAVE IN YOUR BED
MINTS?
WHAT MINTS?
© 2008 PAWS, INC. All Rights Reserved.
JIM DAVIS 3-11
Distributed by Universal Press Syndicate

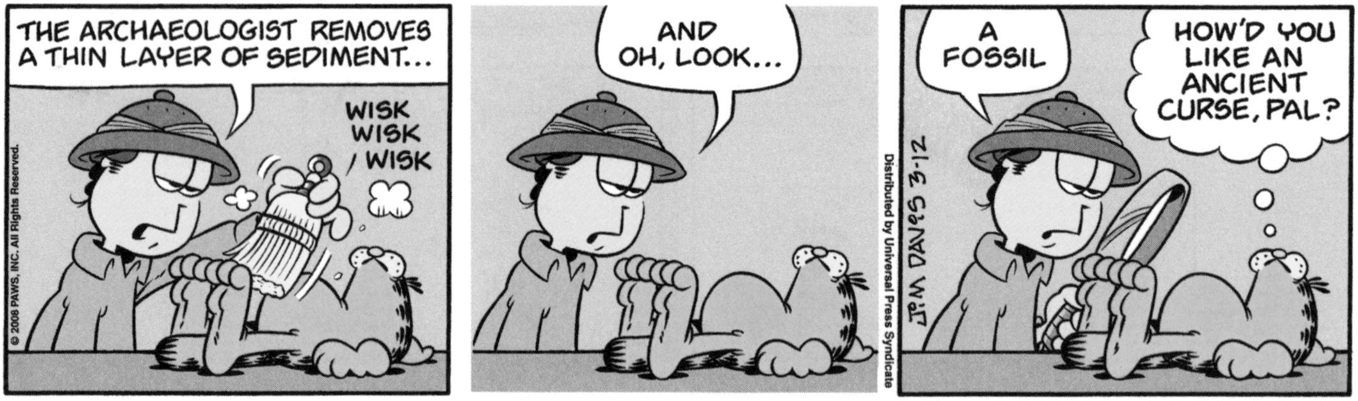
THE ARCHAEOLOGIST REMOVES A THIN LAYER OF SEDIMENT...
WISK
WISK
WISK
AND OH, LOOK...
A FOSSIL
HOW'D YOU LIKE AN ANCIENT CURSE, PAL?
© 2008 PAWS, INC. All Rights Reserved.
JIM DAVIS 3-12
Distributed by Universal Press Syndicate

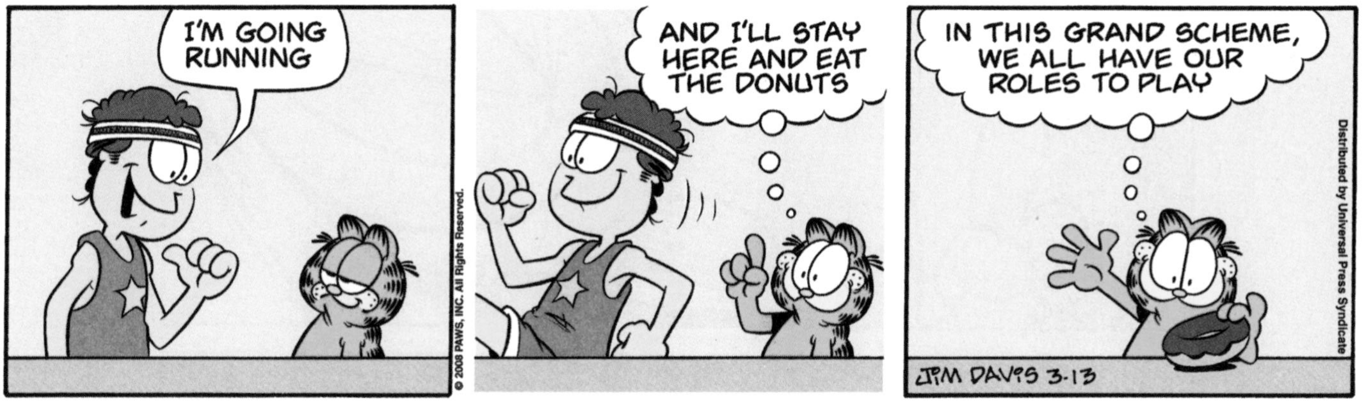
I'M GOING RUNNING
AND I'LL STAY HERE AND EAT THE DONUTS
IN THIS GRAND SCHEME, WE ALL HAVE OUR ROLES TO PLAY
JIM DAVIS 3-13
© 2008 PAWS, INC. All Rights Reserved.
Distributed by Universal Press Syndicate

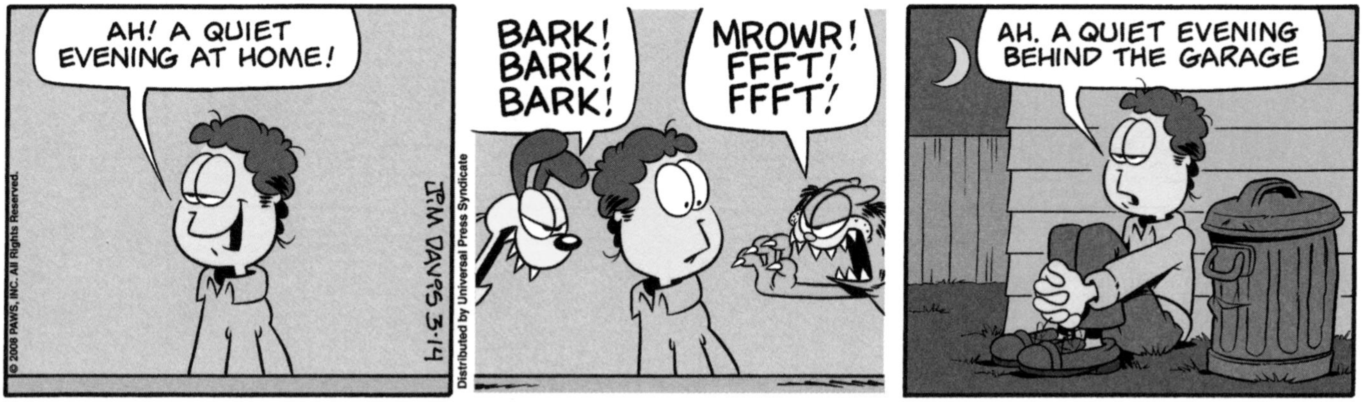
AH! A QUIET EVENING AT HOME!
BARK! BARK! BARK!
MROWR! FFFT! FFFT!
AH. A QUIET EVENING BEHIND THE GARAGE
JIM DAVIS 3-14
© 2008 PAWS, INC. All Rights Reserved.
Distributed by Universal Press Syndicate

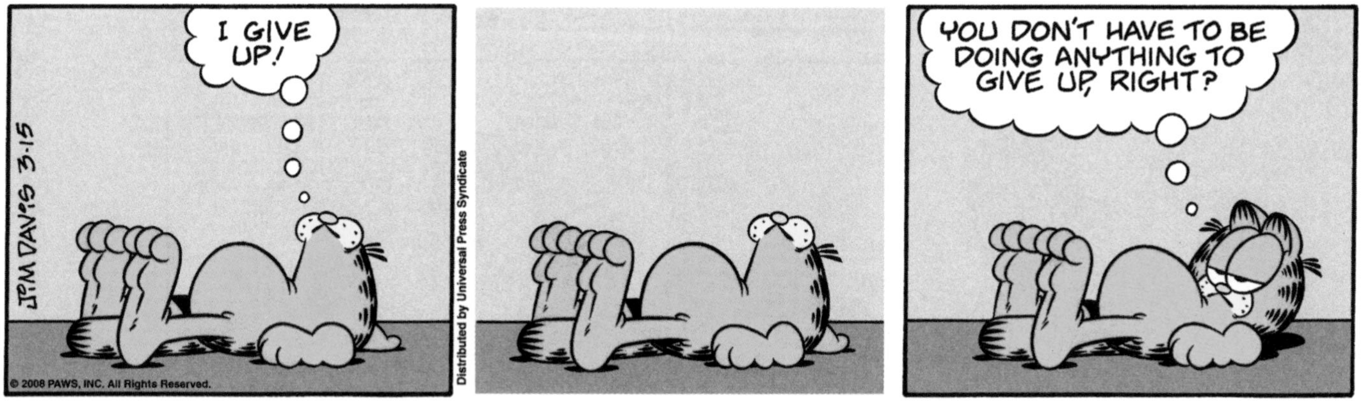
I GIVE UP!
YOU DON'T HAVE TO BE DOING ANYTHING TO GIVE UP, RIGHT?
JIM DAVIS 3-15
© 2008 PAWS, INC. All Rights Reserved.
Distributed by Universal Press Syndicate

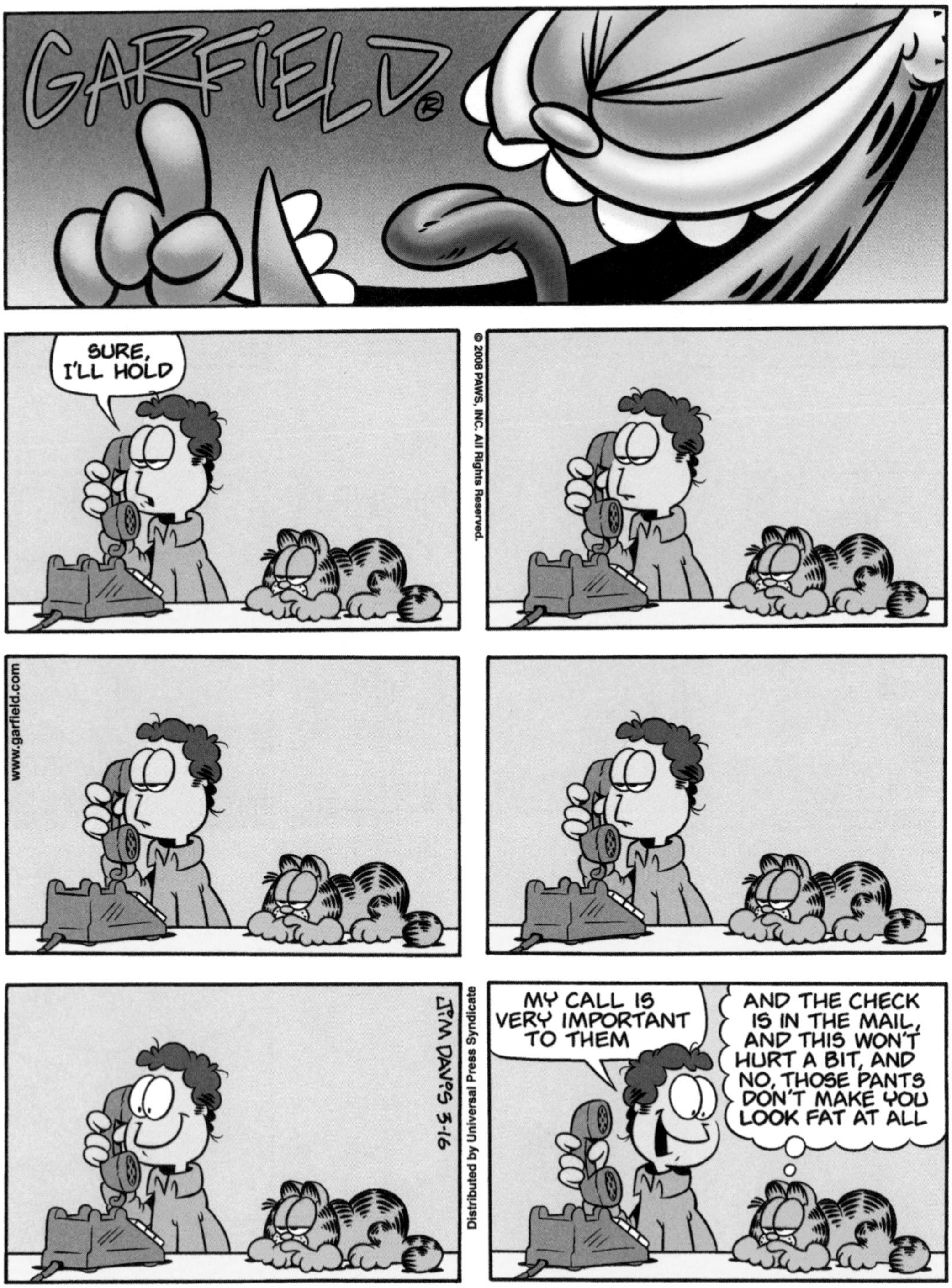
GARFIELD®
SURE, I'LL HOLD
© 2008 PAWS, INC. All Rights Reserved.
www.garfield.com
JIM DAVIS 3-16
Distributed by Universal Press Syndicate
MY CALL IS VERY IMPORTANT TO THEM
AND THE CHECK IS IN THE MAIL, AND THIS WON'T HURT A BIT, AND NO, THOSE PANTS DON'T MAKE YOU LOOK FAT AT ALL

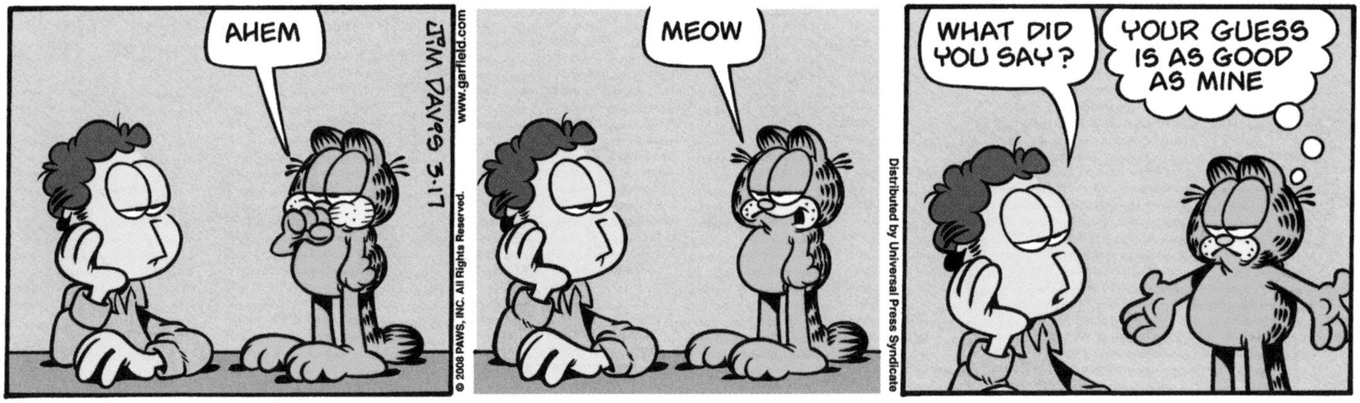
AHEM
JIM DAVIS 3-17
© 2008 PAWS, INC. All Rights Reserved. www.garfield.com
MEOW
Distributed by Universal Press Syndicate
WHAT DID YOU SAY?
YOUR GUESS IS AS GOOD AS MINE

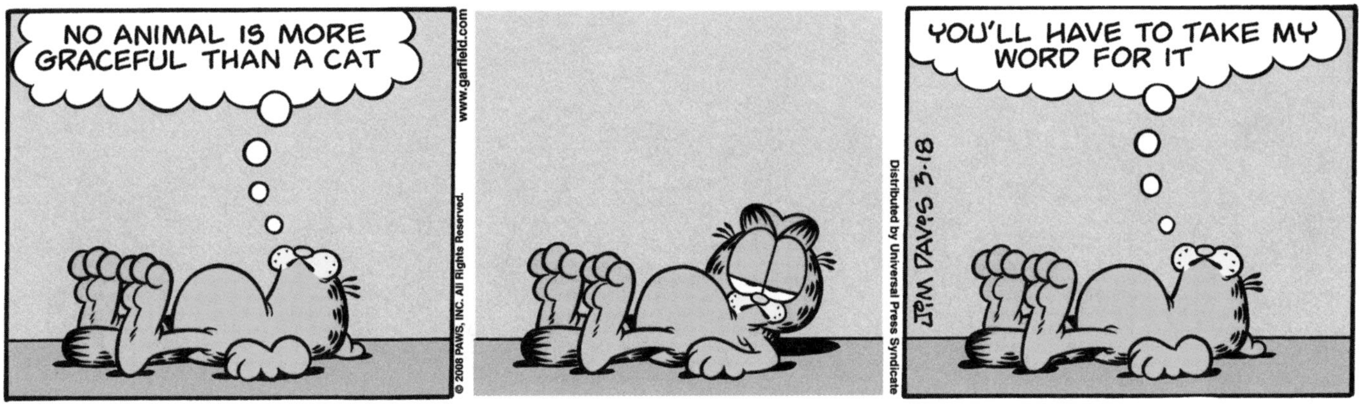
NO ANIMAL IS MORE GRACEFUL THAN A CAT
© 2008 PAWS, INC. All Rights Reserved. www.garfield.com
Distributed by Universal Press Syndicate
JIM DAVIS 3-18
YOU'LL HAVE TO TAKE MY WORD FOR IT

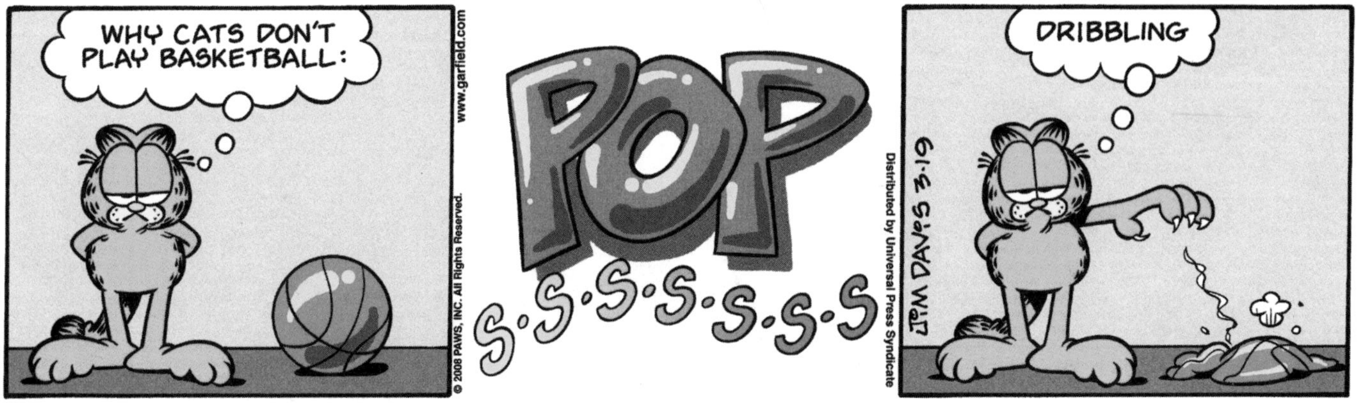
WHY CATS DON'T PLAY BASKETBALL:
© 2008 PAWS, INC. All Rights Reserved. www.garfield.com
POP
S-S-S-S-S-S-S-S
Distributed by Universal Press Syndicate
JIM DAVIS 3-19
DRIBBLING

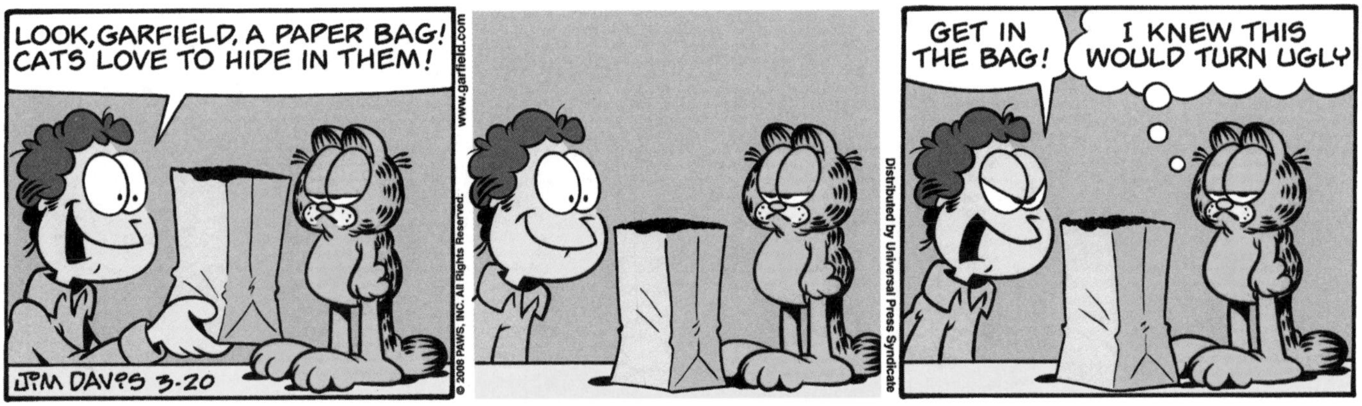
LOOK, GARFIELD, A PAPER BAG! CATS LOVE TO HIDE IN THEM!
JIM DAVIS 3-20
© 2008 PAWS, INC. All Rights Reserved. www.garfield.com
Distributed by Universal Press Syndicate
GET IN THE BAG!
I KNEW THIS WOULD TURN UGLY

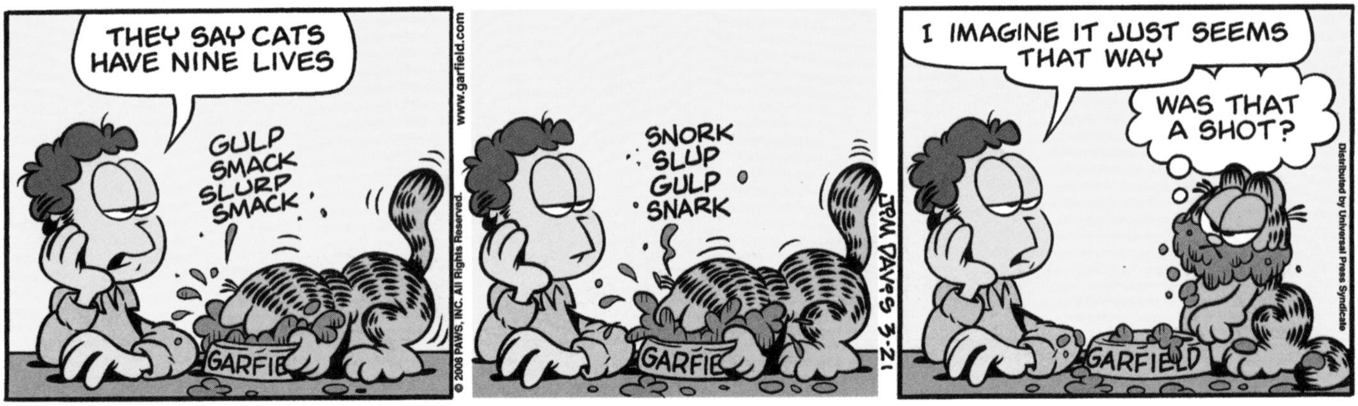
THEY SAY CATS HAVE NINE LIVES
GULP SMACK SLURP SMACK
GARFIE
© 2008 PAWS, INC. All Rights Reserved. www.garfield.com
SNORK SLUP GULP SNARK
GARFIE
JIM DAVIS 3-21
I IMAGINE IT JUST SEEMS THAT WAY
WAS THAT A SHOT?
GARFIELD
Distributed by Universal Press Syndicate

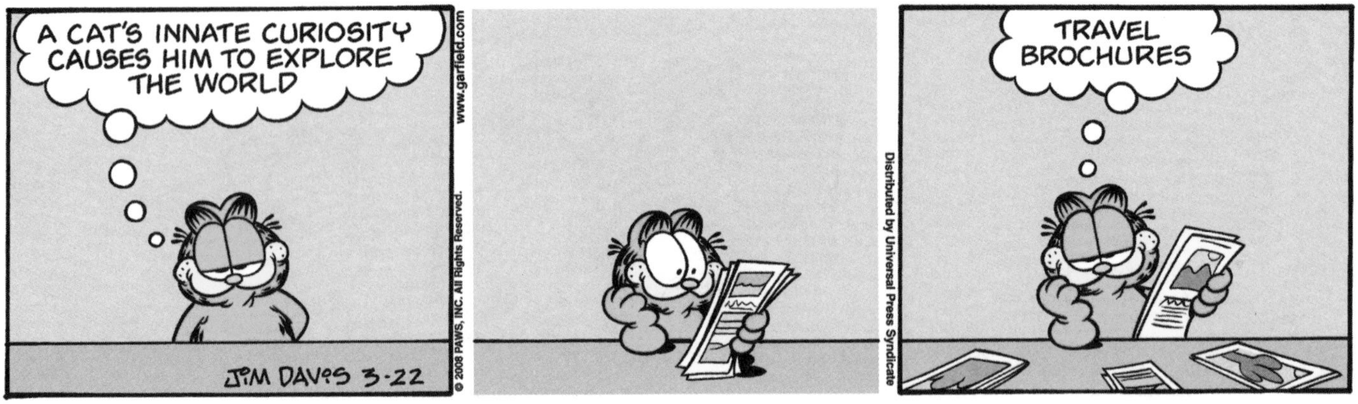
A CAT'S INNATE CURIOSITY CAUSES HIM TO EXPLORE THE WORLD
JIM DAVIS 3-22
© 2008 PAWS, INC. All Rights Reserved. www.garfield.com
Distributed by Universal Press Syndicate
TRAVEL BROCHURES

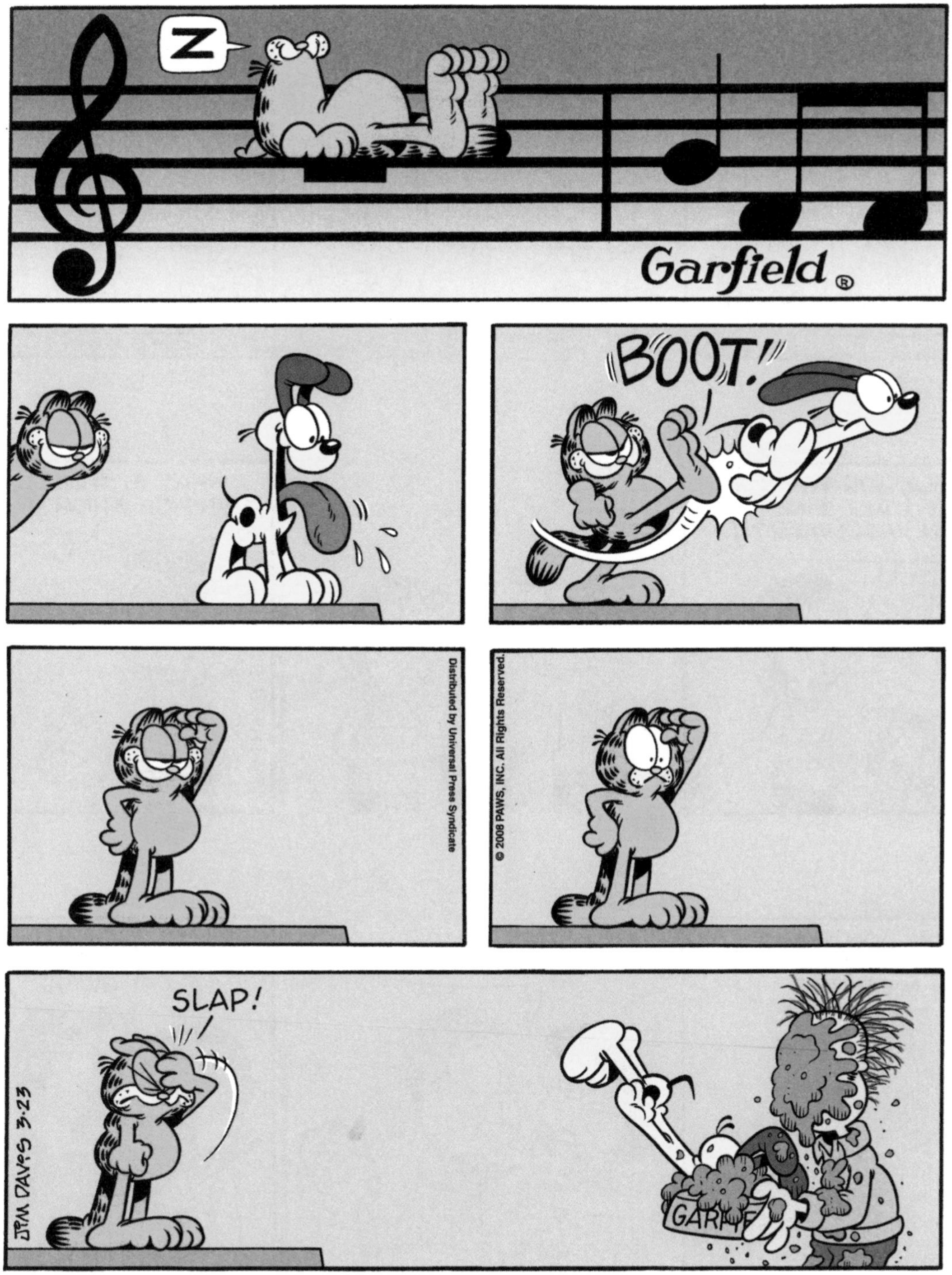
Z
Garfield®
BOOT!
Distributed by Universal Press Syndicate
© 2008 PAWS, INC. All Rights Reserved.
SLAP!
JIM DAVIS 3-23

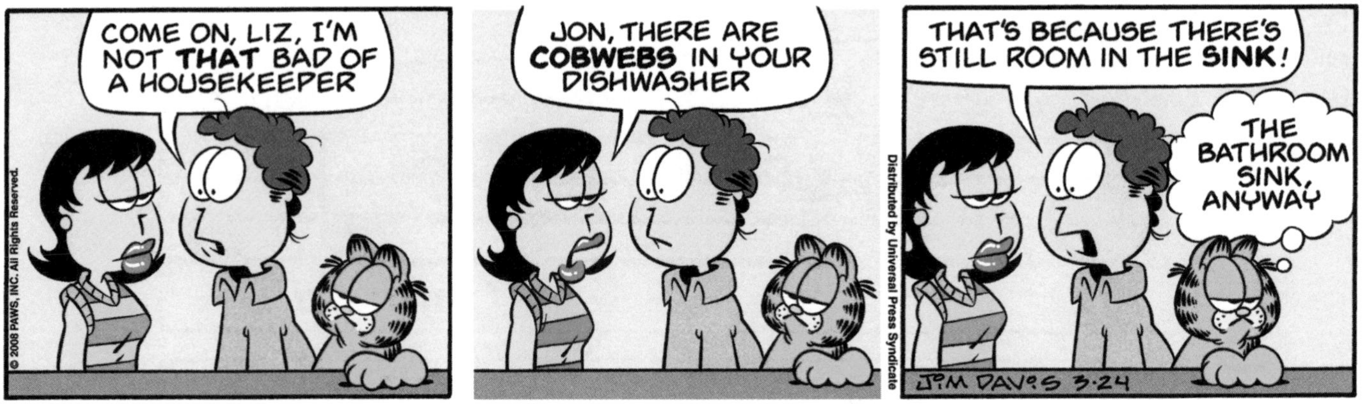
COME ON, LIZ, I'M NOT **THAT** BAD OF A HOUSEKEEPER
JON, THERE ARE **COBWEBS** IN YOUR DISHWASHER
THAT'S BECAUSE THERE'S STILL ROOM IN THE **SINK**!
THE BATHROOM SINK, ANYWAY
JIM DAVIS 3-24
© 2008 PAWS, INC. All Rights Reserved.
Distributed by Universal Press Syndicate

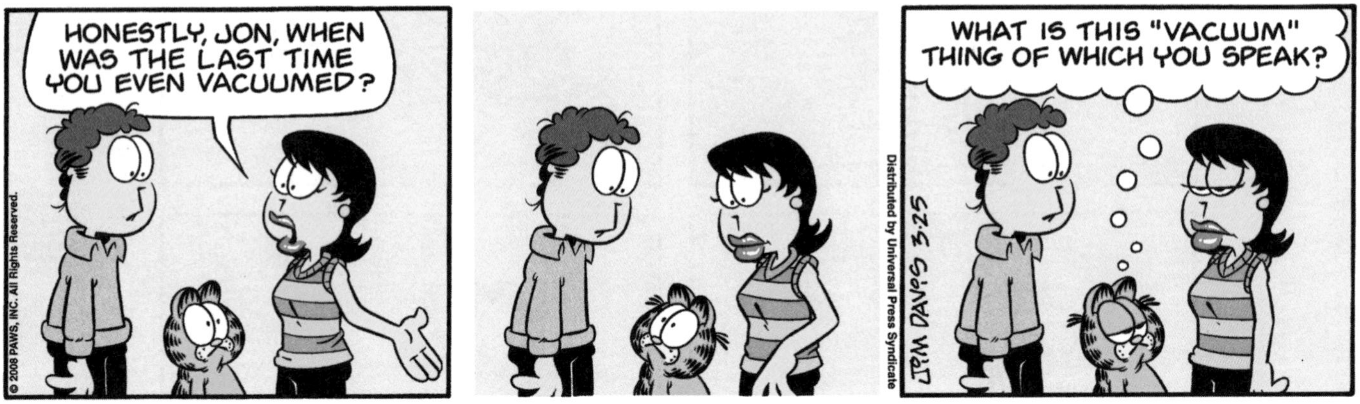
HONESTLY, JON, WHEN WAS THE LAST TIME YOU EVEN VACUUMED?
WHAT IS THIS "VACUUM" THING OF WHICH YOU SPEAK?
JIM DAVIS 3-25
© 2008 PAWS, INC. All Rights Reserved.
Distributed by Universal Press Syndicate

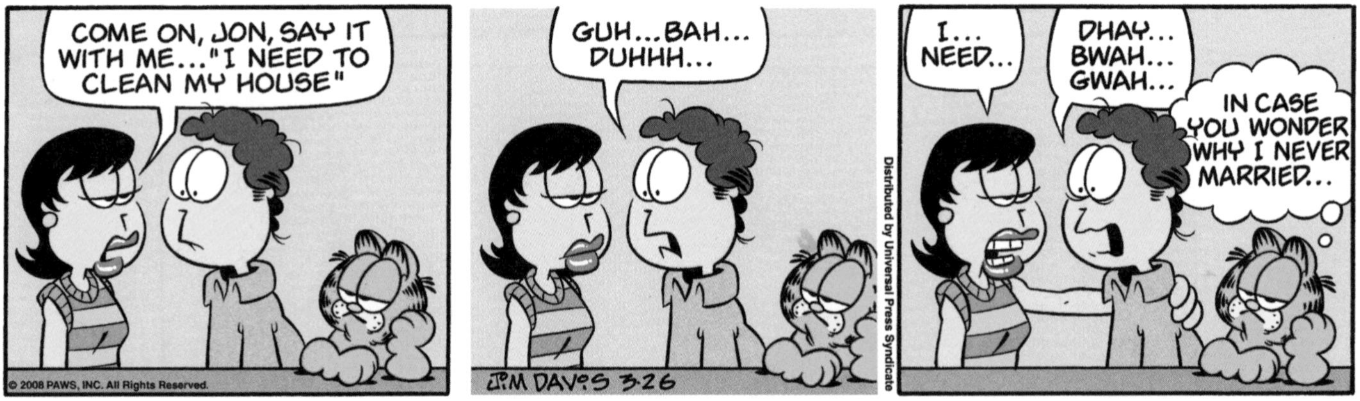
COME ON, JON, SAY IT WITH ME..."I NEED TO CLEAN MY HOUSE"
GUH...BAH... DUHHH...
I... NEED...
DHAY... BWAH... GWAH...
IN CASE YOU WONDER WHY I NEVER MARRIED...
JIM DAVIS 3-26
© 2008 PAWS, INC. All Rights Reserved.
Distributed by Universal Press Syndicate

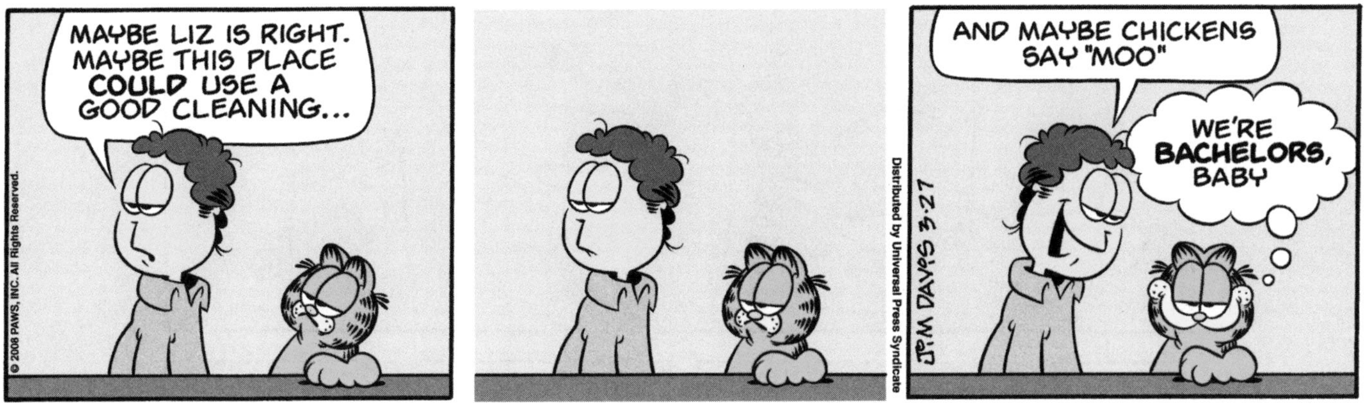
MAYBE LIZ IS RIGHT. MAYBE THIS PLACE **COULD** USE A GOOD CLEANING...
AND MAYBE CHICKENS SAY "MOO"
WE'RE **BACHELORS,** BABY
JIM DAVIS 3-27
© 2008 PAWS, INC. All Rights Reserved.
Distributed by Universal Press Syndicate

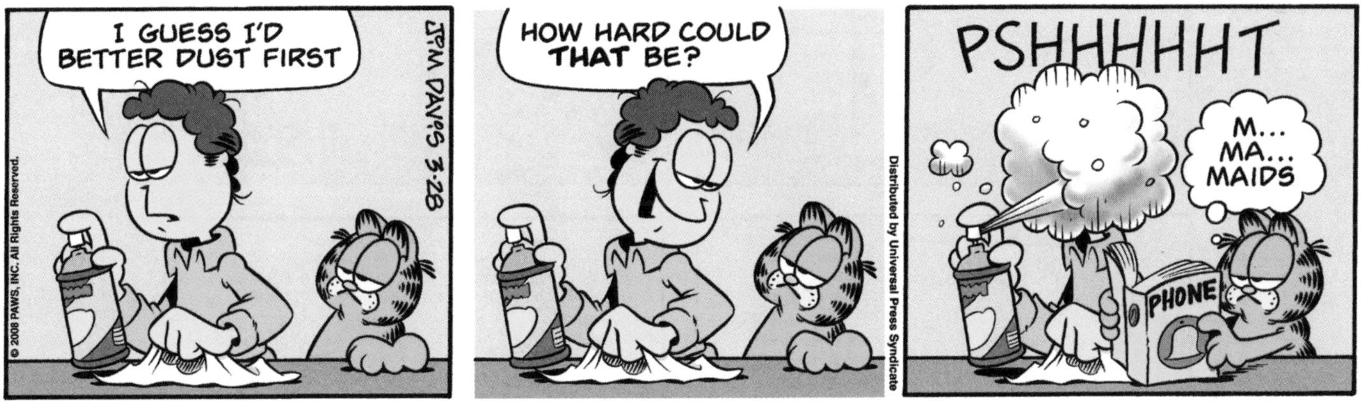
I GUESS I'D BETTER DUST FIRST
HOW HARD COULD **THAT** BE?
PSHHHHHT
M... MA... MAIDS
PHONE
JIM DAVIS 3-28
© 2008 PAWS, INC. All Rights Reserved.
Distributed by Universal Press Syndicate

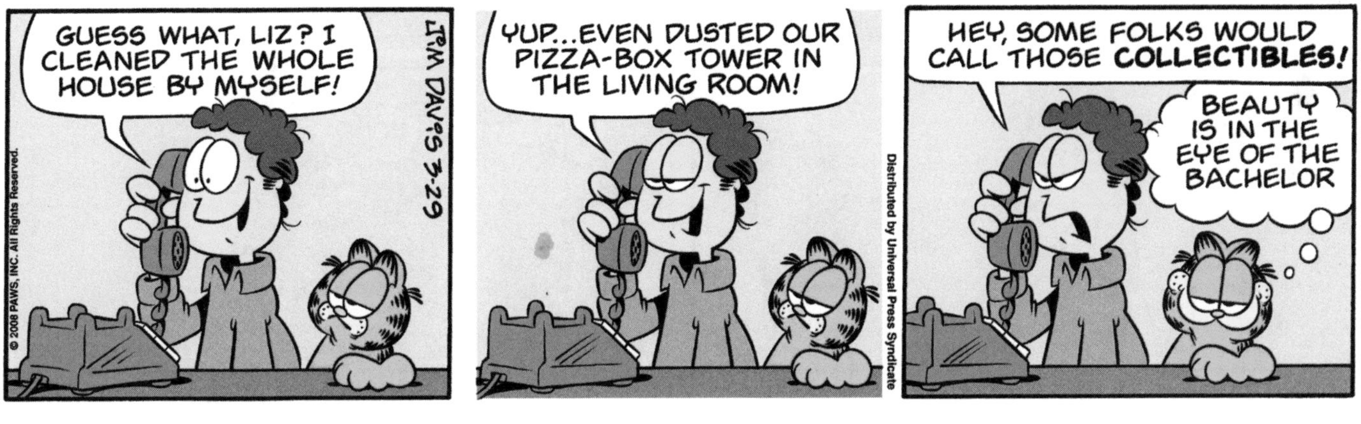
GUESS WHAT, LIZ? I CLEANED THE WHOLE HOUSE BY MYSELF!
YUP...EVEN DUSTED OUR PIZZA-BOX TOWER IN THE LIVING ROOM!
HEY, SOME FOLKS WOULD CALL THOSE **COLLECTIBLES!**
BEAUTY IS IN THE EYE OF THE BACHELOR
JIM DAVIS 3-29
© 2008 PAWS, INC. All Rights Reserved.
Distributed by Universal Press Syndicate

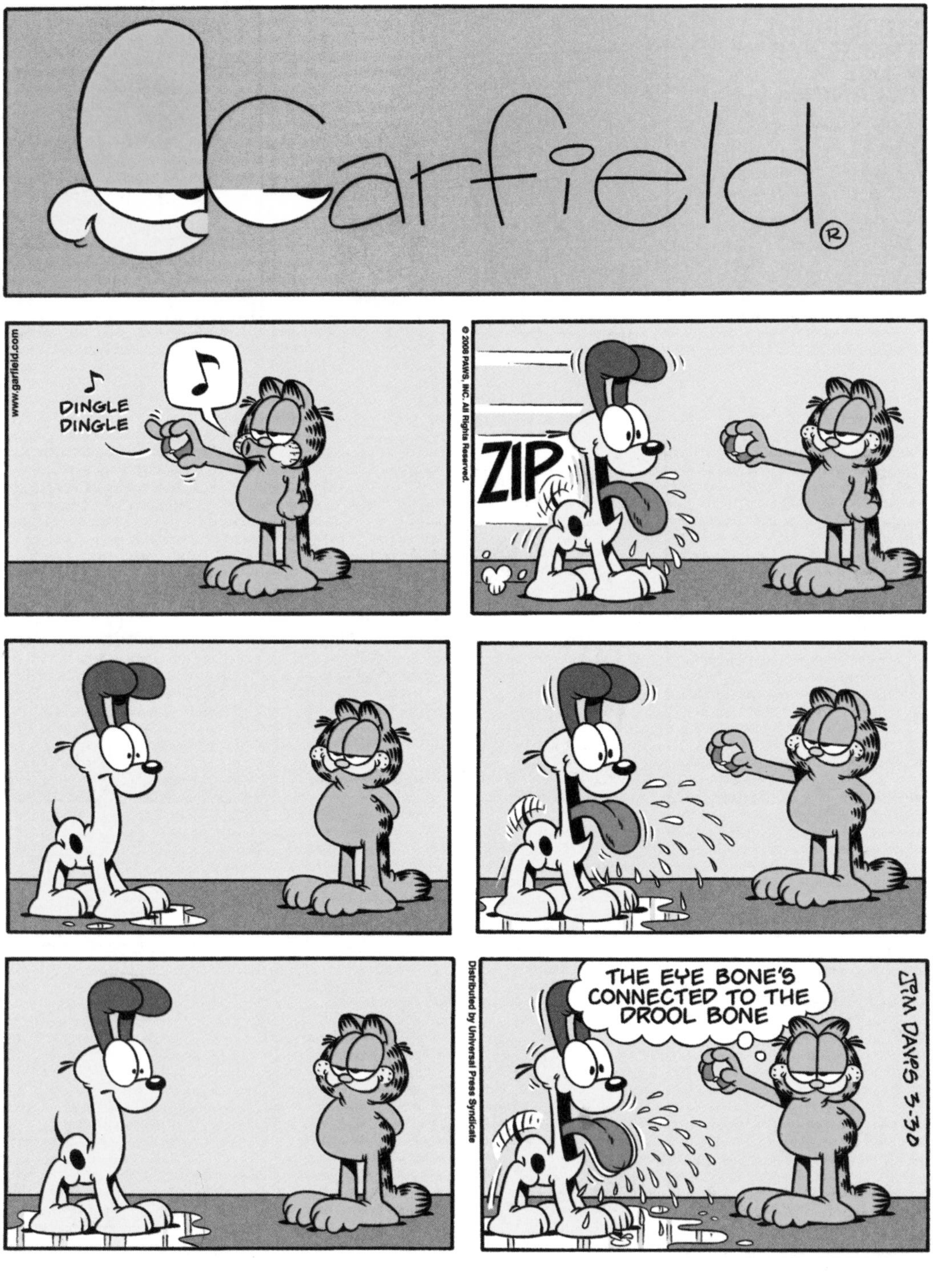
Garfield
www.garfield.com
♪ DINGLE DINGLE
♪
© 2008 PAWS, INC. All Rights Reserved.
ZIP
Distributed by Universal Press Syndicate
THE EYE BONE'S CONNECTED TO THE DROOL BONE
JPM DAVIS 3-30

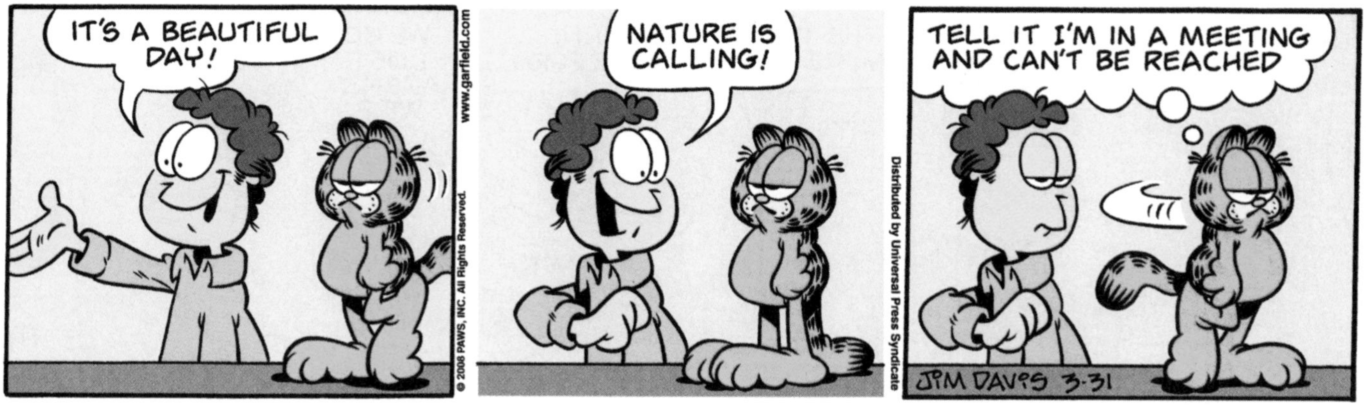
IT'S A BEAUTIFUL DAY!
© 2008 PAWS, INC. All Rights Reserved.
www.garfield.com
NATURE IS CALLING!
Distributed by Universal Press Syndicate
TELL IT I'M IN A MEETING AND CAN'T BE REACHED
JIM DAVIS 3-31

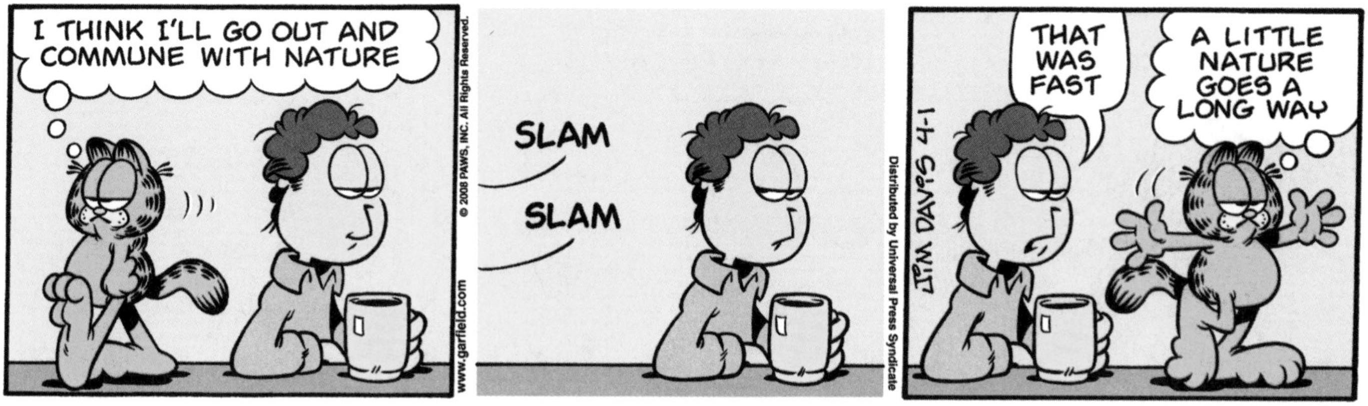
I THINK I'LL GO OUT AND COMMUNE WITH NATURE
© 2008 PAWS, INC. All Rights Reserved.
www.garfield.com
SLAM
SLAM
Distributed by Universal Press Syndicate
JIM DAVIS 4-1
THAT WAS FAST
A LITTLE NATURE GOES A LONG WAY

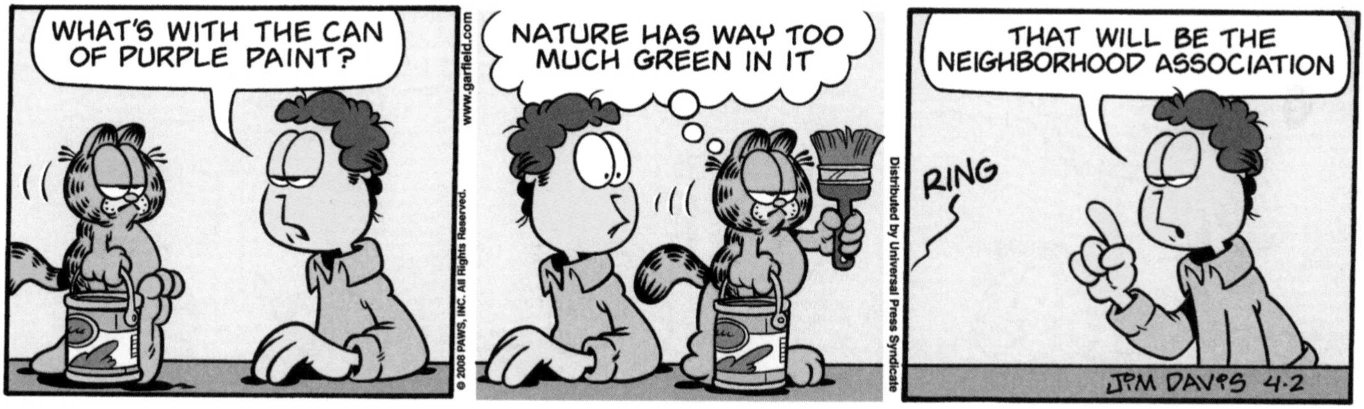
WHAT'S WITH THE CAN OF PURPLE PAINT?
www.garfield.com
© 2008 PAWS, INC. All Rights Reserved.
NATURE HAS WAY TOO MUCH GREEN IN IT
Distributed by Universal Press Syndicate
RING
THAT WILL BE THE NEIGHBORHOOD ASSOCIATION
JIM DAVIS 4-2

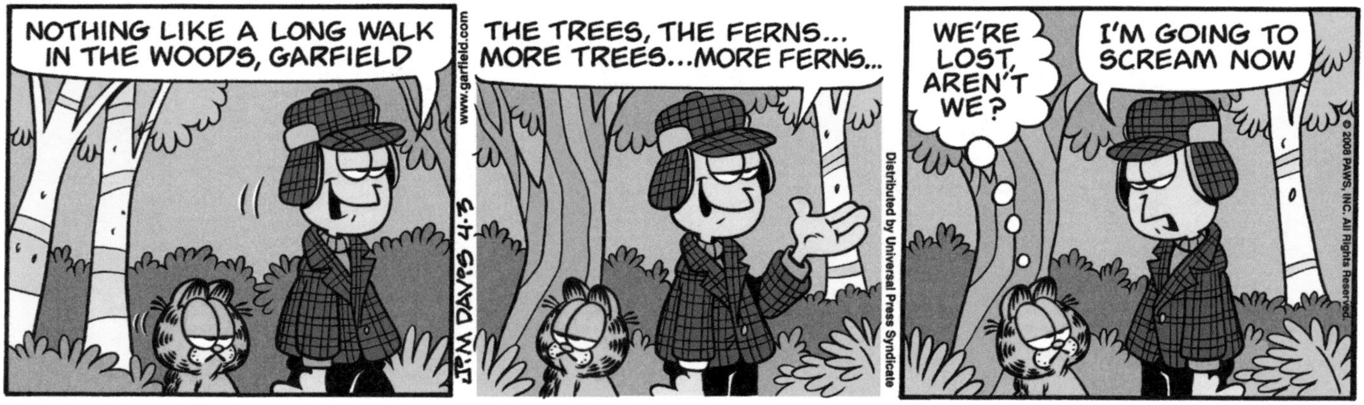
NOTHING LIKE A LONG WALK IN THE WOODS, GARFIELD
www.garfield.com
JIM DAVIS 4-3
THE TREES, THE FERNS... MORE TREES...MORE FERNS...
Distributed by Universal Press Syndicate
WE'RE LOST, AREN'T WE?
I'M GOING TO SCREAM NOW
© 2008 PAWS, INC. All Rights Reserved.

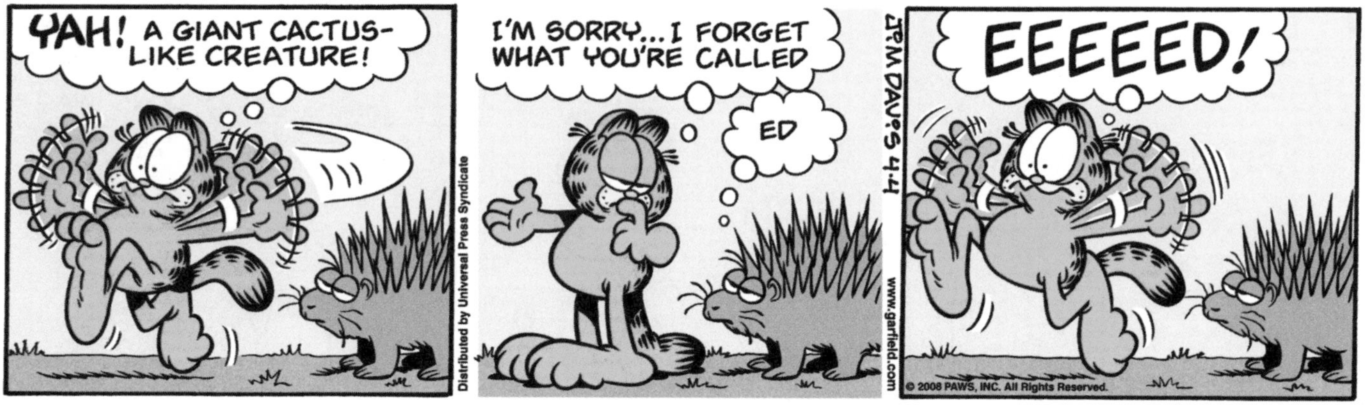
YAH! A GIANT CACTUS-LIKE CREATURE!
Distributed by Universal Press Syndicate
I'M SORRY... I FORGET WHAT YOU'RE CALLED
ED
JIM DAVIS 4-4
www.garfield.com
EEEEED!
© 2008 PAWS, INC. All Rights Reserved.

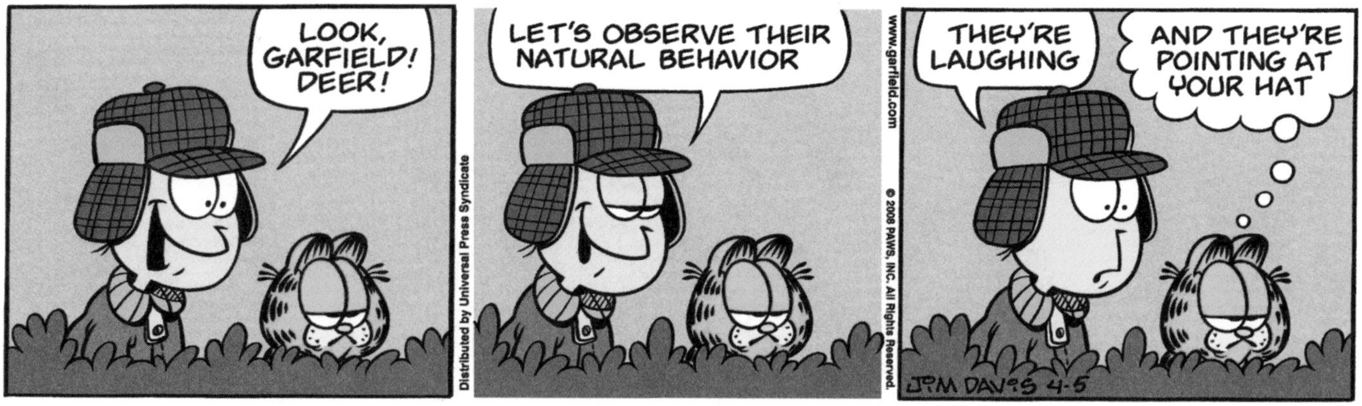
LOOK, GARFIELD! DEER!
Distributed by Universal Press Syndicate
LET'S OBSERVE THEIR NATURAL BEHAVIOR
www.garfield.com
© 2008 PAWS, INC. All Rights Reserved.
THEY'RE LAUGHING
AND THEY'RE POINTING AT YOUR HAT
JIM DAVIS 4-5

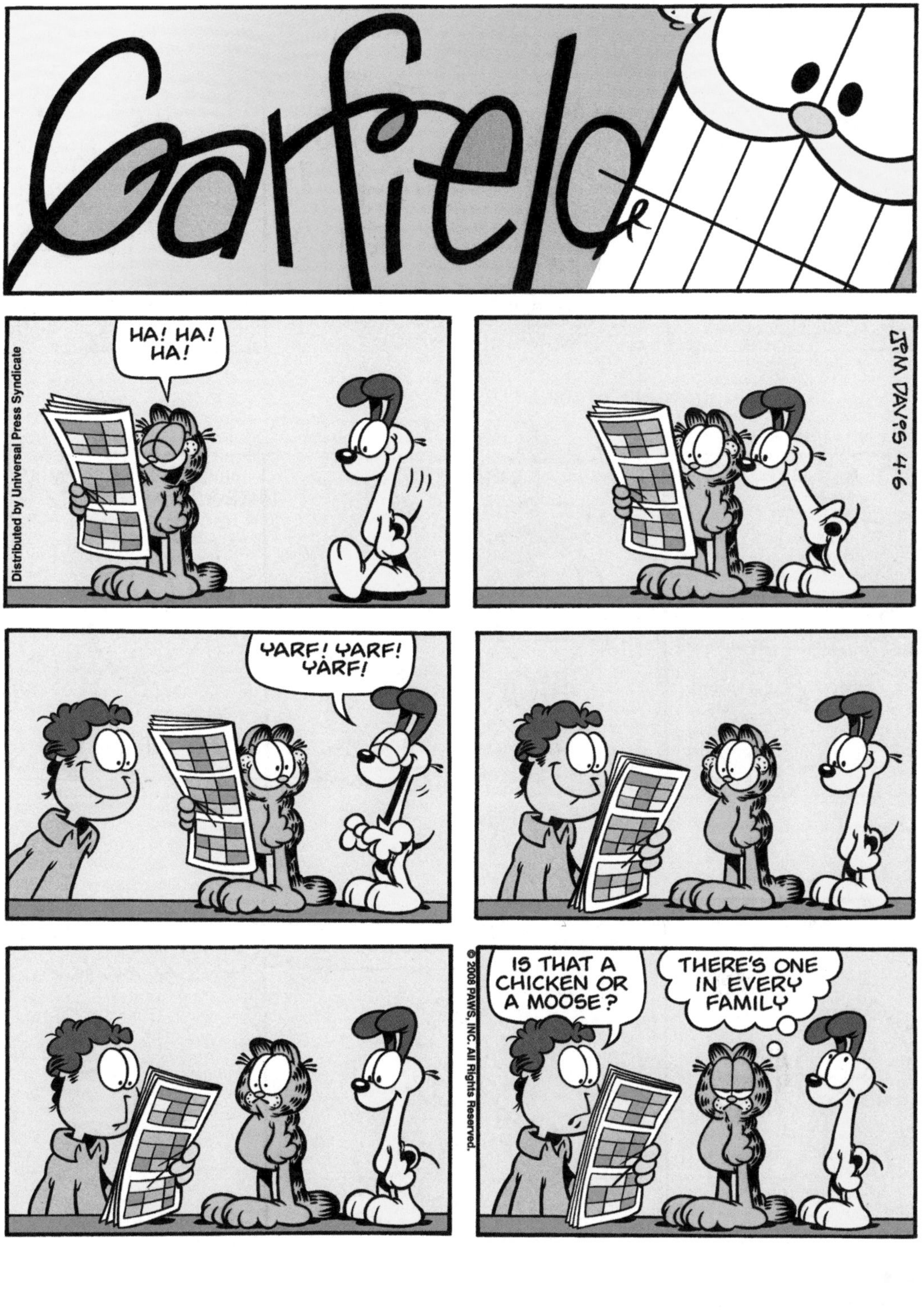
Garfield
Distributed by Universal Press Syndicate
HA! HA! HA!
JPM DAVIS 4-6
YARF! YARF! YARF!
© 2008 PAWS, INC. All Rights Reserved.
IS THAT A CHICKEN OR A MOOSE?
THERE'S ONE IN EVERY FAMILY

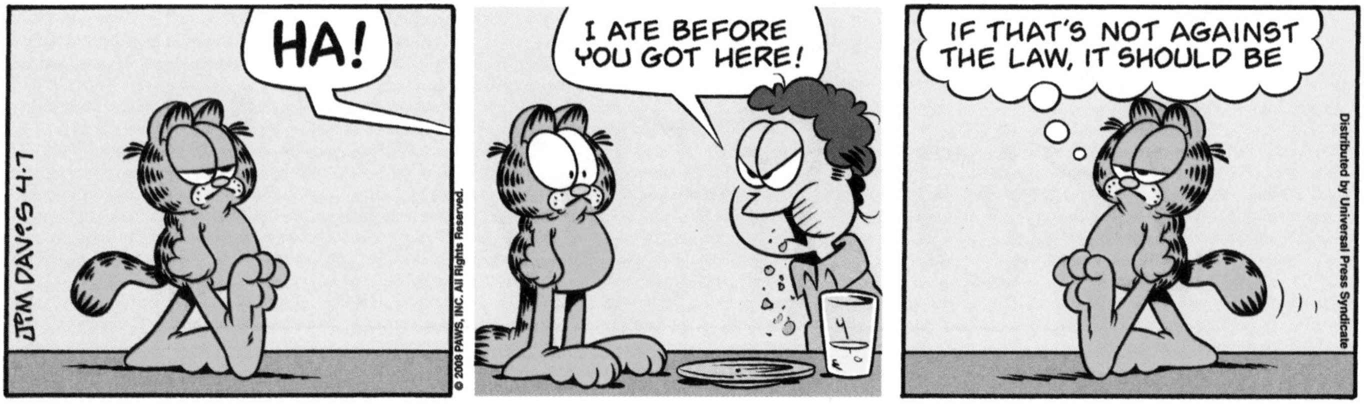
JIM DAVIS 4·7
HA!
© 2008 PAWS, INC. All Rights Reserved.
I ATE BEFORE YOU GOT HERE!
IF THAT'S NOT AGAINST THE LAW, IT SHOULD BE
Distributed by Universal Press Syndicate

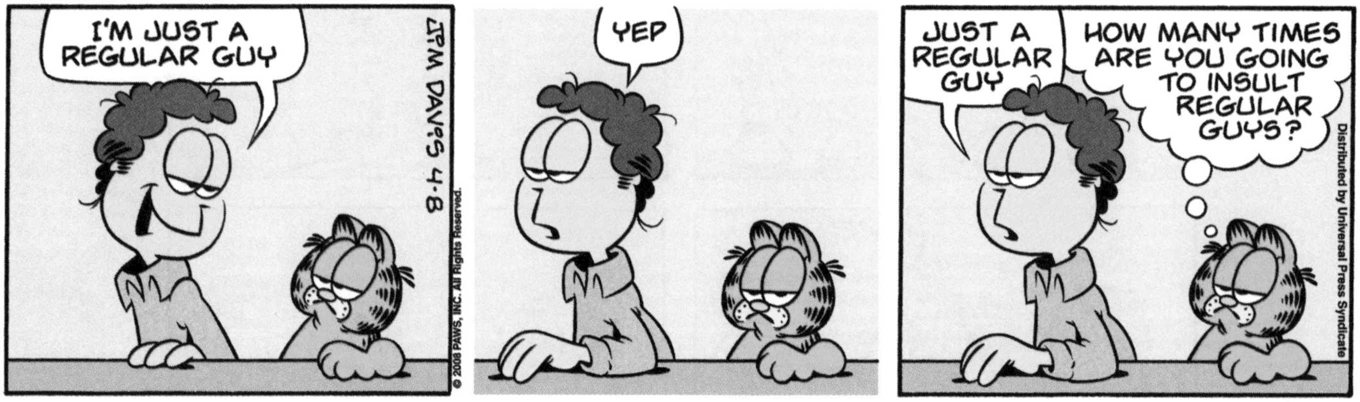
I'M JUST A REGULAR GUY
JIM DAVIS 4·8
© 2008 PAWS, INC. All Rights Reserved.
YEP
JUST A REGULAR GUY
HOW MANY TIMES ARE YOU GOING TO INSULT REGULAR GUYS?
Distributed by Universal Press Syndicate

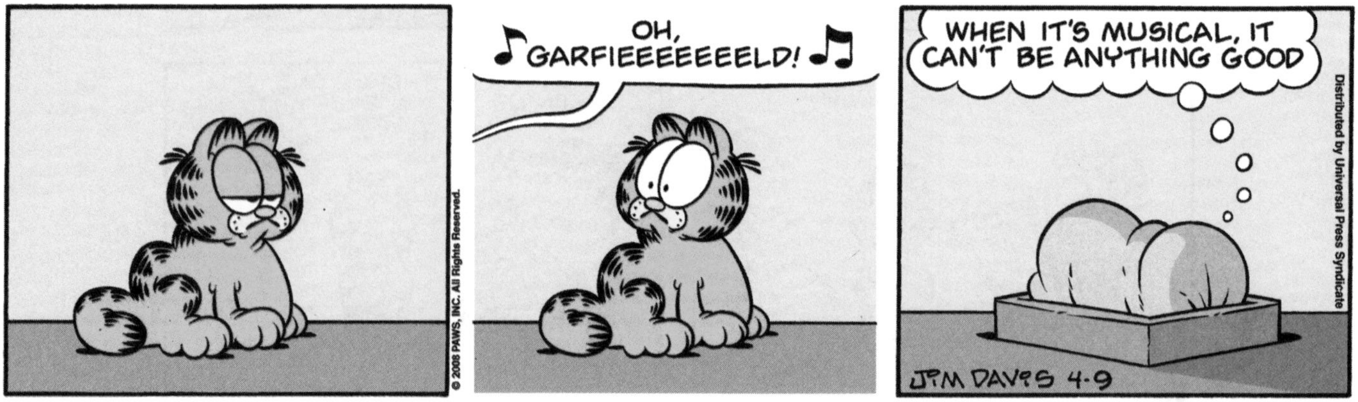
© 2008 PAWS, INC. All Rights Reserved.
♪ OH, GARFIEEEEEEELD! ♫
WHEN IT'S MUSICAL, IT CAN'T BE ANYTHING GOOD
Distributed by Universal Press Syndicate
JIM DAVIS 4·9

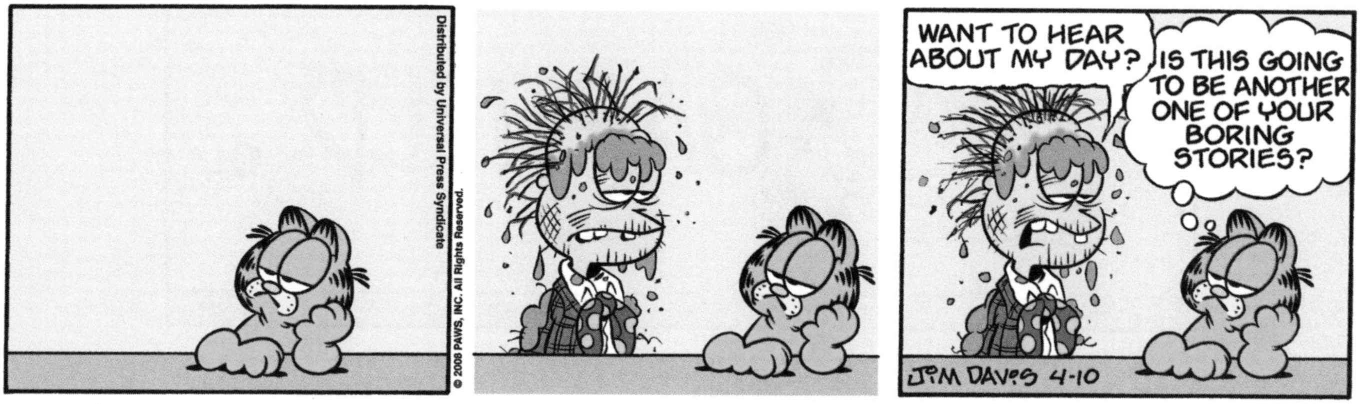
Distributed by Universal Press Syndicate
© 2008 PAWS, INC. All Rights Reserved.
WANT TO HEAR ABOUT MY DAY?
IS THIS GOING TO BE ANOTHER ONE OF YOUR BORING STORIES?
JIM DAVIS 4-10

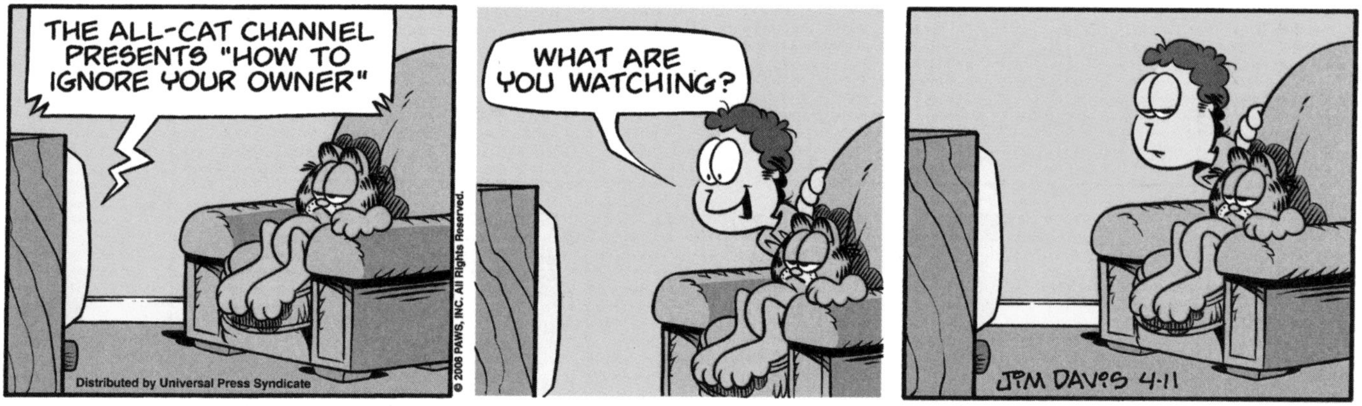
THE ALL-CAT CHANNEL PRESENTS "HOW TO IGNORE YOUR OWNER"
Distributed by Universal Press Syndicate
© 2008 PAWS, INC. All Rights Reserved.
WHAT ARE YOU WATCHING?
JIM DAVIS 4-11

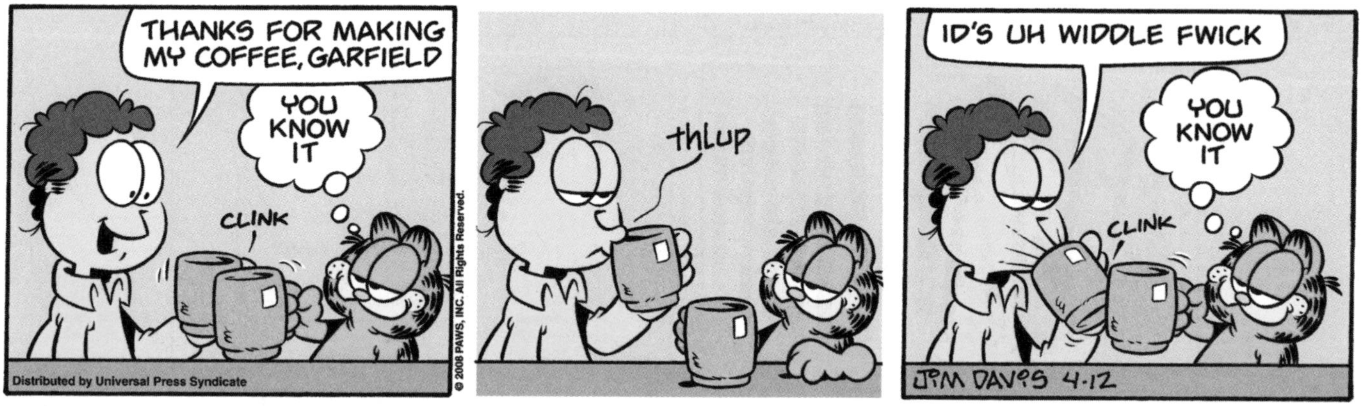
THANKS FOR MAKING MY COFFEE, GARFIELD
YOU KNOW IT
CLINK
Distributed by Universal Press Syndicate
© 2008 PAWS, INC. All Rights Reserved.
thlup
ID'S UH WIDDLE FWICK
YOU KNOW IT
CLINK
JIM DAVIS 4-12

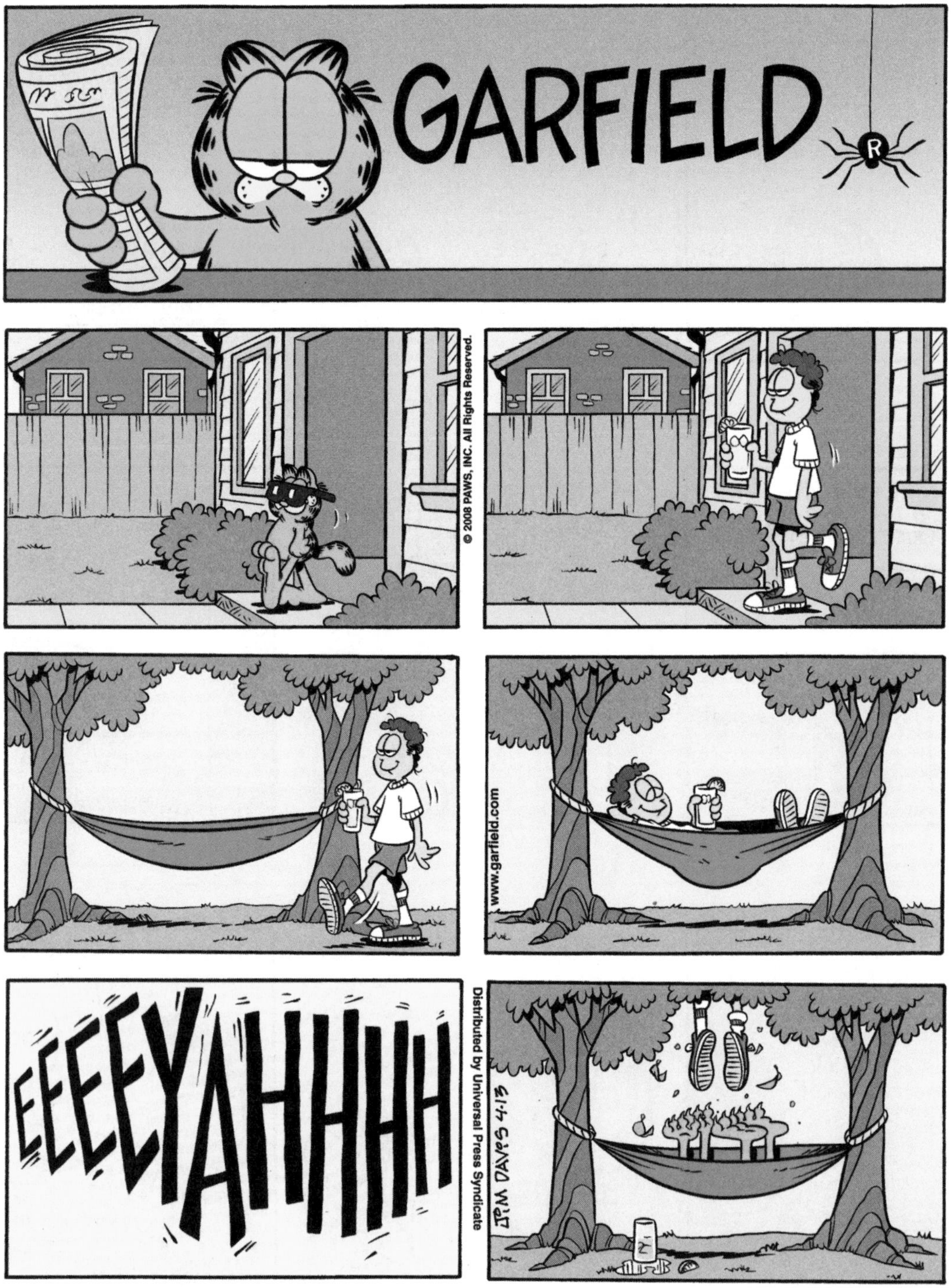
GARFIELD
© 2008 PAWS, INC. All Rights Reserved.
www.garfield.com
EEEEYAHHHHH
Distributed by Universal Press Syndicate
JIM DAVIS 4-13

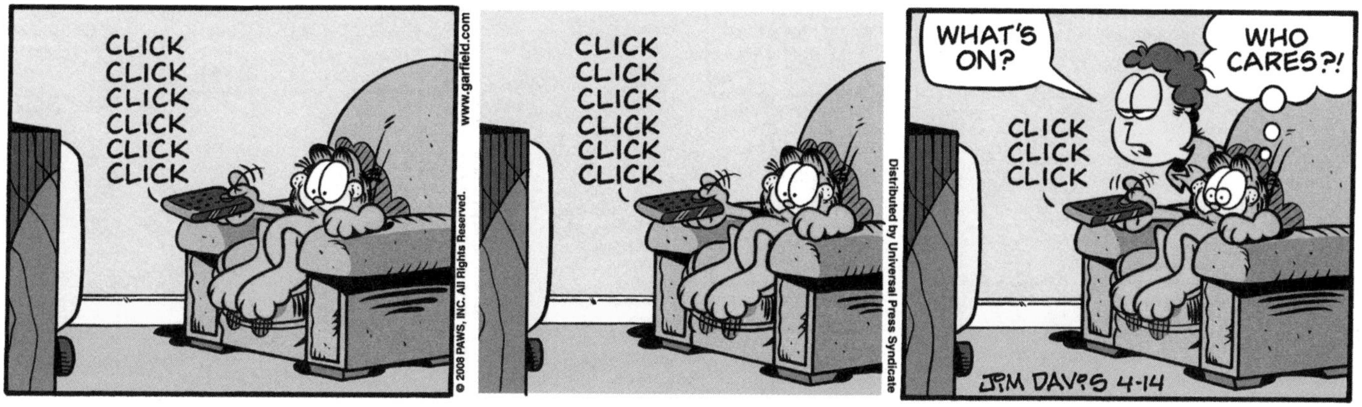
CLICK CLICK CLICK CLICK CLICK CLICK
© 2008 PAWS, INC. All Rights Reserved. www.garfield.com
CLICK CLICK CLICK CLICK CLICK CLICK
Distributed by Universal Press Syndicate
WHAT'S ON?
WHO CARES?!
CLICK CLICK CLICK
JIM DAVIS 4-14

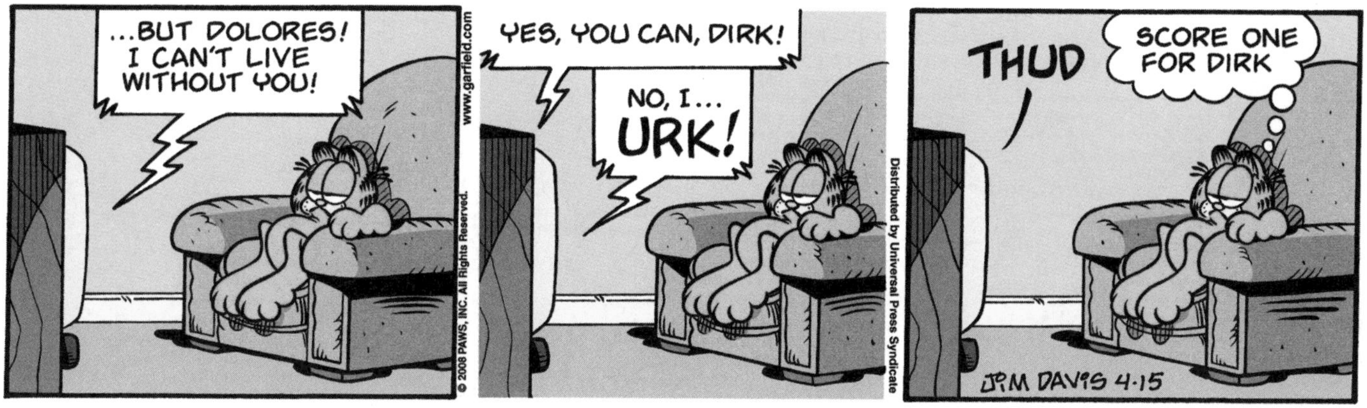
...BUT DOLORES! I CAN'T LIVE WITHOUT YOU!
© 2008 PAWS, INC. All Rights Reserved. www.garfield.com
YES, YOU CAN, DIRK!
NO, I... URK!
Distributed by Universal Press Syndicate
THUD
SCORE ONE FOR DIRK
JIM DAVIS 4-15

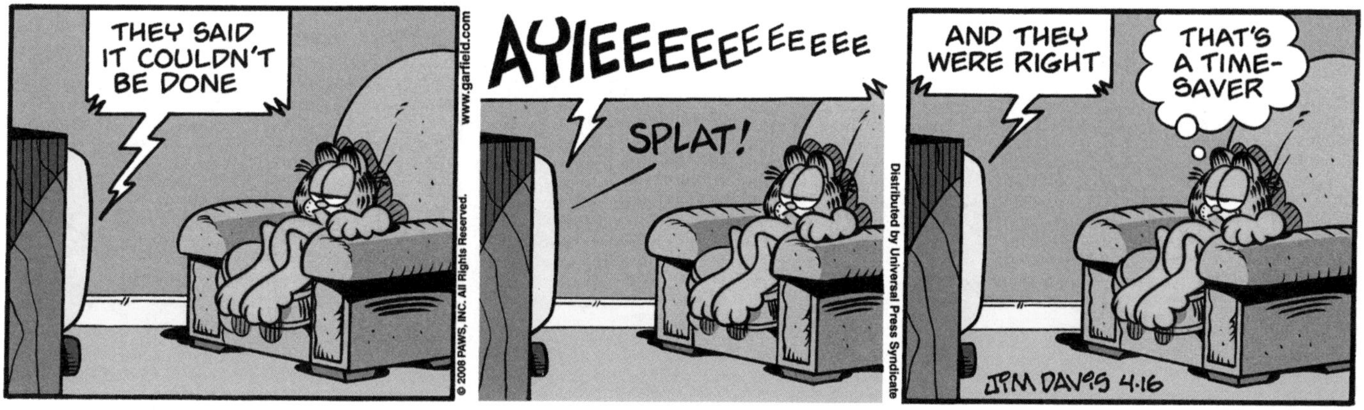
THEY SAID IT COULDN'T BE DONE
© 2008 PAWS, INC. All Rights Reserved. www.garfield.com
AYIEEEEEEEEEEE
SPLAT!
Distributed by Universal Press Syndicate
AND THEY WERE RIGHT
THAT'S A TIME-SAVER
JIM DAVIS 4-16

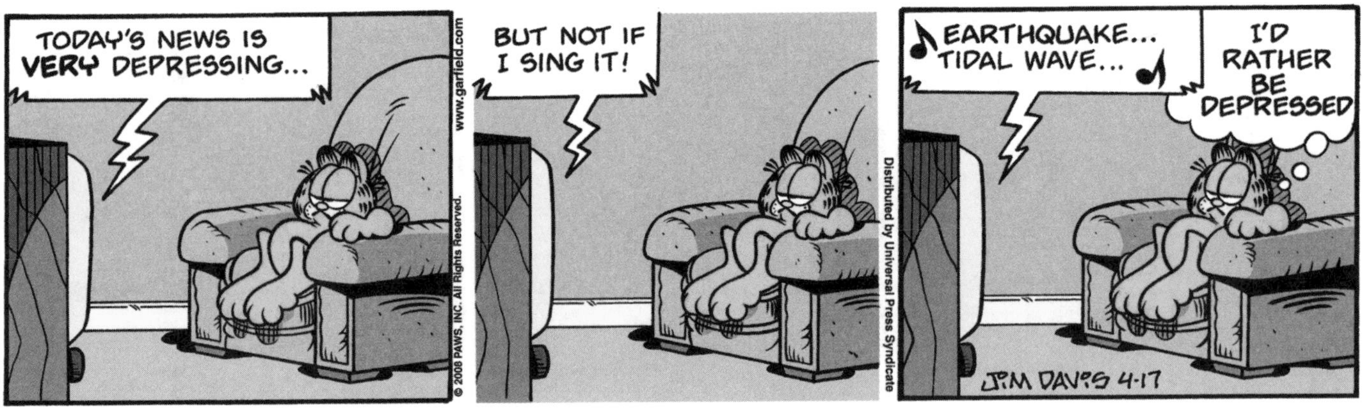
TODAY'S NEWS IS **VERY** DEPRESSING...
BUT NOT IF I SING IT!
EARTHQUAKE... TIDAL WAVE...
I'D RATHER BE DEPRESSED
JIM DAVIS 4-17
© 2008 PAWS, INC. All Rights Reserved. www.garfield.com
Distributed by Universal Press Syndicate

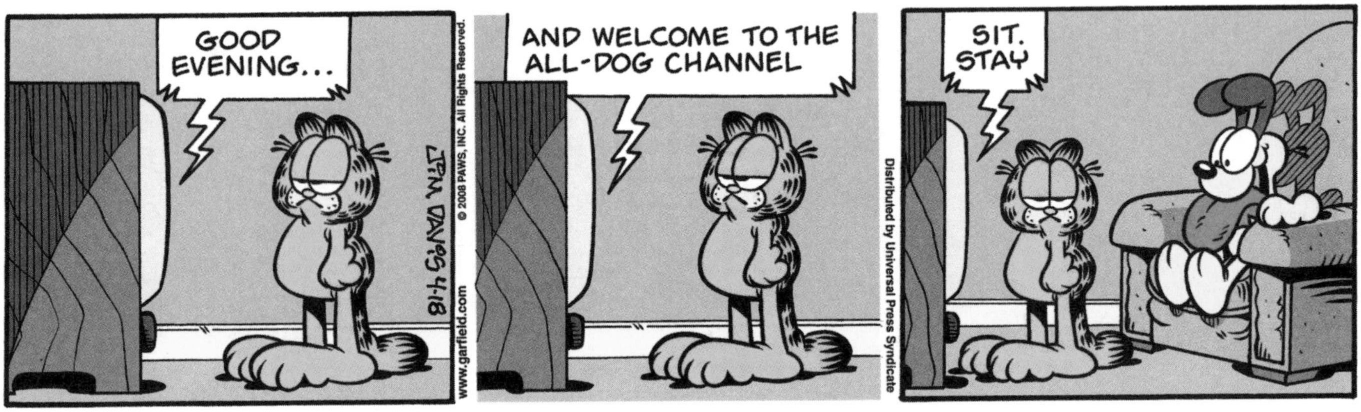
GOOD EVENING...
AND WELCOME TO THE ALL-DOG CHANNEL
SIT. STAY
JIM DAVIS 4-18
© 2008 PAWS, INC. All Rights Reserved. www.garfield.com
Distributed by Universal Press Syndicate

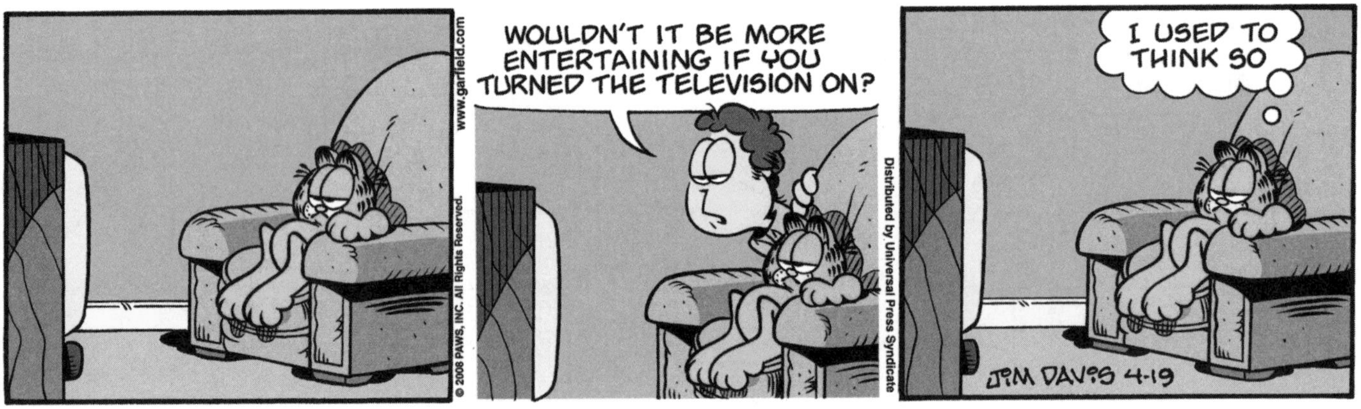
WOULDN'T IT BE MORE ENTERTAINING IF YOU TURNED THE TELEVISION ON?
I USED TO THINK SO
JIM DAVIS 4-19
© 2008 PAWS, INC. All Rights Reserved. www.garfield.com
Distributed by Universal Press Syndicate

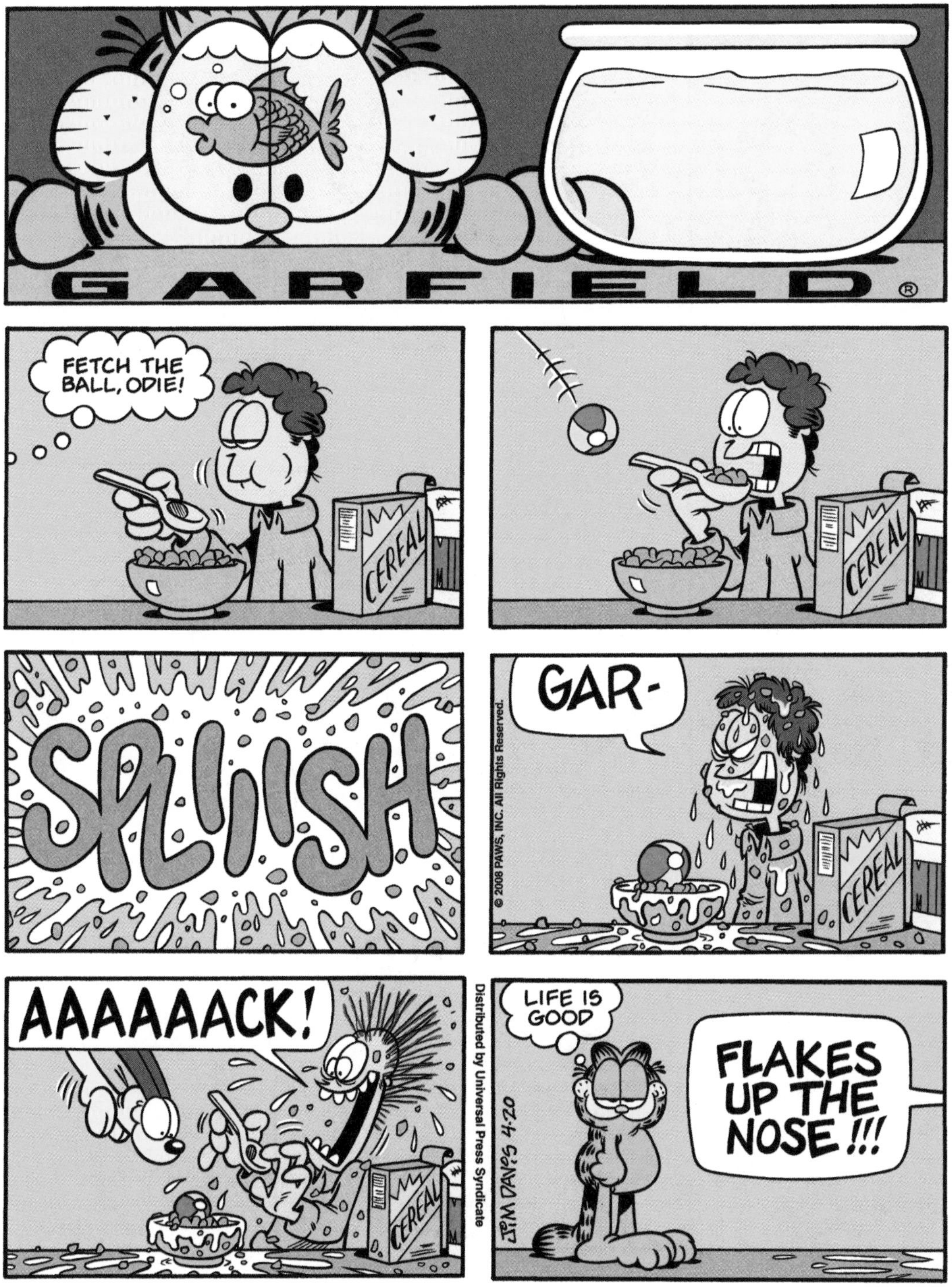
GARFIELD®
FETCH THE BALL, ODIE!
CEREAL
CEREAL
SPLIISH
GAR-
CEREAL
© 2008 PAWS, INC. All Rights Reserved.
AAAAAACK!
CEREAL
Distributed by Universal Press Syndicate
JIM DAVIS 4-20
LIFE IS GOOD
FLAKES UP THE NOSE !!!

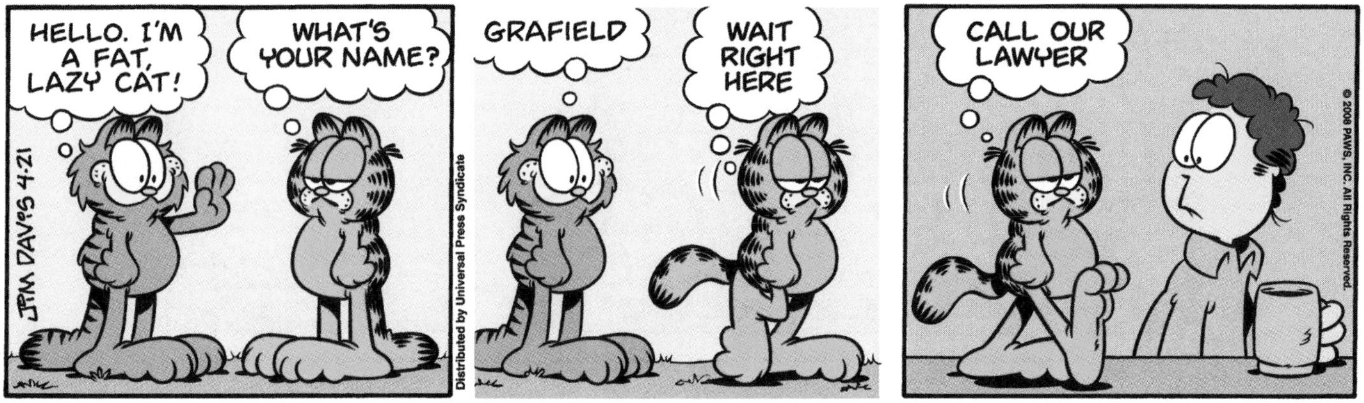
HELLO. I'M A FAT, LAZY CAT!
WHAT'S YOUR NAME?
GRAFIELD
WAIT RIGHT HERE
CALL OUR LAWYER
JIM DAVIS 4·21
Distributed by Universal Press Syndicate
© 2008 PAWS, INC. All Rights Reserved.

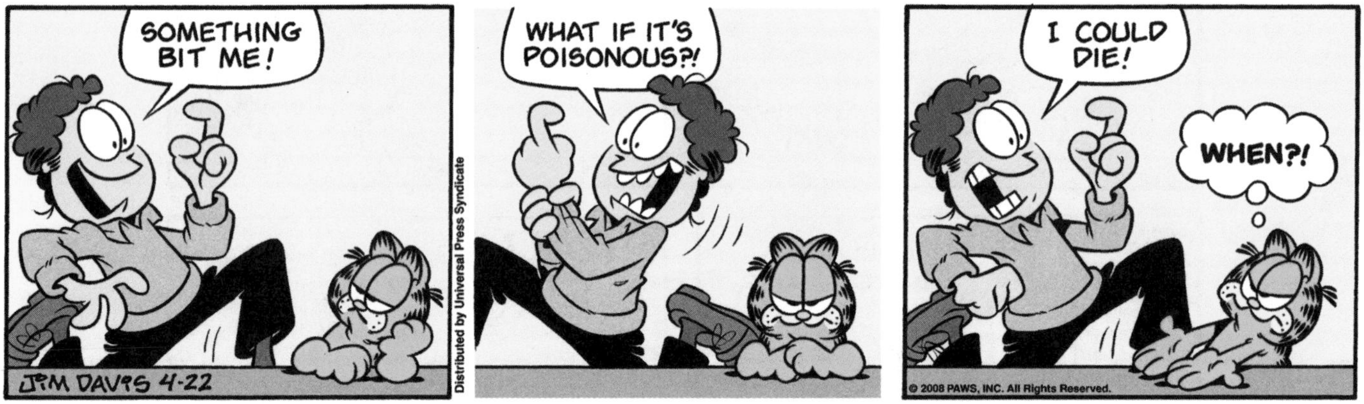
SOMETHING BIT ME!
WHAT IF IT'S POISONOUS?!
I COULD DIE!
WHEN?!
JIM DAVIS 4-22
Distributed by Universal Press Syndicate
© 2008 PAWS, INC. All Rights Reserved.

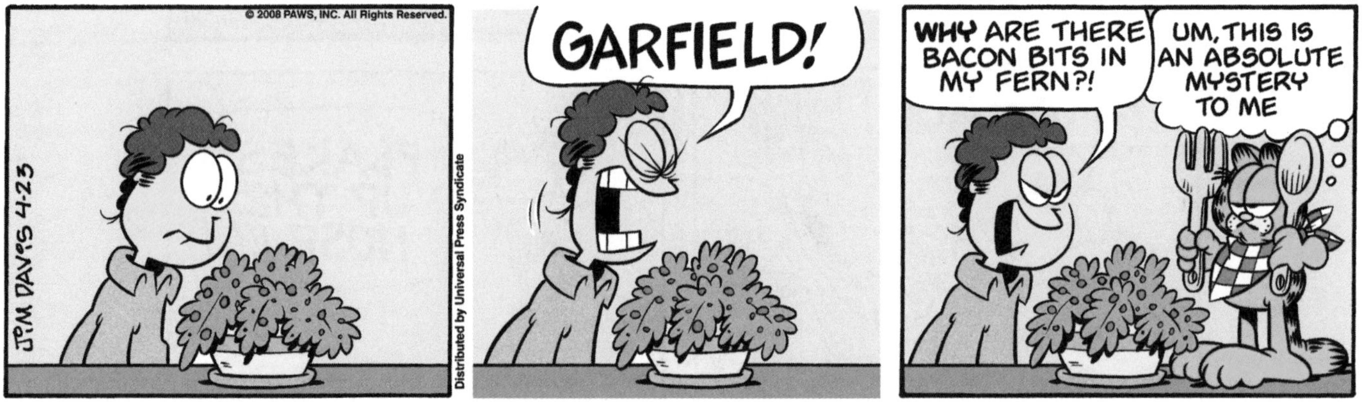
© 2008 PAWS, INC. All Rights Reserved.
JIM DAVIS 4-23
GARFIELD!
WHY ARE THERE BACON BITS IN MY FERN?!
UM, THIS IS AN ABSOLUTE MYSTERY TO ME
Distributed by Universal Press Syndicate

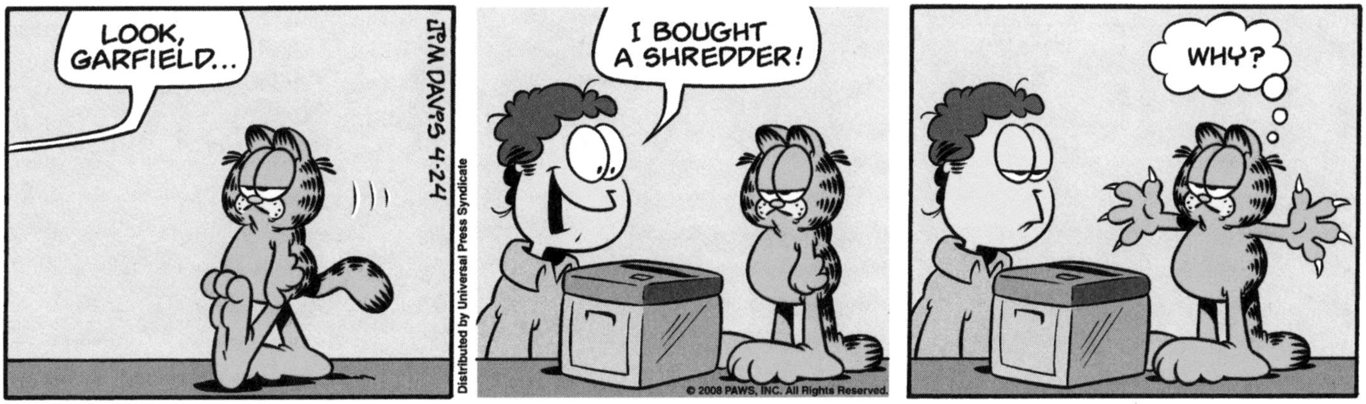
LOOK, GARFIELD...
JIM DAVIS 4-24
Distributed by Universal Press Syndicate
I BOUGHT A SHREDDER!
© 2008 PAWS, INC. All Rights Reserved.
WHY?

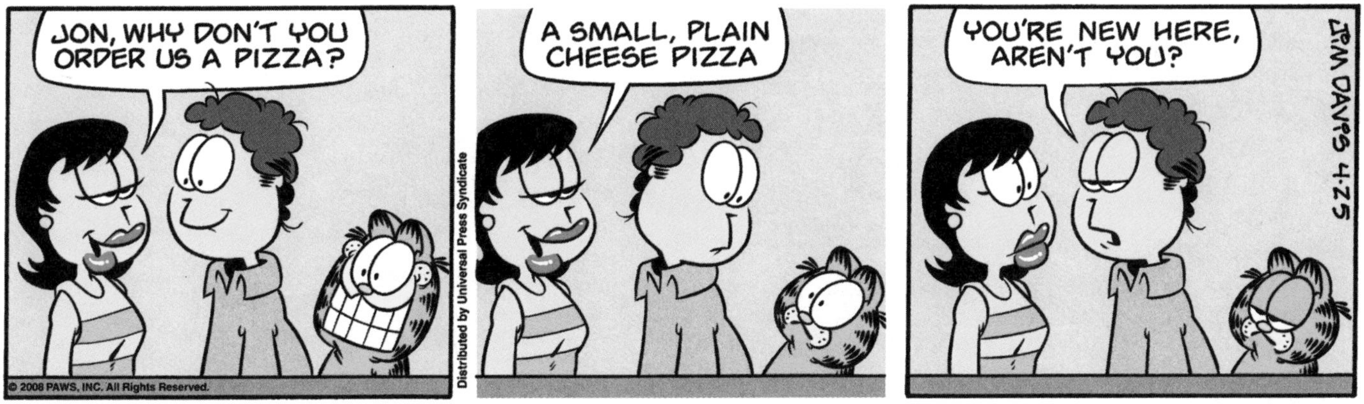
JON, WHY DON'T YOU ORDER US A PIZZA?
© 2008 PAWS, INC. All Rights Reserved.
Distributed by Universal Press Syndicate
A SMALL, PLAIN CHEESE PIZZA
YOU'RE NEW HERE, AREN'T YOU?
JIM DAVIS 4-25

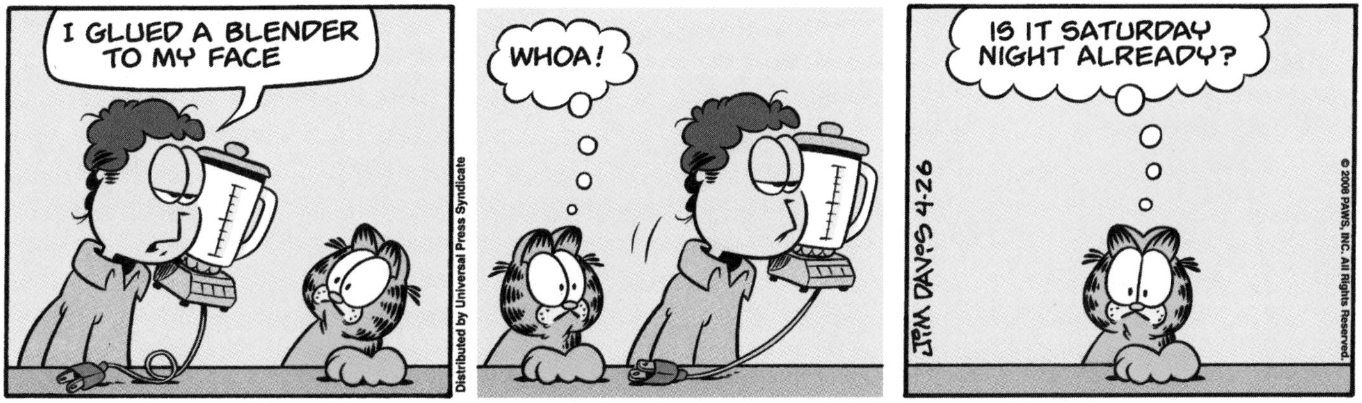
I GLUED A BLENDER TO MY FACE
Distributed by Universal Press Syndicate
WHOA!
JIM DAVIS 4-26
IS IT SATURDAY NIGHT ALREADY?
© 2008 PAWS, INC. All Rights Reserved.

Garfield's KOOKY KLASSICS

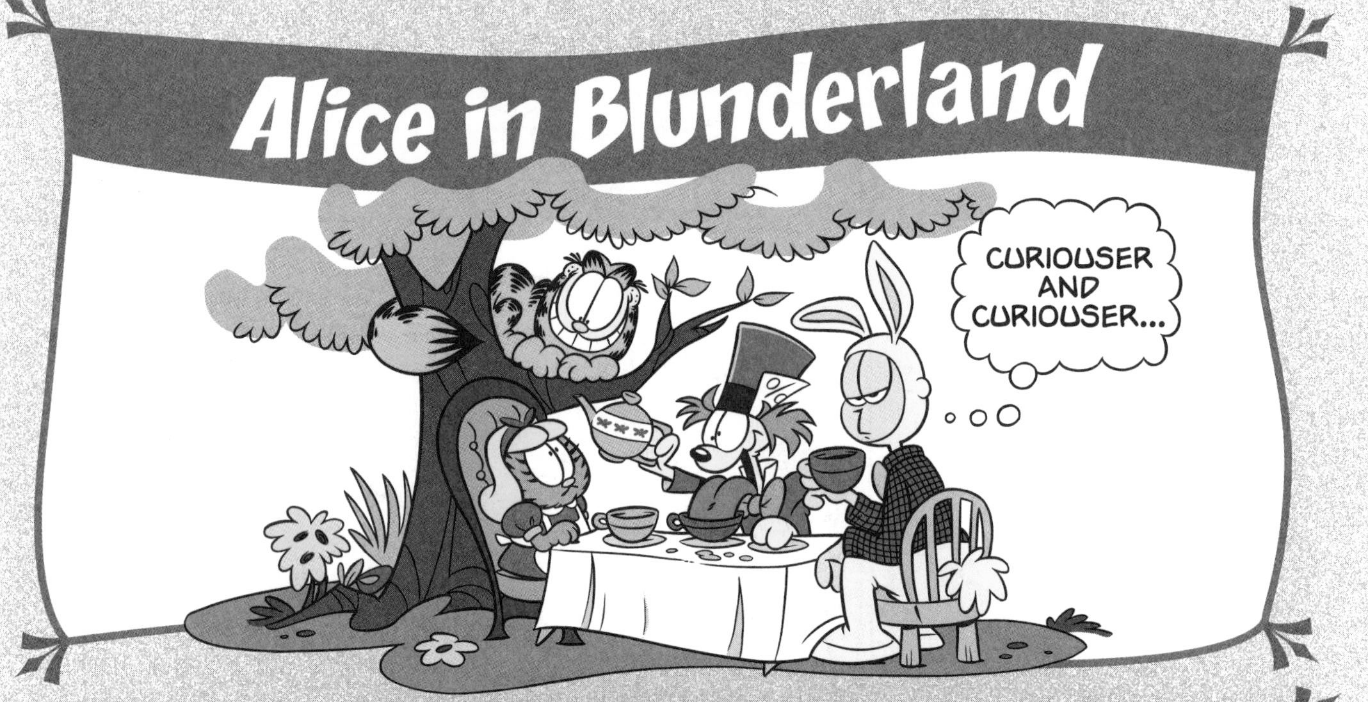
Alice in Blunderland
CURIOUSER AND CURIOUSER...

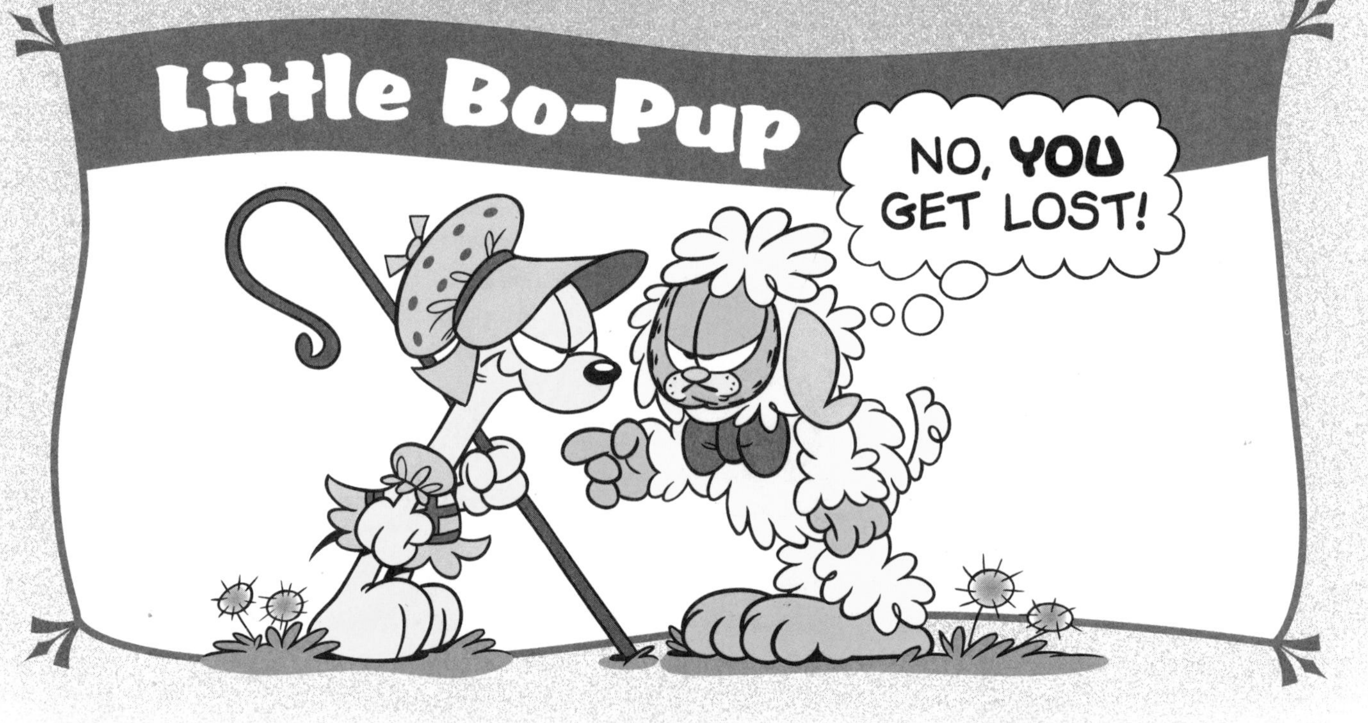
Little Bo-Pup
NO, **YOU** GET LOST!

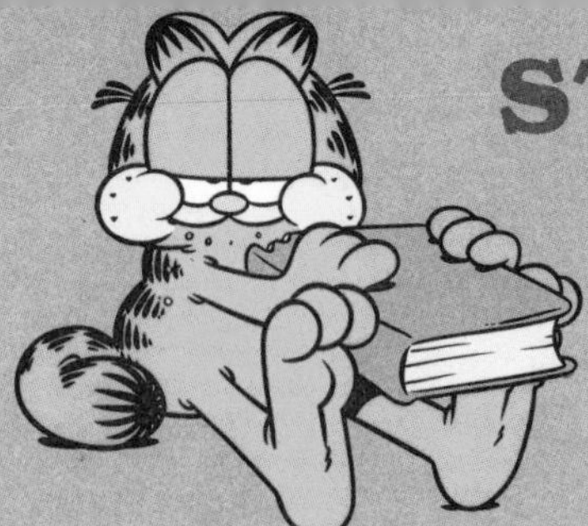

STRIPS, SPECIALS, OR BESTSELLING BOOKS . . . GARFIELD'S ON EVERYONE'S MENU.

Don't miss even one episode in the Tubby Tabby's hilarious series!

🐾 GARFIELD AT LARGE . . . (#1) 978-0-345-44382-3
🐾 GARFIELD GAINS WEIGHT . . . (#2) 978-0-345-44975-7
🐾 GARFIELD BIGGER THAN LIFE . . . (#3) 978-0-345-45027-2
🐾 GARFIELD WEIGHS IN . . . (#4) 978-0-345-45205-4
🐾 GARFIELD TAKES THE CAKE . . . (#5) 978-0-345-44978-8
🐾 GARFIELD EATS HIS HEART OUT . . . (#6) 978-0-345-46459-0
🐾 GARFIELD SITS AROUND THE HOUSE . . . (#7) 978-0-345-46463-7
🐾 GARFIELD TIPS THE SCALES . . . (#8) 978-0-345-46909-0
🐾 GARFIELD LOSES HIS FEET . . . (#9) 978-0-345-46467-5
🐾 GARFIELD MAKES IT BIG . . . (#10) 978-0-345-46468-2
🐾 GARFIELD ROLLS ON . . . (#11) 978-0-345-47561-9
🐾 GARFIELD OUT TO LUNCH . . . (#12) 978-0-345-47562-6
🐾 GARFIELD FOOD FOR THOUGHT . . . (#13) 978-0-345-47563-3
🐾 GARFIELD SWALLOWS HIS PRIDE . . . (#14) 978-0-345-91386-9
🐾 GARFIELD WORLDWIDE . . . (#15) 978-0-345-91754-6
🐾 GARFIELD ROUNDS OUT . . . (#16) 978-0-345-49169-5
🐾 GARFIELD CHEWS THE FAT . . . (#17) 978-0-345-49170-1
🐾 GARFIELD GOES TO WAIST . . . (#18) 978-0-345-49173-2
🐾 GARFIELD HANGS OUT . . . (#19) 978-0-345-49174-9
🐾 GARFIELD TAKES UP SPACE . . . (#20) 978-0-345-49178-7
🐾 GARFIELD SAYS A MOUTHFUL . . . (#21) 978-0-345-49179-4
GARFIELD BY THE POUND . . . (#22) 978-0-345-37579-7
GARFIELD KEEPS HIS CHINS UP . . . (#23) 978-0-345-37959-7
GARFIELD TAKES HIS LICKS . . . (#24) 978-0-345-38170-5
GARFIELD HITS THE BIG TIME . . . (#25) 978-0-345-38332-7
GARFIELD PULLS HIS WEIGHT . . . (#26) 978-0-345-38666-3
GARFIELD DISHES IT OUT . . . (#27) 978-0-345-39287-9
GARFIELD LIFE IN THE FAT LANE . . . (#28) 978-0-345-39776-8
GARFIELD TONS OF FUN . . . (#29) 978-0-345-40386-5
GARFIELD BIGGER AND BETTER . . . (#30) 978-0-345-40770-2
GARFIELD HAMS IT UP . . . (#31) 978-0-345-41241-6
GARFIELD THINKS BIG . . . (#32) 978-0-345-41671-1
GARFIELD THROWS HIS WEIGHT AROUND . . . (#33) 978-0-345-42749-6
GARFIELD LIFE TO THE FULLEST . . . (#34) 978-0-345-43239-1
GARFIELD FEEDS THE KITTY . . . (#35) 978-0-345-43673-3
GARFIELD HOGS THE SPOTLIGHT . . . (#36) 978-0-345-43922-2
GARFIELD BEEFS UP . . . (#37) 978-0-345-44109-6
GARFIELD GETS COOKIN' . . . (#38) 978-0-345-44582-7
GARFIELD EATS CROW . . . (#39) 978-0-345-45201-6
GARFIELD SURVIVAL OF THE FATTEST . . . (#40) 978-0-345-46458-3
GARFIELD OLDER AND WIDER . . . (#41) 978-0-345-46462-0
GARFIELD PIGS OUT . . . (#42) 978-0-345-46466-8
GARFIELD BLOTS OUT THE SUN . . . (#43) 978-0-345-46615-0
GARFIELD GOES BANANAS . . . (#44) 978-0-345-91346-3
GARFIELD LARGE & IN CHARGE . . . (#45) 978-0-345-49172-5
GARFIELD SPILLS THE BEANS . . . (#46) 978-0-345-49177-0
GARFIELD GETS HIS JUST DESSERTS . . . (#47) 978-0-345-91387-6
GARFIELD WILL EAT FOR FOOD . . . (#48) 978-0-345-49176-3
GARFIELD WEIGHS HIS OPTIONS . . . (#49) 978-0-345-49181-7
GARFIELD POTBELLY OF GOLD . . . (#50) 978-0-345-52244-3

DVD TIE-INS

GARFIELD AS HIMSELF . . . 978-0-345-47805-4
GARFIELD HOLIDAY CELEBRATIONS . . . 978-0-345-47930-3
GARFIELD TRAVEL ADVENTURES . . . 978-0-345-48087-3

AND DON'T MISS . . .

GARFIELD AT 25: IN DOG YEARS I'D BE DEAD . . . 978-0-345-45204-7
GARFIELD'S JOKE ZONE/INSULTS . . . 978-0-345-46263-3
GARFIELD FAT CAT 3-PACK/ VOL. 1 . . . 978-0-345-46455-2
GARFIELD FAT CAT 3-PACK/ VOL. 2 . . . 978-0-345-46465-1
GARFIELD FAT CAT 3-PACK/ VOL. 3 . . . 978-0-345-48088-0
GARFIELD FAT CAT 3-PACK/ VOL. 4 . . . 978-0-345-49171-8
GARFIELD FAT CAT 3-PACK/ VOL. 5 . . . 978-0-345-49180-8
GARFIELD FAT CAT 3-PACK/ VOL. 13 . . . 978-0-345-46460-6
GARFIELD FAT CAT 3-PACK/ VOL. 14 . . . 978-0-345-49175-6
SEASON'S EATINGS: A VERY MERRY GARFIELD CHRISTMAS . . . 978-0-345-47560-2
GARFIELD'S GUIDE TO EVERYTHING . . . 978-0-345-46461-3
ODIE UNLEASHED! . . . 978-0-345-46464-4
GARFIELD'S BOOK OF CAT NAMES . . . 978-0-345-48516-8
THE GARFIELD JOURNAL . . . 978-0-345-46469-9
LIGHTS, CAMERA, HAIRBALLS!: GARFIELD AT THE MOVIES . . . 978-0-345-49134-3
30 YEARS OF LAUGHS AND LASAGNA . . . 978-0-345-50379-4
GARFIELD MINUS GARFIELD . . . 978-0-345-51387-8
GARFIELD FROM THE TRASH BIN . . . 978-0-345-51881-1

🐾 **New larger, full-color format!**